Organize for Victory!

Victory!

Principles of the Freedom First Society

By G. Vance Smith
and Tom Gow

The truth is, to be sure, sometimes hard to grasp, but it is never so elusive as when it is not wanted.
— Herman H. Dinsmore (1900–1980)

Freedom First Society
Colorado Springs, Colorado

Published by
Freedom First Society
P.O. Box 15099
Colorado Springs, CO 80935
(719) 380-6962
www.freedomfirstsociety.org

Library of Congress Control Number: 2008924225

Printed in the United States of America

ISBN 978-0-9816161-0-0

Dedicated to

Wayne C. Rickert, C. Walter Ruckel, and
Keith L. Van Buskirk

Without the devotion of these three men to the vision of Robert
Welch and their tireless efforts in the cause of freedom, neither
this book nor the Freedom First Society would exist.

Contents

V: And *Organize* for Victory!

VI: Members in Action

VII: "And So, Let's Act" — Now!

Appendices

Foreword

At no time in history has victory ever come to a disorganized army. But small numbers of warriors — when organized — have won great battles. And many such battles have been won in the final hours of the war in the face of terrifying odds. That is what this book is all about.

The hour is late. The odds are enormous; the stakes are monumental. The enemy has a 200-year head-start undermining the foundations of our country and weakening the moral character of our people. We face not the beginning of a long, difficult war, but we are actually in its final stages. It seems far too late to say, "let's get organized," for who on earth could rally a nationwide body of citizens and lead them to victory against a deeply entrenched, cleverly invisible enemy?

For that matter, how many Americans have the slightest idea that their country is being systematically dismantled by anyone — whether seen or unseen? And if such an insidious power exists, who could identify it, understand it, devise the right strategy, employ the right tactics, or deploy the right troops armed with the right weapons to defeat it?

There are but few men uniquely qualified to accomplish so great a task, and, providentially, they are organized and now established as the Freedom First Society. They are not drawing plans on a tablecloth or probing in the dark for ideas; these men are fully equipped and braced for this very different kind of war.

I am speaking of five individuals: Vance Smith, Tom Gow, Wayne Rickert, Walt Ruckel and Keith Van Buskirk. These men are now prepared to finish the war from which they were abruptly taken by subterfuge and intrigue occurring inside the John Birch Society on October 21, 2005.

The world of mainstream mediocrity will never know these men. They perform not for plaudits, prestige, or a dime's worth of limelight. They have devoted their lives to the freedom of our country. They wear no medals, display no trophies, and take no bows. However, it may well be a reality that the five proven leaders of whom I speak are known, feared, and despised in the highest chambers of elite power. This ruling conspiracy most certainly knows the potential of such men — when organized — to lay bare its backside and leave it no place to hide.

For many years I watched the Birch Society's Chief Executive Officer, Vance Smith, and its Vice President, Tom Gow, at work day and night under the stress of their own unrelenting moral commitment. Uprooted as they were, lesser men might have gone back to the warm and fuzzy cubicles of business and technology where they could sit out the destruction of their country without having to account for it. But at the darkest hour, and by virtue of their fiber, these two dedicated leaders held true and put their country ahead of their personal careers.

Indispensable encouragement and support came from the three top men on the JBS Executive Committee: Messrs. Rickert, Ruckel, and Van Buskirk. When unwise individuals overturned the foundation of the JBS, these three men resigned from the Executive Committee and fought with a determination either to upright the listing Birch Society, or failing that, to launch a new ship.

Effective this past October the new ship has been launched. Its first officers are Vance Smith and Tom Gow. They have a map, a compass, and the inspired plan created by a modern analytical genius, Robert Welch. That brilliant plan — restated in a current context — is laid out in the pages that follow. The security of your life, your family, and your country may well depend upon how seriously you read and respond to the inspired admonitions of this book.

— Don Fotheringham, January 11, 2008

Introduction

As its name suggests, *Organize for Victory!* is a book about solution — the solution to very serious problems confronting our nation and our people.

Rather than championing a unique solution out of thin air, however, *Organize for Victory!* first establishes an essential foundation by identifying the fundamental roots of those problems. After all, the sensible first step toward any elusive solution is to correctly understand the problem.

As we expect the reader will discover, a big part of that problem is that the American public is being *deliberately* misled and confused by the Establishment-controlled media and our educational institutions. As we go to press, the quadrennial presidential campaign cycle, in full swing, provides an excellent illustration.

One reason Americans are misdirected in their thinking regarding politics is that they are generally unaware of how their choices have been restricted. In particular, they are unaware of the grip a group of internationalist Insiders has on the serious contenders for president and the major media of communications (see Chapter 1: A Fact, Not a Theory and Chapter 17: Presidential Politics).

With this concealed grip, media analysts can confine public discussion to a Hobson's choice. For example: "Which candidate is going to *spend the most* or *raise* spending the least on health care?" Carefully excluded from the debate is a critical missing alternative — *no* federal involvement, as mandated by our Constitution and the principle of federalism.

In practice, Americans are not allowed to determine whether the next presidential administration will support the U.S. Constitution or the internationalist/collectivist agenda. Instead, voters are encouraged to decide whether their next president will be a born-again Christian (Huckabee), a Mormon (Romney), a woman (Clinton), a black (Obama), or an aging "maverick" ex-POW (McCain).

Opportunities and Traps

Building on a foundation of clear understanding of the problem, *Organize for Victory!* then spells out the opportunities concerned Americans have to make a difference by following a sound plan. It also warns against some of the common pitfalls that can take those same concerned Americans off course.

Many programs trumpeted as the answer to our nation's problems are able to gain support primarily because adherents fail to evaluate the root problem correctly. Other programs win followers because of the lure of the quick fix.

Freedom First Society is not offering a quick fix, and we cannot. The problem is too deep and long in its creation. Yet our program is not so difficult as many would imagine. Understanding that fact is important for avoiding discouragement and maintaining enthusiasm.

Discouragement with even a sound program can set in because of lack of understanding. For example, few Americans adequately appreciate the opportunity we still have because of inherited layers of strength that have not yet been entirely eroded (see especially Chapter 9: Next, Assess Our Strengths and Enemy Weaknesses).

As the reader will quickly discover, *Organize for Victory!* is not designed to appeal to those who seek superficial answers or a slight variation upon conventional wisdom. Instead, it is intended for concerned Americans who are willing to look deeper than the nightly news for the truth and real solutions. It should resonate with those who agree with these words of Patrick Henry: "For my part, whatever anguish of spirit it may cost, I am willing to know the whole truth, to know the worst, and provide for it."[1]

Moreover, *Organize for Victory!* is designed for responsible Americans who are determined to invest their efforts where they truly count.

Purpose of Freedom First Society

The immediate purpose of Freedom First Society is:

> To build a national network of members and chapters to preserve our liberties as protected by the United States Constitution. Guided by the values and vision of America's Founding Fathers and the great patriot Robert Welch,

Freedom First Society will provide Americans with the organization, programs, campaigns, and educational tools to expose and rout the Conspiracy that is gaining momentum in its diabolical plan to build a tyrannical new world order.

That means we also seek to defend, restore, and support the principles of freedom that made America great. In so doing, we have not invented some new philosophy to guide human affairs. We seek merely the opportunity for new generations to enjoy their heritage and to understand and value its underlying principles so they too can preserve the foundation for freedom and build constructively upon it.

Although our immediate focus is on the *current* threats to our heritage of freedom, we intend for our organization to have value far beyond the immediate fight. The conditions for freedom must always be nurtured and layers of strength built to ward off the next round of threats. In addition, even when current threats have been overcome, the accumulated damage to our layers of strength will require much work to repair.

Members of Freedom First Society come together to preserve freedom. The organization and its leadership merely provide a framework — a tool for inspired, committed volunteers to use in a desperate struggle. We believe it is a good framework, built on the wisdom and experience of a great leader — Robert Welch — and the almost 47-year legacy of the separate organization he started.

But our success will depend on the good people we can persuade to use this vehicle and link arms together in a great cause. When, and if, we are victorious, those who labored in this uphill battle should derive great pride and satisfaction in what they accomplished.

Our Origins
In building a membership organization to accomplish the above, we will be guided by the insights and experience of Robert Welch as reflected in his extensive writings and speeches. The good news is that we are not starting from scratch; we are building on the shoulders of a giant (see the biographical sketch included as Appendix A) and decades of organizational experience in the freedom battle.

A businessman and a great student of history, Robert Welch

became concerned over the direction our nation was headed. He authored several books and toured the nation giving speeches alerting Americans to the dangers of Communism and collectivism. He even launched a national magazine and tested the waters of politics.

But Robert Welch soon realized from his studies that such measures were not sufficient to overcome what he understood was driving America downward. So at the end of 1958, Robert Welch launched a national membership organization, The John Birch Society (JBS), with the purpose of fighting a Conspiracy, preventing its new world order, and preserving our American heritage. Under Mr. Welch's personal leadership for 25 years, The John Birch Society had great impact on the agenda of what he termed the Insiders of this Conspiracy.

For the first 15 years, the JBS enjoyed impressive growth. But then growth became much more difficult and elusive. Compounding the challenge of breathing new life into an aging JBS, from 1983 through 1989 the JBS went through five leadership changes.

Then in 1991 G. Vance Smith became its Chief Executive Officer and Tom Gow its Vice President. A third member of the team, John F. McManus, the Society's official spokesmen, obtained his long sought title of President. For 14 years under that team's leadership, the JBS achieved financial stability, and a revived membership made its influence felt nationally, accomplishing significant victories.

In 2005 that renewed momentum fell apart. Control of the Society fell victim to a whispering campaign of innuendo by several misguided employees and Council members. They sought to topple the leadership outside the procedures Mr. Welch had established for replacing a leader. As we watched the campaign unfold, we saw clearly that the leaders were sacrificing principle on the altar of personal ambition.

Moreover, the authors of this book were convinced that the coup's leaders had no deep commitment to the tough organizational lessons developed under Mr. Welch's leadership and that of his trusted right-hand man for 25 years — Thomas N. Hill.

It soon became apparent that the JBS, under new leadership, would no longer take the point in the fight against the Conspiracy. Nor would it place the necessary top priority on building a volunteer organization. And without these twin pillars, there was simply no way that Mr. Welch's solution could be implemented successfully.

Not willing to see Mr. Welch's plan for leadership in the freedom fight die, a number of dedicated members, including three members of the Society's Executive Committee who resigned over the dispute, joined with us in an attempt to persuade the Council to intervene to repair the damage.

When it became clear that those with a grip on the reins of power at The John Birch Society could not be moved, our team decided that the fight must go on and that there must be a vehicle to provide the leadership that Mr. Welch envisioned.

So, in October of 2007, we formed Freedom First Society, a new principle-centered organization, not built around personality, to carry Mr. Welch's vital plan forward.

From experience we know that careful planning is necessary to ensure that a principle-based organization will stay on course and prosper for even one generation, let alone the many generations for which it is intended. This is particularly the case when that organization promises to play a leading role in a highly contested battle for great stakes.

This book is part of that planning. It lays the foundation stone for the organization by explaining clearly not only what we are about, but also what is *not* our mission and why we proceed as we do.

Although the circumstances leading up to the founding of Freedom First Society are regrettable, the end result will undoubtedly turn out to be a blessing. A new organization, given birth by experienced leadership, has a better opportunity to correct some of the sins that led to the catastrophe.

More importantly, with a fresh start Freedom First Society has the opportunity to cast off cumbersome organizational baggage, enlist new talent, and overcome deficiencies that were making it nearly impossible for its predecessor to grow.

Time will tell.

Section I

There *Is* A Conspiracy

Chapter 1

A Fact, Not a Theory

The first job of conspiracy is to convince the world that conspiracy does not exist.

— Dr. James P. Lucier, 1967

At the time of this writing, the authors recognize that the most powerful and ruthless Conspiracy in the history of mankind has a grip on world affairs and is seeking rapidly to eliminate the last bastions of potential resistance to its world hegemony.

Moreover, the authors believe that the future of freedom is limited unless sufficient numbers of Americans can quickly be brought under strong leadership to expose this Conspiracy and force action to rout it.

Obviously, the above two statements are conclusions. Since the focus of this book is on solution, we can present only a small portion of the mountains of evidence that supports the first conclusion. We expect that many readers will already have some familiarity with that evidence.

However, since the conclusion that there is a Conspiracy is so fundamental to our purpose, we have devoted the first two sections of this book to the issue. The following introductory discussion should help new and prospective members understand our position and perhaps even help them explain it to others.

Definition of Conspiracy

Clarity is essential in describing the Conspiracy. Sometimes we fail to reach people simply because they have been programmed to imagine we are saying something we are not when we use the word Conspiracy. So let's start with the definition of a conspiracy.

> **Definition**: A conspiracy is a secret plot among more than one person to accomplish an unlawful or arguably evil purpose.

The definition has three elements: secrecy, multiple persons acting in concert, and an evil objective. That's it; happens all the time.

Because of the secrecy, planning, and organization, a *conspiracy* to commit a crime increases the threat to society. That's why conspiracy is given special treatment in criminal codes. And political conspiracies have been common throughout history. It's the obvious method corrupt power-seekers would want to use to advance their ends.

Note that it is not necessary, and frequently not the case, that all participants in a conspiracy participate for the same reasons.

Conspiracy With a Capital "C"

But we are not talking about just any conspiracy, we are talking about a particular generations-spanning conspiracy, which we write with a capital "C."

The inner core of this Conspiracy must necessarily be small, restricted to the most trusted and valuable agents to preserve secrecy. But outside this core many more individuals are enlisted to help.[1] Those in the outer circles may or may not understand the full extent of the Conspiracy's objectives or, if they do understand, they may not even care. Some undoubtedly participate for purely selfish reasons and are not especially committed to the ends of the Conspiracy, except as its support helps their positions and their careers.

Much of the Conspiracy's power and influence stems from its ability to reward its followers. Over generations it has expanded its ability to open doors for the ambitious who choose to cooperate with its aims and to close doors to advancement for potential adversaries. This particular enticement appeals to those self-promoters willing to sacrifice any scruples in cooperating with the Conspiracy.

Although we regard the existence of this Conspiracy as indisputable, we freely acknowledge that there is much about its inner workings that we are not in a position to know. In 1966, Robert Welch coined the term *Insiders* to refer to the leaders in an inner core of this conspiratorial power. He wanted a term that would be "as comprehensive as needed, but no more specific than our knowledge can justify."[2]

Not a Theory!
We are eager to point to the more than ample evidence that this Conspiracy exists. That evidence is available for all willing to read. Not only the Conspiracy's existence but its objectives, methods, and principal strategies are well documented.

The evidence is so overwhelming that we regard the Conspiracy's existence as a fact, not a theory. Actually, the common use of the term "theory" to describe what we are alleging as fact serves the Conspiracy well. For who will work hard and organize resistance against something whose existence is only a theory?

In this regard, we draw attention to an observation by Dr. James P. Lucier, a highly regarded journalist and former minority staff director of the Senate Foreign Relations Committee. In 1967, Dr. Lucier insisted: "The first job of conspiracy is to convince the world that conspiracy does not exist."[3] Robert Welch's response was: "And our first job is to show that it does."[4]

Certainly, one way a conspiracy can obscure its existence is to convince the world that any claim of conspiracy is only a theory. Is it just coincidence that so much ridicule has been heaped on "the conspiratorial theory of history?" Mr. Welch claimed that the phrase was a brilliant seizure of advantage by the Conspiracy before the argument even started. He went on to explain:

> For the conspiracy is not a theory, it is a fact. The evidence to prove this fact is so plentiful and obvious, as to be overwhelming. Our whole problem is to get people to stop and look and listen. For the enemy has now spent many decades in cleverly weaving a blanket of obfuscation over the eyes and the ears and the minds of the American people. With a result which sometimes makes us know exactly how the good lady felt when she wrote us "all my friends are idiots."[5]

Nature of the Evidence
Although critics frequently like to dismiss "the conspiratorial theory of history" as the claims of a bunch of hysterical right-wingers, they can get away with that only by refusing to discuss the evidence.

So what evidence is there? All kinds. Enormous quantities of it.

5

Both direct evidence and circumstantial. We have the testimony of eye-witnesses to small pieces and big pieces of the Conspiracy and its activities. Some of these witnesses are hostile to the Conspiracy's aims and others friendly. Some were originally part of the Conspiracy but defected. There are captured secret documents. And there are numerous admissions against interest as the race toward a new world order accelerates.

A popular misconception is that circumstantial evidence is less valid or less important than direct evidence. In fact, an accumulation of circumstantial evidence can be even more powerful than direct evidence. Criminal prosecutions often rely largely on circumstantial evidence, as nearly all criminals are careful not to generate direct evidence, and they try to avoid demonstrating criminal intent. In practice, circumstantial evidence often has an advantage over direct evidence in that it is more difficult to suppress or fabricate. The evidence establishing the Conspiracy's existence falls in both categories.

As the discerning reader might expect, not all of the potential evidence is completely reliable and not all witnesses equally credible. Some judgment in interpreting the evidence is required, and even with good judgment erroneous conclusions regarding specific points are always possible. As an illustration, for a time even the FBI was wrong about who headed the American mafia. Nevertheless, the evidence establishing the existence, objectives, and influence of the Conspiracy is so overwhelming as to defy any other interpretation.

Moreover, when the case is stated properly and conservatively, it squares with reason and human experience. In fact, the opposite contention defies reason. When a free nation's defenses are down, through ignorance, complacency, and growing immorality, corruption is bound to set in, and ambitious men will conspire to gain unrestrained power.

A last comment on evidence in general: People are more inclined to accept uncritically what they first hear, particularly if it's widely and repeatedly reported for an extended time. Against this uncritical acceptance, historical revisionists have an uphill battle to gain an ear for their arguments. This is especially true for those whom the Establishment has labeled as outside the realm of responsible political debate.

Establishment "Authorities"

Now let's take a tour through some of the specific evidence. Our objective with this journey will be not merely to survey some of the quality evidence establishing the existence of this Conspiracy, we will also want to use our journey to provide some insights into the influence, objectives, methods, nature, and strategy of the Conspiracy. Selection of examples here is a matter of personal taste — the options are immense.

Particularly embarrassing to those who seek to dismiss all claims of a dominant Conspiracy is that some of the witnesses and researchers carry Establishment credentials. These Establishment men have spoken out of school and presented evidence counter to the interests of the Conspiracy.

Carroll Quigley

A prime example of a witness with Establishment credentials is the late Carroll Quigley. Quigley gained a reputation as a distinguished professor of history at the Foreign Service School of Georgetown University. He mentored a bright young Bill Clinton who would later become president. Bill Clinton actually paid homage to his mentor in his televised speech accepting the Democratic nomination for president in 1992.

Informed anti-Communists were amazed when they discovered unintended confirmation for their claims in Professor Quigley's monumental 1966 work *Tragedy and Hope: A History of the World in Our Time*. A portion of *Tragedy and Hope* describes the secret maneuvers of a network of international banking families striving to control the finances and affairs of governments. Buried in its 1,348 pages, Quigley provided this gem:

> There does exist, and has existed for a generation, an international Anglophile network which operates, to some extent, in the way the radical Right believes the Communists act. In fact, this network, which we may identify as the Round Table Groups, has no aversion to cooperating with the Communists, or any other groups, and frequently does so. I know of the operations of this network because I have studied it for twenty years and was permitted for two years,

in the early 1960's, to examine its papers and secret records. I have no aversion to it or to most of its aims and have, for much of my life, been close to it and to many of its instruments. I have objected, both in the past and recently, to a few of its policies ... but in general my chief difference of opinion is that it wishes to remain unknown, and I believe its role in history is significant enough to be known.[6]

The international network Quigley described has as its core a secret society established in 1891 by Cecil Rhodes, the South African diamond and gold mogul of Rhodes Scholarship fame. After Rhodes' death in 1902, his successors carried on the conspiratorial activities and established semisecret "Round Table" groups in the chief British dependencies and the United States.

Each semisecret Round Table would then create a public front organization to expand its influence, built around itself as a nucleus. In England the public front was the Royal Institute of International Affairs. According to Quigley, "In New York it was known as the Council on Foreign Relations, and was a front for J.P. Morgan and Company in association with the very small American Round Table Group."[7] These front organizations were able to draw into their scheme some of the most influential men and women from a wide variety of fields.

Not only did the American and British branches of this cabal have "no aversion to cooperating with the Communists," they consistently worked to advance the world Communist revolution. Such action by some of the world's wealthiest capitalists may seem strange until one realizes that both groups are pursuing the same goal — unrestrained power. These very wealthy men are not "free market" capitalists, nor are the Communists genuine representatives of the "downtrodden proletariat."

The Communist revolution has certainly served the Conspiracy by consolidating control in many areas of the world. But more importantly, this militant branch of the Conspiracy has also provided the conflict that the high-level internationalists, described by Quigley, needed to advance their revolutionary goals in the West. The internationalists have used this conflict to persuade nations, most notably the United States, to submit to new international authority controlled by the internationalists from behind the scenes.

So in the previous century, these internationalist schemers worked privately to *help* the Communists and their socialist and even fascist brethren, while *publicly* denouncing them.

Quigley refused to call the secret network he described in *Tragedy and Hope* a conspiracy, as he did not see its work as evil. He claimed to have "no aversion" to this conspiratorial network "or to most of its aims...."

But Quigley had once been more critical. In 1949, Quigley had completed an earlier, and in many respects more revealing, book, *The Anglo-American Establishment*. But he never was able to find a publisher for it. It was published posthumously in 1981.

In *The Anglo-American Establishment*, Quigley wrote:

> No country that values its safety should allow what the Milner Group accomplished in Britain — that is, that a small number of men should be able to wield such power in administration and politics, should be given almost complete control over the publication of documents relating to their actions, should be able to exercise such influence over the avenues of information that create public opinion, and should be able to monopolize so completely the writing and the teaching of the history of their own period.[8]

Quigley's later *Tragedy And Hope* was published by the Macmillan Company of New York in 1966. The revelations in it made the book a big seller, but Macmillan nevertheless stalled in reprinting it, eventually claiming to Quigley that the printing plates had been lost.

After Quigley's death, Edward Hunter, a recognized expert on Communist psychological warfare who had encountered difficulties getting his own books published, told of his friendly relationship with Quigley. Hunter once asked the Georgetown professor, "Surely, you should have known that the Establishment believed that after all those years of contact, it could trust you not to tell tales out of school?" To which Quigley responded, "I told them the kind of a book I was writing. They just did not understand what kind of an Irishman I am." Yet, as Hunter stated, Quigley, "was a deeply worried man, under harassment that he never imagined could befall a professor."[9]

Interestingly, the structure of the Rhodes organization as described by Quigley in *The Anglo-American Establishment* resembled that of the Order of the Illuminati, which preceded the French Revolution. There was an inner circle, known as "The Society of the Elect," and an outer circle called "The Association of Helpers." The real power in the inner circle came from the leader (Rhodes) and a "Junta of Three" — William T. Stead, Reginald Brett (Lord Esher), and Alfred Milner. Alfred Milner acted as leader following the death of Rhodes.[10]

According to Professor Quigley, this organization exercised amazing influence, while remaining largely invisible to the public eye. "[The] power and influence of this Rhodes-Milner group in British imperial affairs and in foreign policy since 1889, although not widely recognized, can hardly be exaggerated," claimed Quigley. Regarding its invisibility, Quigley notes: "This organization has been able to conceal its existence quite successfully, and many of its most influential members, satisfied to possess the reality rather than the appearance of power, are unknown even to close students of British history."[11]

Quigley attributed an extensive list of "accomplishments" in world affairs to the Rhodes-Milner conspiracy (our term). He then suggested how a group wielding such influence could remain hidden from public view:

> It would be expected that a Group which could number among its achievements such accomplishments as these would be a familiar subject for discussion among students of history and public affairs. In this case, the expectation is not realized, partly because of the deliberate policy of secrecy which this Group has adopted, partly because the Group itself is not closely integrated but rather appears as a series of overlapping circles or rings partly concealed by being hidden behind formally organized groups of no obvious political significance.[12]

Milner and Rhodes, states Quigley, "felt that [their group] should pursue its goal by secret political and economic influence behind the scenes and by *the control of journalistic, educational, and propaganda agencies.*"[13] [Emphasis added.]

As the network's influence grew on this side of the Atlantic, it followed a similar strategy for disseminating propaganda. As Quigley notes in *Tragedy and Hope*:

> The American branch of this "English Establishment" exerted much of its influence through five American newspapers (*The New York Times*, New York *Herald Tribune*, *Christian Science Monitor*, the *Washington Post*, and the lamented *Boston Evening Transcript*). In fact, the editor of the *Christian Science Monitor* was the chief American correspondent (anonymously) of *The Round Table*, and Lord Lothian, the original editor of *The Round Table* and later secretary of the Rhodes Trust (1925-1939) and ambassador to Washington, was a frequent writer in the *Monitor*.[14]

In *Tragedy and Hope*, Quigley reveals another dimension that helps explain how the Conspiracy manages the news that Americans regularly receive. While referring to the group of "American experts" that organized through the Institute of Pacific Relations to influence America's Asian policy in favor of the Communists, Mr. Quigley acknowledges:

> It is also true that this group, from its control of funds, academic recommendations, and research or publication opportunities, could favor persons who accepted the established consensus and could injure, financially or in professional advancement, persons who did not accept it. It is also true that the established group, by its influence on book reviewing in *The New York Times*, the *Herald Tribune*, the *Saturday Review*, a few magazines, including the "liberal weeklies," and in the professional journals, could advance or hamper any specialist's career.[15]

Robert Welch Responds

Robert Welch had also researched and studied the evidence of a Conspiracy above Communism. In the same year that Quigley published *Tragedy and Hope*, Mr. Welch would independently summarize his own conclusions in an article entitled "The Truth in Time." But Mr. Welch would later comment on Quigley's revelations:

> Most, though by no means all, of what Quigley tells us in such detail, is true as far as it goes. But he very carefully presents only a part of the horrible truth as if it were the whole truth.... The total Conspiracy is tremendously larger than that part which has financed it.

Mr. Welch took particular aim at Quigley's portrayal of the Conspiracy as practically beginning with Cecil Rhodes. While not discounting the Quigley history about the intrigues of Rhodes, Mr. Welch observed:

> ... it would be very well for the honest student of history to keep in mind that the Master Conspiracy was already three generations old; had brought on the French Revolution and then the various uprisings of 1848; and had founded the Communist movement as one of its tools, long before the ambitious young Cecil Rhodes even entered Oxford.
>
> The Quigley opus is a very scholarly, disingenuous, and monumental work. In most cases — though not all — he misleads you only by omission.[16]

James Billington

Professor James Hadley Billington is another historian with impressive Establishment credentials who has confirmed important history of the Conspiracy. James Billington received his doctorate as a Rhodes Scholar at Oxford, taught history for 17 years at Harvard and Princeton Universities, and directed the Woodrow Wilson International Center for Scholars. In 1987, Professor Billington was sworn in as the 13th Librarian of Congress. For more than three decades, he was a member of the Council on Foreign Relations.

In 1980, Professor Billington published *Fire in the Minds of Men: Origins Of The Revolutionary Faith*. Perhaps the most amazing thing about this book is that its author provides proof of a conspiracy, even though he was at the time himself a member of the conspiratorial CFR. Professor Billington manages to document important history ignored or ridiculed by the "Liberal" Establishment. As an important example, Billington accurately describes the Illuminati and affirms that the Illuminati had more influence following its exposure and alleged death than before. Mr. Welch believed that both Russian Communism and today's Master Conspiracy had their origins in the Illuminati.

In particular, Professor Billington informs his readers:

> The Order of Illuminists was founded on May 1, 1776, by a professor of canon law at the University of Ingolstadt in Bavaria, Adam Weishaupt, and four associates. The order was secret and hierarchical, modeled on the Jesuits (whose long domination of Bavarian education ended with their abolition by the Papacy in 1773) and dedicated to Weishaupt's Rousseauian vision of leading all humanity to a new moral perfection freed from all established religious and political authority.[17]

In *Fire In The Minds of Men*, Billington traces scores of secret organizations that sprouted "from the waning of the French Revolution in the late eighteenth century to the beginnings of the Russian Revolution in the early twentieth."

Of particular interest, Billington documents how an Illuminist-type conspiracy, the League of the Just, arranged for Karl Marx to write the *Communist Manifesto*. However, in a new introduction to a subsequent edition, Billington takes pains to downplay this connection between Illuminism and Marxism.

Clearly, the idea that secret societies have conspired to run the world is not something that exists merely in the imagination of right-wing extremists. This is simply how the world too often has been run.

Order of the Illuminati

Captured or intercepted documents have provided information on the

Conspiracy that is about as authoritative as it gets. We cite here two examples.

A literally providential event led to the exposure, prosecution, and outlawing of the Order of the Illuminati conspiracy in Germany. A courier for the Illuminati was killed by lightning. Incriminating papers found on his body led police to raid the home of one of the conspirators. The 1786 raid uncovered a copy of Weishaupt's writings, which revealed an extensive conspiracy *against the religions and governments* of Europe. Subsequently, copies were distributed to the important monarchs of Europe.

The highly regarded Professor John Robison in England and the Abbé Augustin Barruel in France researched this information, and each authored books warning of the Illuminati conspiracy. Robison's *Proofs of a Conspiracy* was first published in 1798. Some months later in 1799, Barruel's impressive four-volume study, *Memoirs Illustrating the History of Jacobinism*, appeared in French. Initially unaware of each other's work, Robison and Barruel independently came to very similar conclusions.

By the time of its exposure, the Illuminist conspiracy had already spread beyond Germany. Early agents of the Illuminati actually organized insurrectionary and secessionist movements to destroy the newly created American Republic.

This subversive agitation alarmed George Washington sufficiently that he condemned "the nefarious and dangerous plan, and doctrines of the Illuminati...."[18] The same year Robison's book was published (1798), the Reverend G. W. Snyder sent George Washington a copy, to whom Washington replied:

> It is not my intention to doubt that the doctrine of the Illuminati and the principles of Jacobinism had not [sic] spread in the United States. On the contrary no one is more fully satisfied of this fact than I am.[19]

A Century and a Half Later

Another collection of incriminating documents was seized during a police raid of the convention of the Communist Party of America held in Bridgman, Michigan on August 22, 1922. R. M. Whitney examined the Bridgman evidence in his important 1924 book *Reds in*

America. According to Whitney, the raid netted "[n]ames, records, checks from prominent people in this country, instructions from Moscow, speeches, theses, questionnaires — indeed, the whole machinery of the underground organization, the avowed aim of which is the overthrow of the United States Government...."[20]

Reds in America provided shocking documentation of Communist infiltration in America as early as 1922! Among the Bridgman evidence was a detailed plan for Communist Party cells to establish "nuclei" in "all existing Negro organizations" to agitate against racism. Interestingly, the raid also turned up evidence that the Communist Party was playing both sides of the street — a common tactic of revolutionaries seeking conflict to drive their agenda. According to the August 23, 1922 *Herald-Press* of St. Joseph, Michigan, the captured evidence showed that the Party had also been controlling at least one Ku Klux Klan organization.

Congress Looks at the Foundations

Several decades after the Bridgman raid, Congress would turn up evidence of the larger, internationalist Conspiracy that Quigley's books have since described.

In 1953 the House created a special committee chaired by Tennessee Representative Carroll Reece to investigate the tax-exempt foundations. At the time, several major foundations were known to be providing extensive tax-exempt financial support to Communist and left-wing causes clearly hostile to traditional American interests. And back then, Congress wanted to know why.

Louis Budenz, the former editor of the Communist *Daily Worker*, had suggested one explanation for the foundation funding of subversion. Following his defection, Budenz had become a vocal anti-Communist. He claimed that Communists had long realized the importance of the great tax-free foundations. Particular favorites, he reported, "were the Carnegie, Rockefeller, and Guggenheim Foundations...."[21]

A Reece Committee report stated:

> Mr. Louis Budenz testified before the Cox Committee that … a [Communist] commission had been created to penetrate the foundations, and he named names. Mr. Manning Johnson

testified that he was a member of the Party from 1930 to 1940 and gave his opinion that the foundations had been successfully penetrated on both the high and low levels.[22]

As a prime example of that penetration, in 1948 the notorious Soviet spy Alger Hiss had been appointed president of the powerful Carnegie Endowment. One of the concerns of the Reece Committee was Carnegie's funding of the Institute of Pacific Relations (I.P.R.). The Carnegie and Rockefeller foundations had together contributed millions to the I.P.R., a massive, respectable-looking enterprise orchestrating pressure for the U.S. to betray China to the Communists.

The Senate Internal Security Subcommittee later determined that the I.P.R. was "considered by the American Communist Party and by Soviet officials as an instrument of Communist policy, propaganda and military intelligence."[23]

Interestingly, Hiss had been chosen for his position at Carnegie by the Endowment's chairman, Establishment Insider John Foster Dulles. Dulles was a CFR founder and a disciple of the quintessential Insider, Colonel Edward Mandell House (see next chapter). With the help of the Establishment media, Dulles cultivated a phony reputation as a tough anti-Communist while secretary of state in the Eisenhower administration. (See Alan Stang, *The Actor: The True Story of John Foster Dulles, Secretary of State 1953 – 1959*.)

As a result of the exposure of *Communist* penetration of government and the foundations, the foundations were forced to do some housecleaning. However, the exposure didn't significantly change the policy of either the foundations or the White House. In *Tragedy and Hope* (1966) Quigley explained why:

> It must be recognized that the power that these energetic Left-wingers exercised was never their own power or Communist power but was ultimately the power of the international financial coterie....[24]

Historian Arthur M. Schlesinger Jr., a member of the Establishment's Council on Foreign Relations, would seem to agree.

The year prior to Quigley's monumental publication, Dr. Schlesinger published his recollection of the Kennedy years, during which he had served as a special assistant to the president.

In *A Thousand Days: John F. Kennedy in the White House*, Schlesinger wrote of "the New York financial and legal community — that arsenal of talent which had so long furnished a steady supply ... to Democratic as well as Republican administrations. This community was the heart of the American Establishment.... [I]ts front organizations [were] the Rockefeller, Ford and Carnegie foundations and the Council on Foreign Relations; its organs, the *New York Times* and *Foreign Affairs*."[25]

As a "front organization" for the Establishment, one of the ongoing jobs of the Council on Foreign Relations has been to enlist, as members, selected men and women of significant or potential influence. Council gatherings provide the internationalists with a convenient opportunity to rub shoulders with, size up, and influence these individuals.

The CFR membership roster has long functioned as a recruiting ground for important government positions and prestigious appointments. Eventually, the mere possibility of being invited to join this elite group would induce many aspiring ladder climbers to champion the Establishment agenda.

Wild Rumors, Hoaxes, and Sensational Nonsense

Just because we claim that the existence and influence of the Conspiracy is a fact doesn't mean that we recommend accepting *every* story of conspiracy as equally valid. In fact, there is a ton of nonsense promoted as conspiracy theory. And *wild* rumors sometimes spread like *wild*fires.

In 1962, for example, there were multiple reports of Red Chinese troops massing in Baja California. Stories of a domestic system of concentration camps being prepared to intern patriotic Americans circulated for decades. And then there were reports of UN combat troops *discovered* encamped in rural locations in the U.S.

In the mid-1990s, the airwaves were abuzz with tales of sinister, unmarked *black* helicopters flying around (they had to be black to be sinister) and non-English speaking troops in unusual uniforms conducting house-to-house raids and car stops. One source reported that cryptic symbols were being placed on road signs supposedly to guide invading troops.

Such stories range anywhere from the slightly bizarre or outrageous to the simply fantastic (e.g., shape-shifting aliens having infiltrated government).

The Conspiracy Benefits

All this serves the Conspiracy well by helping its compliant media persuade busy Americans that *all* claims of Conspiracy are of this stripe — simply the wild imaginings of wackos. Recall the observation of James Lucier that the first job of conspiracy is to convince the world that conspiracy doesn't exist.

Moreover, any individual or organization gullible enough to give credence to one of these wild stories immediately loses valuable credibility. And just the presence of so much nonsense in the marketplace of information adds to the confusion and makes it more difficult for responsible Americans to determine what is true and what is not.

Fortunately, with a little thought and understanding it should be easy to doubt the legitimacy of many of these rumors. For example, if one understands why the Conspiracy still needs to conceal its aims (see Chapters 8 and 9), then rumors of blatant provocations that risk prematurely waking up the sleeping giant appear silly.

The Conspiracy has quite possibly planted a number of these rumors itself. The Conspiracy has certainly been known to sponsor individuals and groups whose wild irresponsibility should be obvious. For many decades, some disreputable groups and individuals alleged that Communism was a Jewish Conspiracy. The effect was that many Americans came to regard organizations concerned over a threat of Communism as most likely anti-Semitic.

At the very least level of its involvement, the Conspiracy will tolerate outrageous individuals and groups who represent no real threat to it.

One of the effects of repeated doses of these wild rumors is simply to give responsible Americans a bad taste for the topic of conspiracy, essentially inoculating many against wanting to consider the very solid evidence of a real conspiracy.

Similar damage occurs when *disreputable* sources promote *legitimate* evidence mixed in with other nonsense such as racist and anti-Semitic tripe. Such association serves to discredit the legitimate information to anyone who runs across it in such settings.

Cautions and Recommended Action

The responsible patriot seeks to be persuasive, not to be lonely. He is not content to just vent his frustrations by carrying bad news to a "disbelieving world." Our job is to pull together informed opposition to stop the Conspiracy. We have no desire to be able to say "we told you so."

Unfortunately, some of our fellow Americans have difficulty acting responsibly when they begin to see the outlines of the Conspiracy. They have difficulty handling the pressure that comes from understanding something so terrible while few of our friends and neighbors appreciate the danger. But the solution is not to try and gain the attention of the unaware by bombarding them with the most sensational and outrageous.

Effective patriots do not have to be on the cutting edge of every alarming story. Remember that it often takes time for the truth to come out. Why jeopardize our credibility over speculative matters when there is already absolutely solid evidence that should wake up anyone? There simply is no reason to go forward with a losing case, just because the conclusion is sensational.

As we hope the reader will see shortly, there is a ton of alarming, quality evidence. And we will have just scratched the surface. (For even more evidence, please refer to the bibliography. Also see the list of recommended reading on our website, www.freedomfirstsociety.org.)

The responsible patriot learns to discriminate between sources. He or she won't use unverified information from sources with an unknown or flawed track record of reliability and accuracy. And remember the conventional wisdom that if it's almost too good to be true, it very likely isn't. Avoid it. Forget it. Stick with the reliable.

Our recommendation, in summary: Be skeptical, be slow to react, and distinguish between sources. When in doubt, contact someone whose judgment you trust before embracing a sensational news story.

Chapter 2

Premeditated Merger

The substance of [the directives from the White House] is that we shall use our grant-making power so to alter life in the United States that we can be comfortably merged with the Soviet Union.
— H. Rowan Gaither (CFR), 1953

The most important revelation uncovered by the Reece Committee never made it into an official report. As a result of the Committee's determination to investigate the powerful tax-exempt foundations, its director of research, Norman Dodd, was invited in 1953 to the New York City headquarters of the Ford Foundation by its president, H. Rowan Gaither.

According to Dodd's recollection, here is how the interview went. "Mr. Dodd," Gaither told him, "all of us here at the policy-making level have had experience, either in O.S.S. [Office of Strategic Services] or the European Economic Administration, with directives from the White House. We operate under those directives here. Would you like to know what those directives are?"

When Dodd said he would, Gaither continued: "The substance of them is that we shall use our grant-making power so to alter life in the United States that we can be comfortably merged with the Soviet Union."

Taken aback by Gaither's brazen admission, a startled Dodd asked Gaither if he would be willing to repeat that before the Reece Committee. To which the Ford Foundation president replied: "That we would not think of doing."[1]

Tragically, the Reece Committee's investigations were halted soon thereafter. Thanks to political sabotage, the Committee would never have the opportunity to unmask the power structure of internationalists described by Carroll Quigley.

Foundation Influence Prospers

And so the major tax-exempt foundations have continued, even expanded, their support of subversive activities to this day. Prime

21

examples are the foundation grants to organizations seeking to radicalize the Hispanic population, undermine immigration enforcement, and lobby for revolution.

The Ford Foundation has provided funding to the radical Mexican-American Legal Defense and Education Fund (MALDEF). It was litigation by MALDEF that led to the Supreme Court decision requiring state taxpayers to provide free schooling to the children of illegal aliens. MALDEF was also involved with the ACLU in the litigation that allowed a liberal-left federal judge to strike down California's Proposition 187 that would have withheld welfare benefits from illegal aliens.

By examining the flow of funds, one sees that the Ford Foundation virtually created the radical Chicano movement that seeks open borders, uncontrolled immigration from Mexico, and the de facto reconquest by Mexico of the Southwest portion of the United States, termed Atzlan by the radicals.

Back when a few state legislatures still had the courage to investigate subversion, the California Senate Fact-finding Subcommittee on Un-American Activities traced some of this flow of funds. The 1970 report of the Subcommittee said of the Southwest Council of La Raza Unida:

> It is administered by a Board of 26 and its president is Maclovio Barraza. Mr. Barraza has been identified by the Subversive Activities Control Board as a member of the Communist Party, and presides over the Council which recently received a grant of $1,300,000.00 from the Ford Foundation.... The operation of this large and well-financed private concern, with a Communist at its head, obviously exerts a powerful influence on the Mexican-American minority throughout its domain including the Brown Berets.[2]

Moreover, the Southwest Council was *founded* with a $630,000 Ford Foundation grant![3]

Corroboration of "Merger Plan"

Today, a *direct* merger of the United States with the former Soviet Union, as suggested by Ford Foundation President Gaither, does not appear to be in the works. But a more circuitous strategy is moving forward rapidly that would achieve the same objective and unify the world under absolute Insider control.

The Insiders' currently prominent and successful strategy is to achieve world government in steps through regional mergers, such as the European Union, which the Insiders will solidly control from behind the scenes.

The emerging regional governments are designed to encroach on and then destroy national sovereignty, while minimizing public resistance by appealing to regional loyalties and supposed economic benefits. When the entanglements are complete and national resistance impossible, these regional units can be brought under the absolute control of a world superstructure, such as the CFR-built-and-controlled United Nations.

Nevertheless, along the way, several authorities have provided damning evidence and valuable pieces to the puzzle that support the Gaither claim — that pre-meditated merger was the goal of Establishment Insiders. Reasonably, most of these Insiders were not simply secret American Communists loyal to Moscow.

Steps toward such a merger would include building up the Soviet Union into a formidable enemy, weakening the independence of the U.S., and then eventually creating the image that the USSR had reformed and was now our ally.

Those steps would set the stage for a gradual merging of nations under "international" authority. In addition, the internationalists would look to invent crises to provide a pretext for faster integration.

Two Americans, Major George Racey Jordan and Dr. Medford Evans, experienced first hand how helping the Soviet Union to become a nuclear power, or at least to achieve the perception of being a nuclear power, was a policy of leading figures in U.S. administrations. Both Jordan and Evans tried to inform the public as to what they had witnessed. But they encountered a hostile Establishment that attacked their credibility and reduced the reach of their stories.

Major George Racey Jordan
During World War II, Major George Racey Jordan served as a Lend-Lease expediter for materials to Russia and as a liaison officer with

23

the Russians. Initially, Major Jordan was enthusiastic about helping a wartime ally. But he later became concerned by what he saw:

> [T]he tremendous volume of Lend-Lease material going through under "diplomatic immunity," the infiltration of Soviet Agents through the Pipeline, the shipments of non-military supplies and even military secrets, were more than I could stomach.[4]

Major Jordan finally protested through proper channels, but nothing happened. Fortunately, he kept detailed notes on what he observed. He was particularly concerned about several shipments of scientific data and materials destined for Russia. The materials carried unusual names virtually unknown to most Americans at the time. He recorded these shipments and later realized that they were materials needed to build an atomic bomb. Our officials had sent the Soviets uranium, thorium, cobalt, cadmium, and atom bomb data from our own top-secret Manhattan Project.

On at least one occasion, these shipments included the endorsement of Harry Hopkins, Lend-Lease Administrator and Special Assistant to the President [Franklin Roosevelt]. According to Wikipedia, "Hopkins wielded more diplomatic power than the entire State Department. Hopkins helped identify and sponsor numerous potential leaders, including Dwight D. Eisenhower."

When President Harry Truman announced in September of 1949 that a nuclear explosion had been detected in the U.S.S.R., Major Jordan contacted a U.S. senator, and, as a result, his story was investigated by the F.B.I. Two congressional hearings and several interviews by Fulton Lewis Jr. on his radio program followed.

But the Jordan charges did not go unanswered. A vicious attack in the press was unleashed against both Major Jordan and Fulton Lewis Jr. in an attempt to discredit the story. Major Jordan then used his notes to tell his shocking story in *From Major Jordan's Diaries*, first published by Hartcourt, Brace in 1952.

Medford Evans

Dr. Medford Evans, an academic with a Ph.D. from Yale, served as an administrative officer on the U.S. atomic energy project from

1944 through 1952. In January 1951, he was appointed Chief of Training for the Atomic Energy Commission with responsibility for security education and training at all its plants. In that role, Dr. Evans discovered huge lapses in security. Fourteen months later, realizing that his recommendations for tightening security were being ignored, he voluntarily resigned and wrote *The Secret War for the A-Bomb*, published by Regnery in 1953.

In *The Secret War*, Evans argued that despite the atomic bombs allegedly detonated by the Soviets, they had no ability to actually construct one themselves. Evans insisted they didn't need to since, as he later summarized, "the security system of the atomic energy project, including very especially the inventory control of fissionable materials, was and had been so porous that Soviet agents could have stolen enough enriched uranium and plutonium to make, as of the early 1950's, 'perhaps twenty atomic bombs.'"

Nevertheless, the Establishment would use the occasion of the alleged 1949 Soviet atomic bomb detonation as evidence that the U.S.S.R. had become a superpower on a par with the United States. While not discounting a Soviet threat, Evans continued to urge healthy skepticism over undocumented reports of scientific and technical achievements from Russia or China. In "The Emperor's New Bomb" (*American Opinion*, October 1965), Evans observed:

> [E]ven systematic theft could hardly produce in Soviet territory an arsenal equal to what we have in our territory....
>
> It takes, however, more than a few clever scientists to construct a gaseous-diffusion plant [for nuclear weapons production]. It takes a total industrial complex such as that in the United States. But, even if we provided nuclear lend-lease to Red China, where would they get the electric power to operate the thing?

Unintentional support for such skepticism of Soviet (and Chinese) capabilities was provided by *Wall Street Journal* Editor Vermont Royster. In the summer of 1962, he visited Russia and subsequently wrote:

> The Soviet Union is a feudal society, in the true sense of

that word, and measured against any of the advanced nations of the West it is a backward country, whether the test be industry, agriculture, technology, labor skills or the standard of living of the people....[5]

While Royster nevertheless accepted the idea of Soviet leadership in space (and presumably in nuclear weapons), Dr. Evans did not. Somewhat sarcastically, Evans observed:

In a transformation of international power relationships which has perhaps no parallel in history, the Soviet Union has since 1945 risen from such devastation and bankruptcy as made it a quasi-colonial ward of the then uniquely powerful United States to competitive eminence with us in a two-power world.[6]

Regardless of real Soviet military might, the Establishment unquestionably cooperated in supplying the Soviet Union with the superpower image in nuclear weapons and in space. There is even credible evidence that our own government restrained the U.S. military from being first in space so that the Soviets could surprise the world in 1957 with Sputnik.

The need for America to adopt special programs to "catch up" with the supposedly technologically more advanced Soviets would supply H. Rowan Gaither's colleagues with the pretext for more steps to transform the U.S. into a socialist nation. But the efforts to build the U.S.S.R. into a credible enemy continued. We will provide more of this story in Chapter 4.

Security Risks

In the years immediately following World War II, a number of revelations by former Communists and investigations by congressional committees pointed to Communists in sensitive positions in government. Harry Dexter White and Virginius Frank Coe, heading up the Treasury Department, were two of many.

This state of affairs should not have been surprising since during the war years many government officials had put the blinders on regarding the nature and agenda of Communism. In fact, during the war a very friendly image had been crafted for Soviet dictator Joseph Stalin in both Britain and the United States. Later the whole story came out as to what a murderous dictator "Uncle Joe" actually was.

Rather than taking responsible action to clean house, the reaction of the "liberal" Establishment was to join in the Communist-instigated counterattack on the congressional committees uncovering the evidence. Senator Joe McCarthy was made the focus of the counterattack, but the investigations of McCarthy's committee contributed only a piece of what was uncovered. The work of committees led by Congressman Martin Dies, Senator Pat McCarran, and Congressman Francis E. Walter has been erased from public memory by its custodians within the Establishment media.

Unappreciated by most Americans today, in the aftermath of World War II *real* Communists *were discovered* in government, and secret Communist cells working in government *were revealed*, like the Harold Ware cell, the Nathan Silvermaster cell, and the Victor Perlo cell. Moreover, credible testimony regarding the existence of several other cells, never uncovered, was presented.

In the 1990s the NSA released a batch of the decoded "Venona" intercepts — secret Soviet radio traffic collected in the 1940s — confirming that Soviet penetration of our government was even greater than had been previously disclosed. The Establishment has never apologized for its attack on those who were trying to clean house.

However, our security problems were not totally due to a wartime alliance with the Soviets. Significantly, the love affair with Communism started long *before* the outbreak of World War II. Although it was not common knowledge outside of Washington, Earl Browder, head of the Communist party USA, had the run of the White House for years. Browder's shocking access was undoubtedly influenced by the fact that Browder and Eleanor Roosevelt had been close friends and associates years before her husband became president.

Moreover, this "love affair" with Communism was not confined to outright Communists — open or secret. FDR's Secretary of the Interior, Harold L. Ickes, reportedly stated that "I suspect either the motives or the intelligence of those who would have us marshal our forces against a barely imaginary danger of Communism."[7] In his 'secret diary' for July 16, 1935, Ickes claimed that the "Roosevelt Brain Trust" had been "working toward a society of modified Communism."[8]

Adding to the credibility of the Gaither statement was a much earlier admission by Sumner Welles, foreign policy advisor to President Roosevelt. Shortly after FDR extended diplomatic recognition to the Soviet Union (1933), Welles declared:

> [I]f one took the figure 100 as representing the difference between American democracy and Soviet communism in 1917, with the United States at 100 and the Soviet Union at 0, American democracy might eventually reach the figure 60 and the Soviet system might reach the figure of 40.[9]

Colonel Edward Mandell House

It would be difficult to identify anyone who had a more disastrous impact on U.S. policy during the first half of the 20th Century than Edward Mandell House. In Texas, House had developed a reputation as a political kingmaker, helping four governors get elected between 1892 and 1902. But he was only getting started. House relocated to New York City and placed his talent for intrigue and manipulation at the disposal of the New York international bankers.

In 1911, House befriended New Jersey Governor Woodrow Wilson and helped him to the presidency the following year. When Wilson became president, House would exercise tremendous influence over his friend, even taking up residence in the White House for a while. Wilson actually referred to House as his alter ego (his other self). House developed many of Wilson's proposals, including Wilson's famous 14 points, and wrote the first draft of the Covenant of the League of Nations.

House was one of the key players at the 1919 Paris Peace Conference and a driving force for creating the League of Nations, which came out of the conference. When the U.S. Senate wisely refused American entry into the League, House and his Insider co-conspirators regrouped and began laying the groundwork for a future successful attack on U.S. independence.

One of their first steps was to create the exclusive Council on Foreign Relations. The prestige of membership in the CFR was designed to provide the internationalists with the opportunity to indoctrinate America's academic, media, business, political, and foreign policy elite in the necessity for their new world order.

Although House had no official position in government and insisted on staying out of the limelight, his influence would extend far beyond the Wilson years. Decades later his schemes would find significant success in the Roosevelt administration.

Even though House stayed in the background, he had revealed his political agenda in a boring novel he wrote shortly before Wilson became president. In *Philip Dru: Administrator*, House mapped out a subversive plan for socialist revolution in America.

Although the book was first published anonymously, House later admitted that he was its author and that the book represented his political and ethical philosophy. Through his fictional Philip Dru, House would express a desire for "Socialism as dreamed of by Karl Marx" with a "spiritual leavening."[10]

House privately insisted that the U.S. Constitution was seriously outmoded and had become a burden on efficient government. His fictional character Philip Dru would use a military coup to abolish America's constitutional order and remake the mechanism of government.

Philip Dru would foretell the fastening on America of three measures extolled in Marx's Communist Manifesto — the graduated income tax, an inheritance tax, and the Federal Reserve System (a central bank with a monopoly over the issuance of money and credit). All three came about during the Wilson administration.

In July 1937, Thomas W. Phelps, Washington Bureau Chief for the *Wall Street Journal*, provided this assessment of House's amazing impact on America:

> As Congress puts the finishing touches on the legislative program for the first four years of the Roosevelt Administration, Col. E.M. House, confidant of President Roosevelt, emerges as the prophet, if not the real brain trust of the New Deal. Almost 25 years ago, House wrote of a revolution led by a young West Pointer, who triumphed in one brief but bloody battle; became a benevolent dictator and proceeded to reshape the American Government. In its large

outlines, almost the entire revolutionary program has been put through or is in process of being realized under two Democratic Presidents who have served since House turned novelist for a few weeks.[11]

Zbigniev Brzezinski

Like Colonel House, Zbigniev Brzezinski was another presidential advisor with a Marxist bent. Significant facts in Brzezinski's career reveal a huge gap between public perception of prominent leaders, such as Jimmy Carter, and the reality. Examining Brzezinski's career also confirms the Conspiracy's subversive nature and its influence over current affairs.

By 1970 Zbigniev Brzezinski, then a professor at Columbia University, had been a CFR member for almost a decade. Writing in *Foreign Affairs* that year, Brzezinski would articulate a strategy to create "a community of the developed nations." Specifically, Brzezinski suggested:

> A council representing the United States, Western Europe and Japan, with regular meetings of the heads of governments as well as some small standing machinery, would be a good start.[12] [Emphasis added.]

Brzezinski would expand the concept in a book published that same year. In *Between Two Ages: America's Role in the Technetronic Era*, Brzezinski repeatedly praised Marxism[13] while outlining a plan for the transition to world government in stages.

In defense of his plan, Brzezinski argued that "[n]ational sovereignty is no longer a viable concept...."[14] He then proposed the "[m]ovement toward a larger community of the developed nations ... through a variety of indirect ties and already developing limitations on national sovereignty."[15]

According to the proposal, this community would eventually "embrace the Atlantic states, the more advanced European Communist states, and Japan."[16] But the ultimate goal was to merge all nations in a world government, controlled of course, by the Insiders.

To carry this strategy forward, David Rockefeller, Chairman of the

Council on Foreign Relations, formed the Trilateral Commission three years later (in 1973) and made Brzezinski its first director.

To give life to their new Commission, Rockefeller and Brzezinski set out together to recruit leading internationalists from the United States, Western Europe, and Japan to their subversive group. One of their approximately 100 recruits from the United States was a little-known governor from the state of Georgia. At the time, Jimmy Carter had no significant national following.

Immediately, Rockefeller and Brzezinski began grooming Carter as a presidential candidate. Aided by the CFR's grip on the media, they succeeded, in less than three years, in giving Carter national credibility and propelling him clear to the White House. In the process, the Establishment media deceived the American people by presenting Jimmy Carter as a simple man of the people with no Establishment ties.

In 1976, Leslie Gelb of the *New York Times* wrote: "For the better part of three years, Brzezinski (along with Prof. Richard N. Gardner of Columbia) had Carter virtually to himself...."[17]

In his own campaign booklet, Carter strove to put a nice face on a clearly subservient relationship: "Membership on this Commission has provided me with a splendid learning opportunity, and many of the members have helped me in my study of foreign affairs."[18]

After winning the 1976 presidential election, Carter made his Establishment ties obvious by appointing more than a dozen Trilateralists and CFR heavyweights to top posts in his administration. Zbigniew Brzezinski became Carter's National Security Advisor, Cyrus Vance — chairman of the board of trustees of the Rockefeller Foundation — was tapped for secretary of state, and Harold Brown earned the nod as secretary of defense.

In addition, Michael Blumenthal received appointment as secretary of the treasury and Paul Volcker became chairman of the Federal Reserve Board. Each of the mentioned appointments were members of both the Trilateral Commission and the Council on Foreign Relations. Oh, yes, and Jimmy Carter's running mate, Walter Mondale, also came with both credentials.

There should be little doubt that each of these men was expected to support Insider agendas advancing the cause of world government. Certainly, in the years since the formation of the Trilateral

Commission, the attack on national sovereignty has accelerated.

Confirming his agenda, at a 1995 Gorbachev State of the World Forum, Brzezinski would assert to the assembled internationalists:

> We cannot leap into world government in one quick step....
> [T]he precondition for eventual globalization — genuine
> globalization — is progressive regionalization, because
> thereby we move toward larger, more stable, more
> cooperative units.

Indeed, these larger regional units will be "more cooperative," because they will have been designed by the Insiders, who will also control them.

Admiral Chester Ward

In 1959, Admiral Chester Ward accepted an invitation to join the CFR. Since 1956, Admiral Ward had served as Judge Advocate General for the U.S. Navy. In 1975, after 16 years as a member, instead of supporting the CFR's goals, Admiral Ward denounced the CFR for "promoting disarmament and submergence of U.S. sovereignty and national independence into an all-powerful one-world government."

Admiral Ward further charged that "this lust to surrender the sovereignty and independence of the United States is pervasive throughout most of the membership.... The majority visualize the utopian submergence of the United States as a subsidiary administrative unit of a global government...."[19]

The admiral's claims agreed with the earlier findings of the Reece Committee. In its 1954 report, the Reece Committee concluded that CFR publications "are not objective but are directed overwhelmingly at promoting the globalist concept" and that it had become "in essence an agency of the United States Government ... carrying its internationalist bias with it."[20]

Those who regarded the "merger plan" as merely a wild story back in the 1960s must have done a double take when U.S. and Russian military forces began to train alongside each other at American military bases.

What will be the consequences if the Conspiracy succeeds with its plans to gain total unrestricted power over the planet? In the next section, we will take a look at that question and present some principles for projecting the lines.

Far Fewer Surprises!

Robert Welch compiled an amazing track record for predicting events that baffled many of his contemporaries. However, he claimed that no special talent was required, only a willingness to be guided by hard evidence. We cite here one particularly impressive example.

In April 1961, Robert Welch audaciously predicted the outcome of the anticipated Bay of Pigs invasion of Cuba. He offered his prediction at a public meeting in Los Angeles two or three days *before* the actual invasion took place.

At the time it was an open secret that the invasion was "in the works." Because Mr. Welch had studied the careers of the actors involved, understood the script, and knew to ignore the hype, he did not hesitate to predict to the assembled audience that the invasion would fail.

But Mr. Welch made three further predictions about what would become apparent after the dust had settled:

> First, Castro would have been made tremendously stronger and safer within Cuba itself, because of the anti-Castro patriots who would have been killed or captured. The latent resistance to Castro would have been so discouraged and broken, by the defeat and the reprisals, that Castro would not have to do any serious worrying again about insurrection for a long time to come....

> Second, the United States would have lost immeasurably in prestige, and in damage to any position of moral, political, or military leadership it still had left. For we would not only be publicized and criticized everywhere for having tried to "meddle in the internal affairs of a small nation," but even more because we had completely and pitifully failed in the attempt — so far as our *supposed* purpose of helping the anti-Communists was concerned....

> Third, Castro's prestige would have been greatly enhanced everywhere throughout Latin America, because he would be glorified as the wonderful little Cuban David, who had stood up to, and defeated, that great gringo Goliath, the United States.[1]

Section II

Absolute Evil

Chapter 3

Betrayal of Allies

[H]e that thinks absolute power purifies men's blood and corrects the baseness of human nature need read but the history of this or any other age to be convinced of the contrary.[1]
— John Locke (1632-1704)

Okay, so there is a generations-spanning Conspiracy that seeks total power over the planet. What can Americans expect should this Conspiracy reach its goal? In this section, we'll look at that question. It is an important question, because a solid understanding of the seriousness of the threat is fundamental to the commitment Americans can be expected to bring to a solution.

Although no one has a crystal ball, there are principles of projection that have proven reliable throughout history. One is the famous axiom expressed by Lord Acton: "Power tends to corrupt and absolute power corrupts absolutely."[2]

Another reliable standard is to judge future performance by past performance, especially when it comes to tyranny. Patrick Henry would use that standard in his famous "Give me liberty or give me death speech" to help propel America toward independence:

> I have but one lamp by which my feet are guided; and that is the lamp of experience. I know of no way of judging the future but by the past. And judging by the past, I wish to know what there has been in the conduct of the British ministry for the last ten years to justify those hopes with which gentlemen have been pleased to solace themselves and the House? — March 23, 1775

In the case of the Conspiracy, the projection should be even more clear cut. We are not dealing with a group that has heretofore had a responsible, even neutral track record. The Conspiracy has already perpetrated enormous crimes on other nations spanning centuries. And, as we shall show in Chapters 4 and 5, the American people, who are the Conspiracy's most formidable target, have already suffered from the Conspiracy's designs, even if they are unaware of the source of the damage.

Early Victims

Perhaps, the first significant victims of the Conspiracy were the people of France. The French revolution and its reign of terror did not result from a spontaneous uprising, as is widely taught. Warnings dating *well before* the event point to Illuminist planning. And Lord Acton observed in his *Lectures on the French Revolution*:

> The appalling thing in the French Revolution is not the tumult, but the design. Through all the fire and smoke we perceive the evidence of calculating organization. The managers remain studiously concealed and masked; but there is no doubt about their presence from the first.

Lord Acton's comment notwithstanding, the tumult and atrocities were indescribable. The barbarism that became commonplace during the French Revolution served as prototypes for modern totalitarian experiments in terror of both the Communist and Nazi varieties.

The Illuminist conspiracy, which precipitated the French Revolution, was conceptually, and quite likely organizationally, the grandparent of the modern Conspiracy, including its Communist branch.

Of course, the French Revolution was evil ran amok. One would reasonably demand a good deal of evidence before putting America's smiling, well mannered leaders and TV personas in the same category as a Stalin, a Mao, a Hitler, or those who generated the barbarism of the French Revolution. Such harsh judgments do not play well to reasonable people.

Our task is not to render judgment on individual participants, but rather to be honest about the character of the Conspiracy itself, and not, as Patrick Henry warned, "shut our eyes against a painful truth" or find ourselves among "those who, having eyes, see not, and having ears, hear not...." Nevertheless, it may be helpful to remember that most of those involved in political conspiracies do not themselves pull the triggers or even have a taste for such violence.

One *can* be corrupted by evil and decide to serve evil, while separating oneself, in one's own mind, from the consequences and the excesses.

Regardless of how they might rationalize their actions, some American leaders do have a great deal of innocent blood on their hands, albeit indirectly. That track record is what we will look at next.

Track Record Abroad

In the previous century, unbeknownst to most Americans, the U.S. government, under the influence and grip of the Insiders, repeatedly betrayed nations, even allies, into Communist hands. The track record starts with the Russian revolution itself.

Contrary to popular history, the Communists didn't overthrow the Czar in March 1917. Lenin and Trotsky had been exiled and were not even in Russia at the time. The Czar was overthrown by a combination of liberal and social revolutionaries who sought political revolution not a complete remaking of society. Alexander Kerensky, a social democrat, headed up the new provisional government.

The Kerensky regime lasted only a few months. Lenin and Trotsky returned, and with outside aid, organized the Bolsheviks to overthrow the provisional government in November.

Up to that time, Russia had been a U.S. ally in World War I. American Insiders, in particular Colonel Edward Mandell House, played a role in Trotsky's return to assist Lenin in the Communist conquest of Russia.[3] And others helped to bankroll the revolution.[4]

In his 1994 book, *Death by Government*, University of Hawaii Professor R. J. Rummel estimates that the Soviets, during six decades, murdered nearly 62 million human beings. By way of comparison, Rummel notes that this death toll is more than four times the battle dead for all nations during World War II.[5]

What few Americans recall from history is how fragile the Red regime was from the outset. But the Communist government had friends among America's Insiders.

In the 1920s, American enterprise was encouraged to invest in building up Soviet industry. Then, in 1933, President Roosevelt rescued the Soviet Union from financial collapse by extending it diplomatic recognition. Overt aid from the West has continued ever since.

At every critical juncture, when the Soviet regime got into serious trouble, U.S. policymakers moved to bail the Soviets out. What few Americans understand is that the Soviet Union would likely have collapsed without such aid. During this time, Russia would begin to gobble up its neighbors and commit genocide on its own and neighboring peoples.

"I Saw Poland Betrayed"

American Insiders also betrayed Poland and Eastern Europe into Soviet hands at the end of World War II. Arthur Bliss Lane, U.S. ambassador to Poland from 1944 to 1947, witnessed the betrayal by U.S. leaders first hand. He resigned his post and attempted to alert the American people to what was happening with his book entitled *I Saw Poland Betrayed*. Many other countries friendly to the U.S. would see their governments and peoples similarly betrayed.

Operation Keelhaul

What became officially known in Pentagon records as "Operation Keelhaul" was arguably one of the most heartless mass betrayals *of friends* in modern history. Yet amazingly, this gigantic crime is almost entirely unknown to Americans, except for the soldiers still living who had been ordered to take part.

Operation Keelhaul refers to the forced repatriation of somewhere between two and five million refugees from Communist slavery back into Stalin's hands at the close of the World War II. These refugees included not only civilian women and children who had fled Soviet territory, but tens of thousands of men who had fought valiantly with us in *our* uniform against the Germans.

In addition, millions of soldiers from several anti-Communist armies were disarmed, deceived, and delivered to the Communists for execution or slave labor.

Stalin was very interested in the fate of these refugees, because he knew that, if left where they were, they would provide strong opposition to his plans to annex Central Europe. So he demanded that all refugees from Soviet rule since 1939 be returned to Russia.

Incredibly, General Eisenhower agreed to make it the job of the armies of occupation to carry out Stalin's demand. Reluctant British and American soldiers had to force the refugees into trucks and cattle cars at bayonet point.

The refugees, largely white European Christians who had escaped Stalin's horror, were then transported to Soviet territory. There are film records of mothers tossing their babies off a bridge into freezing waters and then jumping to their deaths rather than return to Communism. Many of the American and British soldiers tasked with this work broke under the strain and refused to participate. Others drove their trucks into forests and let the refugees escape.[6]

"May God Forgive Us"

In the years immediately following World War II, American Insiders with the help of American Communists would betray China into Communist hands. China, under Chiang Kai-shek, had been our ally during World War II, but at the end of the war he faced a revolutionary Communist insurgency led by Mao Tse-tung. Mao's guerilla terrorist war was given a huge boost when our Russian "allies" allowed Mao to gain control of Japanese arms surrendered in China.

However, the Russian support was not sufficient to ensure Chiang's defeat and the delivery of China into Communist hands. Incredibly, our government turned the tide against Chiang by repeatedly undermining our former ally: We forced cease-fires upon Chiang just when his military was making progress. General George Marshall put pressure on Chiang to form a coalition government with the Communists. And then, in March of 1946, the U.S. implemented a 10-month embargo on the sale or shipment of arms to Chiang, even holding up arms Chiang had paid for.

When instituting the embargo, General George Marshall would boast: "As Chief of Staff I armed 39 anti-Communist divisions; now with a stroke of the pen I disarm them." Stockpiles of arms on their way to Chiang were actually destroyed in India.

The struggle in China was constantly misrepresented to the American people to prevent them from understanding the betrayal. Chiang's government was portrayed as corrupt, and Mao was described as an agrarian reformer rather than a Communist.

The secretly pro-Communist U.S. State Department cooperated in this disinformation and covered up news that would have revealed the true character of Mao's revolution. When the Chinese Communists murdered a young U.S. army war hero, Captain John Birch, while on an official U.S. mission after the surrender of the Japanese, the State Department swept his murder under the rug. The State Department even lied to Captain Birch's parents about what had happened to their son.

A number of books have recorded these tragic and treasonous events.[7] In 1952, the Henry Regnery Company published Robert Welch's *May God Forgive Us*, summarizing this incredible betrayal by our own government.

There have been numerous estimates of the death toll from the resulting Communist genocide. From his research, Professor Rummel offered a conservative estimate of more than 35 million deaths — approximately one of every 20 Chinese.[8] A Senate subcommittee had estimated the death toll at 64 million, almost double this figure.

The undeniable Chinese genocide has not prevented globalist-minded Insiders in this country from supporting their Communist agents in Beijing. Returning from a 1973 trip to China, David Rockefeller had the gall to claim: "Whatever the price of the Chinese Revolution, it has obviously succeeded.... The social experiment in China under Chairman Mao's leadership is one of the most important and successful in human history."[9]

Henry Kissinger, Nelson Rockefeller's protégé and secretary of state under Richard Nixon, undoubtedly reaped enormous profits for the Insider team from the opening up of China. The *Wall Street Journal* claimed that Kissinger Associates had obtained a $7 million contract with the Chinese government.[10] And David Rockefeller's Chase Manhattan became the first Western bank to open in Communist China.

But it would be a mistake to suppose that profits were the primary motive behind Insider support for the Chinese Communists.

The "unfortunate publicity" of Chinese troops mowing down student protestors in the 1989 Tiananmen Square massacre caused nary a blip in U.S.-Chinese relations. In his newspaper column, Kissinger described the massacre as "inevitable," insisting that "[n]o government in the world would have tolerated having the main square of its capital occupied for eight weeks by tens of thousands of demonstrators...."[11]

Within a few weeks of that massacre, U.S. officials Lawrence Eagleburger (formerly of Kissinger Associates) and Brent Scowcroft (former chairman of the CFR's membership committee) would travel to China to reassure the Chinese leaders of continued U.S.-Chinese relations.

Recall Carroll Quigley's claim that the international network he had studied and been close to "has no aversion to cooperating with the Communists ... and frequently does so."

"Arch-capitalist" David Rockefeller has been a welcome guest in Moscow and Beijing. During a 1982 visit to Communist Zimbabwe, he made it clear that "[w]e [Chase Manhattan bank] have found we can deal with just about any kind of government, provided they are orderly and responsible."[12] And the people be damned!

Clearly, the lives of all of us would be at great risk should Rockefeller and his fellow Insiders gain total control of the planet.

Genocide in Tibet

The Chinese people were not the only casualties of the U.S. betrayal of China. In 1950 China would invade the peaceful mountain kingdom of Tibet and begin a campaign to eradicate all vestiges of Tibetan civilization. According to the Dalai Lama, the religious leader of Tibet, the Communists have murdered in the neighborhood of 1.2 million Tibetans.[13]

The State Department refused to recognize the Dalai Lama as the political leader of Tibet or his government in exile. China's forcible occupation of Tibet continues to this day. Apparently, American Insiders, who have no problem cooperating with "responsible governments," do not want to rock their China boat.

The Hungarian Revolt

In 1956, the peoples of several of the captive nations of Europe were restless and demanding independence from Moscow. Especially so in Hungary. With the encouragement of U.S. broadcasts behind the Iron Curtain, Hungarian freedom fighters came out in the open and courageously fought Soviet tanks with home-made Molotov cocktails. Some of the tank commanders, sympathizing with the

Hungarian people, joined the freedom fighters. Incredibly, the Hungarians managed to seize control of their capital city, Budapest. The events were recorded and broadcast in inspiring news footage.

Soviet reinforcements were poised on the borders to invade Hungary. But the Soviets, not wanting a confrontation with the West, waited to see whether the U.S. would support the freedom fighters with more than words.

The courageous freedom fighters knew their situation was desperate and eagerly looked for aid from the West. A few cargo planes landed, but the disappointed freedom fighters found food supplies rather than arms. Then came the betrayal.

On November 2, 1956 the U.S. State Department sent an incredible message to Tito, the Communist dictator of Yugoslavia. The message reaffirmed U.S. support for Tito's allegedly moderate regime. But amazingly it also betrayed the Hungarian revolution by signaling our opposition to the creation of anti-Communist governments in Eastern Europe: "The Government of the United States does not look with favor upon governments unfriendly to the Soviet Union on the borders of the Soviet Union."[14]

With this reassurance, Soviet tanks rolled across the border and crushed the revolt.

Several years later, a *New York Times* editorial would blatantly advocate a reprehensible "moral" standard that supposedly justified such betrayals:

> [W]e must seek to discourage anti-Communist revolts in order to avert bloodshed and war. We must, under our own principles, live with evil even if by doing so we help to stabilize tottering Communist regimes, as in East Germany, and perhaps even expose citadels of freedom, like West Berlin, to slow death by strangulation.[15]

Patrick Henry must have turned over in his grave.

Cuba, Nicaragua, and Iran

A string of U.S. betrayals of friendly anti-Communist governments followed a generally common pattern. Globally orchestrated media campaigns would target a pro-Western government as unworthy of support. Then the U.S. State Department, reminiscent of its campaign against Chiang Kai-shek, would withdraw assistance and pressure the pro-Western leader to resign or reach accommodation with Communist-led insurgencies.

As one example, the *New York Times* repeatedly disparaged Cuban President Fulgencio Batista and praised Fidel Castro as the George Washington of Cuba, the Robin Hood of the Sierra Maestra, while concealing Castro's Communist credentials from the American public. Our ambassador to Cuba at the time, Earl E. T. Smith, would complain to the State Department about the pro-Castro CIA men in the U.S. embassy in Havana.[16]

Fidel Castro ascended to power on January 1, 1959. In the years immediately following, the Senate Internal Security Subcommittee would uncover evidence that forces within the U.S. State Department had aided Castro's conquest of Cuba.[17]

With Cuba as a base, Soviet Communism would begin to create insurgencies throughout Latin America. One of the principal targets was the government of Anastasio Somoza, president of Nicaragua. Incredibly, the Sandinista Nationalist Liberation Front took over the country in July of 1979 after defeating the National Guard in a civil war that lasted only seven weeks.

But there was more to the story. According to Somoza, a West Point graduate, it was President Jimmy Carter who gave the orders that forced Somoza out of Nicaragua and put the Sandinista Communists in power. To confirm his claim, Somoza had taped conversations with Carter's official representatives. Transcripts were included by Jack Cox in his 1980 book, *Nicaragua Betrayed*, based on extensive interviews with Somoza.[18]

When President Somoza resigned in 1979, he fled to Miami, where he was denied the sanctuary promised by the Carter administration.[19] Somoza then fled to Paraguay, where he was killed by a Communist assassination team the following year.

To help destabilize the Somoza government, the U.S. government had delayed loans agreed to by the World Bank and successfully embargoed all shipments of ammunition to Somoza's army. In contrast, the Sandinista forces were well supplied by Cuba and the Soviet Union. A few weeks before Somoza's capitulation, then-Secretary of State Cyrus Vance reportedly told representatives of the

Organization of American States that "the government of Anastasio Somoza should be replaced."[20]

Similarly, the U.S. helped to overthrow Shah Pahlevi of Iran, who was very friendly to the West. The American people are now being lobbied on the necessity of going to war with Iran.

These betrayals of America's allies, the resulting massive death and suffering, the purges of religion and values of truth and decency, all demonstrate clearly the evil nature of the Conspiracy.

Chapter 4

The War *Against* U.S. Independence

If it be the pleasure of Heaven that my country shall require the poor offering of my life, the victim shall be ready. But while I do live, let me have a country, or at least the hope of a country — and that of a free country. But whatever may be our fate, be assured ... this declaration will stand. It may cost treasure, and it may cost blood, but it will stand, and it will richly compensate for both.... And live or die, survive or perish, I am for the declaration. It is my living sentiment, and, by the blessing of God it shall be my dying sentiment. Independence now, and independence forever.[1]

— John Adams, 1776

The betrayals discussed in the previous chapter should provide sufficient warning as to what Americans can expect if these internationalists ever achieve unaccountable power. But there is even clearer evidence of the evil that directly threatens Americans.

Since the Conspiracy's principal goal is to build a totalitarian order over the entire planet, it must destroy America's constitutional order — in particular, it must eliminate U.S. independence and sovereignty. And it is well along in doing so.

As a matter of strategy, the Conspiracy's attack has also included steps to centralize power in the federal executive at the expense of the other two branches — the judicial and legislative — and at the expense of the states and the people.

Let's examine this attack on our constitutional order and see what it means to Americans.

The Constitution implements a philosophy of limited government. It very carefully spells out which branches will have what specific authority. And those branches are clearly limited to those functions. Nothing in the Constitution empowers the federal government to delegate any authority over the U.S. to international institutions, such as the UN, even through treaty. Only an amendment could properly do this.

But obviously the clear language of the Constitution cannot

enforce itself. And in the absence of sufficient public alarm, serious usurpations of constitutional authority are being strengthened through precedent. In fact, the greatest long-term threat to our constitutional order is the *unconstitutional* subordination of the U.S. to institutions set up by the internationalists — institutions such as the UN, the World Trade Organization, UNESCO, NAFTA, many others, and others in development yet to come.

The Goal of World Government

In the April 1974 issue of *Foreign Affairs*, the journal of the Council on Foreign Relations, future Trilateralist Richard N. Gardner openly admitted that world government was the objective of his fellow internationalists. But he endorsed the deception of the salami approach for destroying national sovereignty:

> In short, the "house of world order" will have to be built from the bottom up rather than from the top down. It will look like a great "booming, buzzing, confusion," to use William James' famous description of reality, but an end run around national sovereignty, eroding it piece by piece, will accomplish much more than the old-fashioned frontal assault.[2]

So what would the loss of our national sovereignty mean?

Our constitutional order provides the foundation that has allowed America to enjoy the blessings of unprecedented prosperity and freedom. Under a UN-managed order, Americans would be conscripted freely to fight in UN wars, and we would lose the protection of our Bill of Rights, to name just two consequences. America would be in essentially the same shape as if we had been conquered by a foreign power.

Empowering the UN

Although the Insiders have patiently followed the strategy of gradualism described by Richard Gardner through a dizzying array of international ties and agreements, a more direct attack has long been underway on an essential element of any nation's sovereignty — the control if its military.

In 1961, the Kennedy State Department under the leadership of CFR-Insider Dean Rusk developed an incredibly subversive program to transfer control of America's military might to the United Nations. The program carried the full title of *Freedom From War: The United States Program for General and Complete Disarmament in a Peaceful World*. The full text was published as Department of State Publication 7277.

President Kennedy actually presented *Freedom From War* personally before the 16th General Assembly of the United Nations on September 25, 1961. This official plan maps out a program for the *transfer* of arms to the United Nations in three stages:

> In Stage III progressive controlled disarmament ... would proceed to a point where *no state would have the military power to challenge the progressively strengthened U.N. Peace Force*. [Emphasis added.]

Clearly, "no state" includes the United States. If this plan succeeded, then in Stage III the United States would no longer have the military power to challenge any action taken against it by the "friendly, benevolent" world authority and would have to comply fully with UN decisions.

Freedom From War also makes it clear that the term "General Disarmament" in its title is a serious misrepresentation. While *nations* would disarm, a new superpower controlled by the Insiders — the United Nations — would be armed:

> The progressive steps to be taken during the final phase of the disarmament program would be directed toward the attainment of a world in which:
>
> (a) States would retain only those forces, non-nuclear armaments, and establishments required for the purpose of maintaining internal order; they would also support and *provide agreed manpower for a U.N. Peace Force....* [Emphasis added.]
>
> (d) The peace-keeping capabilities of the United Nations *would be sufficiently strong* and the obligations of all states

under such arrangements sufficiently far-reaching as to assure peace and the just settlement of differences in a disarmed world. [Emphasis added.]

This is essentially the same dream that drove Colonel House and his colleagues to create the League of Nations. When the U.S. "failed" to join the League, the Insiders regrouped and created the CFR whose brainchild was the United Nations. But the UN accepted by the Senate following World War II was a watered-down version, just a foot in the door, of what the Insiders really wanted. *Freedom From War* outlines steps to take it to the next stage of authority.

Incredibly, this so-called disarmament plan, presented at the height of the Cold War, would have placed supreme military power in the hands of the UN's Undersecretary for Political and Security Council Affairs. This was the UN post overseeing all UN military activity. By secret agreement at the founding of the UN, this post had always been in the hands of an official from the Soviet bloc!

As a public document, *Freedom From War* still tried to camouflage its full intent with high-sounding appeals to international cooperation and security in a peaceful world. It even referred to "independent nations" — a ridiculous contradiction:

The over-all goal of the United States is a free, secure, and peaceful world of *independent states* adhering to common standards of conduct and subjecting the use of force to the rule of law, a world which has achieved general and complete disarmament *under effective international control,* and a world in which adjustment to change takes place in accordance with the principles of the United Nations. [Emphasis added.]

Not surprisingly, the Establishment media never sought to explain the details and implications of "7277" to a trusting public. For a brief time, the document could be purchased from the Government Printing Office by anyone knowledgeable enough to ask for it, but when demand rose, it was allowed to go out of print.

At the same time as the Kennedy State Department unveiled *Freedom From War*, a classified study was being prepared for the

State Department that candidly discussed the objective of establishing a world government.

Lincoln P. Bloomfield

We are speaking of a secret study prepared under contract with the State Department by the private Institute for Defense Analyses.[3] On March 10, 1962, the Institute delivered Study Memorandum No. 7, *A World Effectively Controlled By the United Nations*, written by MIT professor Lincoln P. Bloomfield.

Dr. Bloomfield had served as an adviser to various administrations and just prior to the study he had served with the State Department's disarmament staff. It is safe to say that he understood the thinking at State. As a member of the Council on Foreign Relations, he also held Establishment credentials. While writing the report, Dr. Bloomfield was director of the Arms Control Project at the Center for International Studies, Massachusetts Institute of Technology.

As a classified document, the Bloomfield report was clearly intended for an exclusive, trusted audience of fellow internationalists. Here is the document's opening paragraph, under the heading SUMMARY:

> A world effectively controlled by the United Nations is one in which "world government" would come about through the establishment of supranational institutions, characterized by mandatory universal membership and some ability to employ physical force. Effective control would thus entail a preponderance of political power in the hands of a supranational organization.... [T]he present UN Charter could theoretically be revised in order to erect such an organization equal to the task envisaged, thereby codifying a radical rearrangement of power in the world.

Bloomfield repeatedly emphasizes a key point: "[I]t is world government we are discussing here — inescapable." Under "Definitions" he notes: "Finally, to avoid endless euphemism and evasive verbiage, *the contemplated regime will occasionally be referred to unblushingly as a 'world government.'*" [Emphasis added.]

Bloomfield also makes it clear that the United States would be trapped in this "contemplated regime":

> National disarmament is a condition sine qua non for effective UN control....
> The essential point is the transfer of the most vital element of sovereign power from the states to a supranational government....
> The overwhelming central fact would still be the loss of control of their military power by individual nations.

The Bloomfield study further advocates:

> The appropriate degree of relative force would, we conclude, involve total disarmament down to police and internal security levels for the constituent units, as against a significant conventional capability at the center backed by a marginally significant *nuclear* capability. [Emphasis added.]

Unfortunately, Dr. Bloomfield's study is not just some utopian pipe dream. As we shall see, the study outlines what has become the fixed and determined policy of the U.S. government, regardless of the administration and regardless of party politics.

War Powers

These "disarmament" policies clash head on with our Constitution. Simply put, the U.S. Constitution authorizes no such delegation of military force and authority. Let's pause for a moment to review the plan of our Founding Fathers for a U.S. military and how it was to be used. This is the plan — our Constitution — that was accepted by the required nine States in 1788. These features have never been amended.

Don Fotheringham has testified before more than a dozen state legislatures on constitutional matters. In his studies, he has intensely reviewed the records of the 1787 Convention. In a recent article Fotheringham noted that "more time and deliberation went into the question of executive power — and the means of restraining it — *than any other consideration at the Convention.*"

Alexander Hamilton had made a similar observation. Regarding executive power, Hamilton wrote: "There is hardly any part of the system which could have been attended with greater difficulty in the arrangement of it than this."[4]

Fotheringham further observes:

> Many are surprised to learn that the Constitution makes no allowance for executive war powers or presidential emergency power of any kind. No, the president cannot commence or declare war, suspend the Constitution, ignore the Bill of Rights, declare martial law, or circumvent any restraint on his proper authority in times of exigency. This deliberate, carefully considered omission of power applies at all times to all U.S. presidents. Their power to *manage* military operations does not include power to *determine or initiate* war.
>
> Our nation's founders delegated the power to make war and all provisions for war entirely to Congress. Only Congress is authorized to declare war; raise and support our military forces; call up the national guard; appropriate the money for war; make all rules concerning captures on land and sea; provide and maintain a navy; make rules for the government and regulation of the armed forces; to provide for organizing, arming, and disciplining the national guard, and for governing such part of them as may be employed in the service of the United States.... (See Article I, Section 8.)
>
> From records of the Convention, we learn that "the Executive should be able to repel and not to commence war." As commander in chief of U.S. military forces he is to conduct the operations of war in defense of our country. He is our top military leader authorized to engage the enemy in response to a declaration of war issued by Congress, and he must look to Congress for the men, money, and materiel needed in such times of national emergency.[5]

Ever since World War II, Congress has shirked its responsibility to declare war and has allowed presidents to usurp its authority. Although our men have fought in several wars since that time, not once has Congress provided the constitutionally required declaration. Congress has realized that an uninformed public would base its support for a president's action based on his popularity ratings, rather than on poorly understood constitutional principles.

James Madison, often referred to as the Father of the Constitution, explained why the Constitution was written the way it was:

> Of all the enemies to public liberty war is, perhaps, the most to be dreaded, because it comprises and develops the germ of every other. War is the parent of armies; from these proceed debts and taxes; and armies, and debts, and taxes are the known instruments for bringing the many under the domination of the few.... No nation could preserve its freedom in the midst of continual warfare....[6]

> The constitution supposes, what the history of all governments demonstrates, that the Executive is the branch of power most interested in war, and most prone to it. It [the Constitution] has accordingly with studied care, vested the question of war in the Legislature.[7]

Alexander Hamilton further elaborated the principle in the first Pacificus essay:

> In this distribution of powers the wisdom of our Constitution is manifested. It is the province and duty of the Executive to preserve to the Nation the blessings of peace. The Legislature alone can interrupt those blessings, by placing the Nation in a state of War.

Much later, Abraham Lincoln would write a particularly insightful summary of the Founders' intent in a letter to his law partner:

> The provision of the Constitution giving the war-making power to Congress was dictated, as I understand it, by the following reasons: Kings had always been involving and impoverishing their people in wars, pretending generally, if not always, that the good of the people was the object. This

our Convention understood to be the most oppressive of all Kingly oppressions, and they resolved to so frame the Constitution that no one man should hold the power of bringing this oppression upon us.[8]

Scamming the American People

Ever since *Freedom From War* was introduced in 1961, its agenda has remained the fixed policy of the U.S. State Department. CFR members in both Republican and Democrat administrations have labored to advance this treasonous agenda. However, their success in moving such a significant revolution forward has often depended on help from "external" events, also orchestrated by the Conspiracy. Here is an example.

The following sequence of events begins in 1992 during the final year of the presidency of George Bush (the senior). Bill Clinton would deny President Bush a second term in the November elections that year. It would be a busy year for the Insiders in their attempt to speed up the arming of the UN to function "as envisioned by its founders" — a vision never advertised to the public when the Senate agreed to U.S. membership back in 1945.

- On January 31, 1992, the UN Security Council convened for the first time ever at the level of heads of state. At that meeting the Security Council ostensibly directed UN Secretary General Boutros Boutros-Ghali to report back by July 1st with recommendations for strengthening the UN's peacekeeping capabilities.

- In June of that year, Boutros-Ghali delivered the requested recommendations in a report entitled *An Agenda for Peace*. Boutros-Ghali's report called for UN members to designate troops to be kept on standby for use by the Security Council and for "permanent" arming of the UN. It also came up with a list of "new risks" to the world's "stability," demanding UN attention.

- In August, presidential candidate Bill Clinton indicated his support for "a new voluntary U.N. rapid deployment force."[9]

- In his September 21, 1992 address to the United Nations, President Bush pledged U.S. support for expanded UN peacekeeping operations and applauded Boutros-Ghalis' call "for a new agenda to strengthen the United Nations' ability to prevent, contain, and resolve conflict across the globe."

- The CFR's *Foreign Affairs* and editorials in the *New York Times* greeted these proposals with great enthusiasm.[10]

- The Winter 1992/93 issue of *Foreign Affairs* published "Policymaking for a New Era," an open memorandum to president-elect Clinton from a "bipartisan" commission co-sponsored by the Carnegie Endowment for International Peace and the Institute for International Economics. The memorandum stated:

> This commission believes that greater American support for both U.N. peacekeeping and peacemaking efforts is a national security objective in which policy and a reorganizational effort should move forward together.

Here are two of the proposals offered by the "bipartisan" commission:

> [E]stablish a major military command, headed by a three- or four-star officer, to support U.N. military operations and, if necessary, U.S. participation in them....
> [D]esignate one or two U.S.-based brigades for support of U.N. operations.

What a farce! The entire sequence was orchestrated to appear as the consensus of independent leaders coming to the same conclusion — that it was imperative to empower the UN. The CFR-Insider hand is visible at every stage: The UN secretary-general is simply a stooge for the CFR. And the Establishment's Carnegie Endowment is Alger Hiss's old stomping ground investigated by the Reece Committee.

In addition, the Institute for International Economics (IIE) is a Washington, D.C. Trilateralist group. David Rockefeller, formerly

Chairman of the Council on Foreign Relations, served on the board of IIE. The IIE director was C. Fred Bergsten, a prominent member of David Rockefeller's Trilateral Commission and assistant secretary of the treasury under Carter.

After he was sworn in as president, Clinton would appoint more than a half dozen members of this "bipartisan" advisory commission to top level spots in his administration.[11]

Presidential Decision Directive 13

Once in office, President Clinton wasted little time in moving the CFR's UN agenda forward. His administration issued a secret presidential decree concerning U.S. involvement in UN military operations. The decree was known as Presidential Decision Directive 13. Portions of PDD-13 were leaked to the press.

According to the *New York Times*, PDD-13 envisioned "an expanded role in United Nations peacekeeping operations that would include having Americans serve under foreign commanders on a regular basis."[12]

The news prompted considerable opposition from the public and Congress. But President Clinton remained undeterred. In his September 27, 1993 speech to the United Nations, the president argued:

> The United Nations must also have the technical means to run a modern world-class peacekeeping operation. We support the creation of a genuine UN peacekeeping headquarters with a planning staff, with access to timely intelligence, with a logistics unit that can be deployed on a moment's notice, and a modern operations center with global communications.

But the Somalia fiasco further served to fuel the opposition. A few days following the president's UN speech, Senator Trent Lott addressed the controversy on the floor of the Senate:

> The Clinton Administration appears dedicated to sending the U.S. military into the dangerous seas of multilateral peacekeeping in an effort to elevate the status of the United

Nations into the guardian arbiter of the new world order.

Key to this new vision of the world is creation of a new world army whose singular purpose is to enforce the whims of the arcane United Nations Security Council. The Administration's effort to create a new vision for the U.S. military is embodied, I fear, in a new Presidential Decision Directive, called PDD-13. Under PDD-13, the United States becomes the trainer and bill-payer of an effort to create a military command structure for the Secretary-General of the United Nations.[13]

Responding to the controversy, President Clinton issued another Presidential Decision Directive, PDD-25. An "unclassified" 15-page summary of PDD-25 was released to the public. The ostensible summary was calculated to reassure the public and Congress that the U.S. would not give up its decision-making role over the use of its troops.

Clipping the Eagle's Wings

Since World War II, the Conspiracy has undertaken many steps to clip the wings of the American eagle. The object is clearly to limit America's ability to act independently and increase her *dependence* on other nations and international authority.

In recent decades, America has suffered from deindustrialization and manufacturing flight. Our steel factories have shut down, while the U.S. has helped to build China's steel production. America is even importing raw materials from abroad.

Over the last several decades, America has lost military bases in Iran, the Philippines, and at the Panama Canal. In Vietnam, the U.S. built a seaport at Cam Ranh Bay and an air base at Da Nang, and then with our pullout allowed these facilities to fall into Soviet hands.

In 1978, CFR-members Henry Kissinger, Ellsworth Bunker, and Sol Linowitz arranged (with Senate approval, following a hard-fought battle) to give the U.S. canal in Panama to the Marxist dictatorship of Omar Torrijos Herrera. In addition, the U.S. gave the Panamanian government $400 million to take the world's most strategic waterway off our hands. As part of the deal, we agreed to abandon our military defense installations adjacent to the Canal.[14]

Two of our largest military installations were the Subic Bay Naval Station and Clark Air Force Base located in the Philippines. The lease arrangement was due to expire in 1991. After helping to destabilize the friendly Marcos regime, by joining in the Communist-instigated propaganda campaign over human rights abuses, the United States found it could not renew the bases agreement.

"The Best Enemy Money Can Buy"

The betrayal of American interests to build up the Soviet Union went far beyond providing the Soviets with nuclear capability, real or otherwise. It included the formation, nurturing, and frequent rescuing of the U.S.S.R from economic collapse (until the cost got too high and it was time for a new deception — the demise of Communism so that Russia could become a so-called ally of the West).

Our next story starts at the Republican Convention in Miami Beach in 1972. This was the convention that would nominate Richard Nixon to run for a second term as president. A little known research fellow at Stanford University's Hoover Institute addressed the Party's National Security Subcommittee.

The testimony of Dr. Antony C. Sutton was a blockbuster. But it gathered little public attention. Apparently, someone influential got wind of what the professor was going to say and realized that the Insiders would not be pleased. Before Dr. Sutton could address the Subcommittee, the television cameras were removed from the hearing room, the press was excluded, and the press conference, which the Subcommittee had scheduled for Mr. Sutton afterwards, was canceled.[15]

Nevertheless, Dr. Sutton's testimony was later published to much more limited audiences. What Sutton had to say was not only political dynamite, but he had impeccable credentials to back up his statements. For more than a decade the professor had researched the connection between Western technology and Soviet economic development. At that point in his research, Dr. Sutton had written three dry, very scholarly and technical volumes on the subject, each covering a different span of years.

Here are excerpts from Dr. Sutton's blockbuster address to the

Subcommittee summarizing his research:

> I have 15 minutes to tell you about this work. In a few
> words: there is no such thing as Soviet Technology. Almost
> all — perhaps 90-95 percent — came directly or indirectly
> from the United States and its allies. In effect the United
> States and the NATO countries have built the Soviet Union.
> Its industrial *and* its military capabilities. This massive
> construction job has taken 50 years.... It has been carried out
> through trade and the sale of plants, equipment and technical
> assistance....
>
> The history of our construction of the Soviet Union has
> been blacked out — much of the key information is still
> classified....
>
> The United States is spending $80 billion a year on
> defense against an enemy built by the United States and
> West Europe. Even stranger, the U.S. apparently wants to
> make sure this enemy remains in the business of being an
> enemy. Now at this point I have probably lost some of you.
> What I have said is contrary to everything you've heard from
> the intellectual elite, the Administration, and the business
> world, and numerous well-regarded Senators — just about
> everyone.[16]

Sutton went on to present specific examples and to show how we
had continued to build up that enemy during the Vietnam war and
how substantial aid was continuing right along under the Nixon
administration. He pointed in particular to U.S. aid that was then
helping the Soviets to build the massive Kama River truck factory.[17]
Trucks from this factory would support the Soviet invasion of
Afghanistan.

In following years, Sutton would update his research and
summarize the situation in two much more readable books designed
for public consumption: *National Suicide: Military Aid to the Soviet
Union* and *The Best Enemy Money Can Buy.*

This secret policy of building up the Soviet Union continued. In
1982, when discussing the proposed Reagan defense budget, fellow
Republican Senator William Armstrong from Colorado would

complain that the American taxpayer was being asked to shoulder two defense budgets — ours and the Soviets:

> The great irony for Americans who will be asked to tighten their belts in order to pay for our defense needs is that much of the additional money that must be spent on defense is required to offset Soviet weapons that probably could not have been built without our assistance.

In that same speech on the Senate floor, Senator Armstrong also explained: "Most trade with the Communist bloc is financed by loans from Western banks, often at absurdly low interest rates guaranteed by Western governments." [18]

Because of managed news, the public at large got little of this perspective.

Even when pieces of the news did leak out, they were rarely combined to build a complete picture. And then, of course, genuine leadership would have been required to force appropriate action. As an example of news that should have set off alarm bells, during the build-up of the Vietnam War the *Chicago Tribune* reprinted the dispatch of a West German newspaper:

> Weapons of the Polish armed forces are being shipped from Stettin harbor in Poland in ever increasing quantities to ... North Vietnamese harbors.... While on one side of the Stettin harbor American wheat is being unloaded from freighters, on the other side of the same harbor weapons are loaded which are being used against American soldiers.... The Poles receive the wheat [from the U.S.] on credit and they in turn ship their weapons to North Viet Nam on credit. [19]

During that same era, members of The John Birch Society would make use of a filmstrip, *The Great Pretense: How to Finance Communism While Ostensibly Opposing It*, in an attempt to make Americans aware of the treachery that was taking place.

ORGANIZE FOR VICTORY!

Chapter 5

The Conspiracy's War on America

We are fighting against the most cruel, amoral, cunning, ambitious, extensive, powerful, and successfully organized gang of completely merciless criminals the world has ever seen....
— Robert Welch, August 1961 *JBS Bulletin*

Although the Conspiracy has not consolidated its power here, the United States has not escaped the Conspiracy's ravages. In fact, it is hard to imagine a significant problem in our society that the Conspiracy has not *intentionally* made worse for its own subversive purposes.

Yet to blame the Conspiracy credibly for any specific problem would generally require extensive arguments and evidence. That is because the Conspiracy has often succeeded in unleashing other apparently non-conspiratorial forces to perpetuate the damage. So we will examine here only two examples — America's drug problem and international terrorism.

Of course, our primary reason for this examination is to shed light on the character of those we are being asked to trust for leadership and solutions, even if those solutions ultimately mean revolution. What should immediately alarm Americans is the willingness of our leaders to conceal and accept what is really going on, while cynically misdirecting and scamming the public with dangerous non-solutions.

Our War Against Drugs
Everyone knows that the profit motive drives the illegal drug trade. But would any other agenda benefit from seeing America saddled with a growing drug problem? The answer is yes.

The Communists have long been in the business of producing and selling drugs. Their objective: Corrupt the Free World and obtain funding to sponsor other activities such as terrorism.

During the war in Vietnam, heroin was sold to our soldiers at ridiculously low prices in order to get them hooked, undermine their combat effectiveness, and saddle America with the drug habits of returning soldiers.[1] Similarly, the top planners in the Conspiracy chain have long realized that an indulgent or drug-crazed society is easier to subdue.

The Chinese Connection
The Chinese drug trade resulted from a conscious decision of the Communist government, not from Chinese entrepreneurs. By the time that Nixon opened up doors to China, China was the number one producer of drugs in the world.

During the 1950s Harry Anslinger served as the U.S. Commissioner of Narcotics. In response to misleading press reports, he would often explain: "The Mafia was not the biggest drug dealer. This was a false impression. By far the biggest drug dealer was Peking."[2] Anslinger worked tirelessly to get this story out, providing extensive data to the UN and to Congress. He retired in 1962.

In March 1970, John E. Ingersoll, director of the Bureau of Narcotics and Dangerous Drugs, told a House subcommittee: "[T]he countries of Burma, Thailand, Laos, and China (Yunan Province) are sources of opium which moves to Bangkok, Macao, and Hong Kong to be made into heroin which enters the West Coast of the United States."[3]

Dr. Joseph Douglass is an expert on national security issues, who has taught at the Naval Postgraduate School and John Hopkins School of International Relations. Before becoming a consultant to various government agencies, he also served in the government as deputy director, Tactical Technology Office, Advance Research Projects Agency.

In 1984, Dr. Douglass began his research into the origin of drug trafficking. Out of that research came his 1990 book *Red Cocaine: The Drugging of America*, with an introduction by Ray S. Cline, former deputy director for intelligence, CIA. Regarding the Chinese connection, Dr. Douglass reports that Mao began developing a strategy based on drugs long before the Communists took control of mainland China:

> In 1928 Mao Tse-tung, the Chinese communist leader, instructed one of his trusted subordinates ... to begin cultivating opium on a grand scale. Mao had two objectives:

obtaining exchange for needed supplies and "drugging the white [i.e., non-communist] region"....

Mao's strategy was simple: use drugs to soften a target area. Then, after a captured region was secured, outlaw the use of all narcotics and impose strict controls to ensure that the poppies remained exclusively an instrument of the state for use against its enemies....

As soon as Mao had totally secured mainland China in 1949, opium production was nationalized and trafficking of narcotics, targeted against non-communist states, became a formal activity of the new communist state, the People's Republic of China.[4]

For the distribution and smuggling of drugs, Mao would rely heavily on the contacts of the Chinese underworld to connect to organized crime in Europe and the Americas.

During a visit to Egypt in 1965, Chou En-lai boasted of one role for China's expanded poppy production:

The more troops they [the U.S.] send to Vietnam, the happier we shall be, for we feel we shall have them in our power, we can have their blood.... Some of the American soldiers are trying opium, and we are helping them. We are planting the best kinds of opium especially for American soldiers in Vietnam. We want them to have a big army in Vietnam which will be hostage to us and we want to demoralize them. The effect which this demoralization is going to have on the United States will be far greater than anyone realizes.[5]

The Cover-Up
Despite mountains of evidence known to government officials, the facts were withheld from the American public. The cover-up of China's involvement in the drug trade had begun long ago. In a study of Chinese narcotics trafficking, Dr. Stefan T. Possony of Stanford's Hoover Institute observed:

Beginning in the early 1960s, the subject [Communist

China's drug offensive against the United States], which originally had attracted great attention, became an "unsubject," to paraphrase Orwell.[6]

Dr. Douglass confirms the U.S. government's efforts to conceal the evidence:

[N]otwithstanding the overwhelming evidence on the role of China, the White House ... issued instructions in 1972 to U.S. Government officials telling them that the rumors about Chinese drug trafficking were without substance and should be disregarded....[7]

While China has been, and likely remains, the most important producer and organizer in the Golden Triangle, China is rarely listed as a producing country in any of the reports issued by the State Department, the Drug Enforcement Administration, or U.S. Customs.[8]

Soviet, Cuban Connections

Meanwhile, the Soviets were also supporting the world narcotics trade. One of the best sources of information on the Soviet drug offensive was General Major Jan Sejna, who defected to the West in 1968. Sejna was a high official in the Czech government who had worked regularly with top officials of the Soviet Union and other Soviet bloc nations.

Unfortunately, as Douglass points out, General Sejna defected at a time when *detente* was riding high. Rather than welcoming him as a hero, U.S. officials sought to minimize Sejna's significance and eventually to discredit him. Douglass, however, saw the story quite differently:

General Sejna had also turned over to the CIA secret and top secret documentation he had brought with him, carefully selected by him for its wide-ranging importance. He was never asked one question about these documents or the material they contained. While the documents were translated, the translations were never made available to the intelligence community.[9]

What was some of the information Sejna brought with him? Sejna told Douglass that Cuban and East European intelligence services, under the direction of the Soviets, had succeeded in creating a massive narcotics network throughout Latin America by 1965.[10]

On several occasions, Sejna had worked directly with Raul Castro, Fidel's brother, to help set up the network. Several defectors from the Cuban Intelligence Service, the DGI, would confirm that Fidel Castro was working to "load up the United States with drugs." According to DGI officer Rene Rodriguez-Cruz, Fidel Castro believed that "drugs are the best way to destroy American society without troops or guns."[11]

Yet the Clinton administration would accept Castro's claim that his regime was making every effort to stop drug shipments through Cuban airspace and territorial waters. Florida Representative Lincoln Diaz-Balart disagreed:

> The participation of the [Castro] tyranny in narco-trafficking has not diminished, but has increased. And the Clinton Administration continues systematically covering up that participation in spite of the fact that the North American intel community knows the details of said participation very well.[12]

Our New "Allies" in the Drug War

In recent years, the executive branch has gone far beyond covering up Chinese and Russian involvement in the drug trade. Incredibly, the principal drug-pushers have now been embraced as *allies* in the war on drugs.

In November 1996, China hosted a forum sponsored by the UN Drug Control Program. A few months later, Zhu Entao, head of the Chinese Interpol bureau, announced that China "has joined the global fight against drug crime" and that it supports international cooperation "in battling international and regional drug trafficking."[13]

America's policymakers and the Establishment media eagerly accepted the disinformation. In 2000, the Clinton administration took steps to form an "alliance" with Beijing to fight drug trafficking. General Barry McCaffrey, head of the U.S. Office of National Drug

Control Policy, traveled to Beijing in June to sign a drug-control pact with the Chinese.

Reporting on the events in Beijing, the *Associated Press* would wax enthusiastically that "the pact opens the door for a broader common fight against drugs."[14]

Yang Fengrui, a top Chinese official in the Ministry of Public Security (MPS) and China's point man on fighting drugs, told foreign reporters: "Drugs are a great problem. It is the source of all evil. It is the enemy of all humanity." AP claimed that Yang's involvement was a "sign of Beijing's commitment to working with Washington."[15]

In a stateside interview, Dr. Douglass responded:

> Red China's security services have been involved for 50 years in implementing the Chinese Communist Party's drug offensive against the West, and are still leading that effort. It's absurd to claim that these official drug pushers mean genuinely to cooperate in curbing their own strategic plans.[16]

However, such pacts will give the "unreformed" Reds new access to U.S. law enforcement practices and information.

A "No-win War"

Michael Levine became the most highly decorated undercover agent in the history of the Drug Enforcement Administration (DEA). His experience and audacity allowed him to penetrate the highest levels of the Latin American drug trade. Yet he retired from the DEA in 1989, a disillusioned man still determined to make a difference. In his 1990 exposé *Deep Cover*, Levine writes:

> It is both sobering and painful to realize, after twenty-five years of undercover work, having personally accounted for at least three thousand criminals serving fifteen thousand years in jail, and having seized several tons of various illegal substances, that my career was meaningless and had had absolutely no effect whatsoever in the so-called war on drugs. The war itself is a fraud....[17]

One of the favorite inside jokes of John Lawn (DEA

administrator and chief narcotics enforcement officer in the U.S.) is to quote ex-President Reagan: "We've turned the corner in the war on drugs." It's a line that always gets a laugh among the suits. Well, the time has come for the American public to be let in on the joke.[18]

New Pretexts for World Government

For several decades following World War II the greatest pretext for empowering the UN was the fear of a nuclear holocaust. For example, the introduction to *Freedom From War* (1961) reads:

> The revolutionary development of modern weapons within a world divided by serious ideological differences has produced a crisis in human history. In order to overcome *the danger of nuclear war now confronting mankind*, the United States has introduced at the Sixteenth General Assembly of the United Nations a *Program for General and Complete Disarmament in a Peaceful World*. [Emphasis added.]

However, the threat of a nuclear confrontation with the Soviets failed to resolve what Lincoln Bloomfield, in his confidential study, termed the "central dilemma in world politics today":

> [G]iven a continuation unabated of communist dynamism, the subordination of states to a true world government appears impossible; but if the communist dynamic were greatly abated, the West might well lose whatever incentive it has for world government.[19]

In other words, Bloomfield argued that for the West to accept world government, the Soviets would need to be transformed and provided a tamer image, but then the paradox — the driving pretext for such a radical plan would be gone.

Unless, Bloomfield postulated in his confidential "study," there was "a crisis, a war, or a brink-of-war situation so grave or commonly menacing that deeply-rooted attitudes and practices are sufficiently shaken to open the possibility of a revolution in world political arrangements."

He further postulated that accelerated world government "may be brought into existence as a result of a series of sudden, nasty, and traumatic shocks.... The transforming experience, whether evolutionary or revolutionary, must, to achieve the foundation of consensus requisite for community, be enough to reach and move great masses of people...."[20]

By the middle of the 1980s, the Insiders were ready to give the Soviets the desired facelift through *glasnost* and *perestroika*. Of course, that meant that they could no longer use the Soviet Union, through the Cold War, as a threat to drive the movement toward world government. Now the Insiders would have to rely on alternate threats. But with its new face-lift, the former Soviet Union could be enlisted as *our partner* in combating these new threats.

Several of the selected threats, such as *drugs, terrorism,* and allegations of *impending environmental catastrophe,* had been around for a time, but the Insiders now moved them to the front burner as *global* crises. The UN, the Establishment media, and cooperating politicians argued that these threats could not be addressed by any one nation but would require global action. This meant that the UN would need new authority to deal with these crises and national governments would need to submit to that new authority.

"The Terror Network"

More than a century and a half ago, Karl Marx wrote: "Only one means exists to shorten the bloody death pangs of the old society and the birth pangs of the new society, to simplify and concentrate them — revolutionary terrorism."[21] Marx's disciples began to apply that principle in the last century, although they generally avoided using the word "terrorism."

The actual beginning of the modern-day international terrorist movement can be traced to a 1964 decision of the Soviet Politburo. Following that decision, the Soviet Union began recruiting terrorists from around the world and training them in Moscow at the Lenin Institute and at Lumumba University and at various camps in the USSR, Czechoslovakia, East Germany, and Cuba.

By January 1966, Fidel Castro would host the Tricontinental Conference, an international gathering of 513 representatives of 83 terrorist groups. Tricontinental would map out a "a global revolutionary strategy to counter the global strategy of American imperialism."[22]

Before the year was out, terrorist training camps in Cuba, under the direction of a colonel in the Soviet KGB, would be training recruits from throughout Latin America. Among the first graduates were the Sandinista Communists who would seize power in Nicaragua in 1979.

Claire Sterling, an American foreign correspondent for several major publications, including the *Reader's Digest* and the *Washington Post*, researched these developments. She discovered that "Castro was training the advance guard of the coming European fright decade — Palestinians, Italians, Germans, French, Spanish Basques — and forming guerrilla nuclei in practically every Western Hemisphere state south of the American border."[23]

More training camps would appear in Eastern Europe, the Middle East, and Asia. But the instructors generally came from the Soviet Union, Cuba, and East Germany. And that's where the thousands of ruthless terrorists were born who could, seemingly in a moment, command the world's attention.

Claire Sterling documented the Soviet hand in this network in her important 1981 book *The Terror Network: The Secret War of International Terrorism*, published jointly by Holt, Rineheart and Winston and Reader's Digest Press.

However, her exposé was ignored in government circles. Insider plans required that the Soviets not be exposed as the orchestrators of modern terrorism. The world's "superpowers" and the major players among nations had to appear clean for the authority of the "international community" to be respected. Nations who did not fit the required image of responsibility were described as "rogue states" in need of *international* supervision.

So, with the aid of the Establishment media, an effective blackout regarding the Soviet hand in terrorism (and drugs) has been maintained. Nevertheless, the evidence of Soviet sponsorship has never been in doubt, nor has it been unknown to the intelligence community or to American presidents and their advisors.

In *The Terror Network*, Ms. Sterling refers to the response of former CIA director William Colby to questions from an Italian reporter. In that exchange, Colby admitted that Moscow and Prague were supporting the Italian terrorists.[24]

And Ms. Sterling also quotes Dr. Hans Joseph Horchem of West Germany's antiterrorist Office for the Defense of the Constitution, "considered one of the West's best informed intelligence analysts." In 1979 Dr. Horchem was particularly blunt regarding Soviet involvement: "The KGB is engineering international terrorism. The facts can be proven, documented, and are well known to the international Western intelligence community."[25]

The important lesson, however, was Ms. Sterling's follow-up comment: "Both men could speak with authority.... But neither was speaking for his government. No Western government has gone so far to indict the Soviet Union. Some have gone pretty far to avoid doing so."[26]

Ray S. Cline, former Deputy CIA Director for Intelligence (1962–1966) and coauthor of the 1984 book *Terrorism: The Soviet Connection*, also summed up the clear evidence:

> It's important to realize that when you say the Soviet Union supports terrorism, you do not mean that they direct and command each terrorist activity. That would be impossible and not very useful. What they do is supply the infrastructure of terror: the money, the guns, the training, the background information, the communications, the propaganda that will inspire individual terrorist groups.[27]

Contrary to the misleading sanitized news regularly offered to the public, there have been no really significant stand-alone terrorist groups. Virtually all the notable groups receive their funding and direction from Russia, China, Cuba, and thinly deniable assets such as Iran, Iraq, Syria, and Libya.

Yet U.S. presidents, influenced by the Insiders, have persisted in covering up the Soviet connection. Moreover, since the "collapse" of the Soviet Union, the disingenuousness and willful blindness have reached new heights. Now the former Soviet Union is supposedly our friend and ally in the war against terrorism.

In January 1989, a few months before the Berlin Wall came down, Secretary of State George Shultz joined representatives of 34 other nations in Vienna to condemn "as criminal all acts, methods, and practices of terrorism, wherever and by whomever committed" and agree that "terrorism cannot be justified under any circumstances."[28]

What a show of contempt for the public! Among the signers of the anti-terrorist agreement were representatives from the Soviet Union, Bulgaria, Czechoslovakia, East Germany, and Hungary — all *supporters* of international terrorism.

That same year, former CIA Director William Colby headed up a joint U.S.-Soviet Task Force to Prevent Terrorism, a public relations ploy. The task force was ostensibly intended to find ways to cooperate in dealing with the growing threat of terrorism.

As far back as the late 1970s, several notable figures and groups tried valiantly to inform the public of the threat of terrorism and move the government to appropriate action. As one example, Congressman Lawrence P. McDonald offered outstanding leadership in the battle to strengthen America's internal security. His Western Goals Foundation produced as its first video documentary — *No Place to Hide: The Strategy and Tactics of Terrorism.*

No Place to Hide aired on CNN eight days following the Soviet shootdown of KAL flight 7. Ironically, Congressman McDonald was aboard that flight. He, along with 268 other defenseless passengers, became victims of a Soviet terrorist act — an event hastily swept under the rug by the Establishment.

The Action Is in the Reaction

Congressman McDonald's video documentary explained that terrorism was to be feared not only for its action but also for the expected *reaction*. In fact, it is the reaction of the target government that sponsors of terrorism seek.

Governments normally respond to terrorist acts by cracking down on liberties to try to achieve order. For the Conspiracy, this dramatic pretext for a crackdown provides an ideal opportunity for consolidating power.

Within hours of the September 11, 2001 terrorist attacks, CFR members began preparing the public for the "revolution in world political arrangements," described by Bloomfield. They insisted that the crisis demanded actions that had long been part of the globalist agenda.

The public was repeatedly told that the U.S. can fight terrorism only through the terrorist-loving United Nations. That the attacks demonstrated the need for the UN's International Criminal Court. And that Americans might have to sacrifice some of their liberties to achieve security.

Lawmakers rushed to show bipartisan support for every Insider objective that could be portrayed as fighting terrorism, including the payment of "back dues" to the UN.

The insanity, or rather duplicity, in counting on the UN to fight a war against terrorism was highlighted a few weeks later when the General Assembly voted overwhelmingly to elect Syria to a two-year term on the Security Council! The Bush administration chose not to oppose Syria's election even though our own State Department had included Syria on its list of state sponsors of terrorism.

On January 31, 2001, a few days after the inauguration of President George W. Bush, the CFR-dominated Hart-Rudman Commission delivered its proposal for an independent National Homeland Security Agency to the new president and his cabinet. This was several months *before* the nation-shaking attacks of September 11, 2001.

And *just three days* after the attacks, the CFR hosted a meeting in Washington, D.C., which publicized the Commission's recommendation. Six days later, President Bush announced the creation of a new Cabinet-level post, the Office of Homeland Security.

To build and maintain an Orwellian security state, there must be a never-ending stream of enemies. The planned "war on terrorism" fills that role to a tee. Secretary of Defense Donald H. Rumsfeld, in a *New York Times* op-ed, predicted that the war on terrorism:

> ... will be a war like none other our nation has faced.... [I]t will involve floating coalitions of countries, which may change and evolve.... This is not a war against an individual, a group, a religion or a country. Rather, our opponent is a global network of terrorist organizations and their state sponsors.... Forget about "exit strategies"; we're looking at a sustained engagement that carries no deadlines.[29]

Rumsfeld could just as easily have promised "perpetual war for perpetual peace." It was difficult not to recall Alexander Hamilton's warning in *The Federalist No. 8*:

> Safety from external danger is the most powerful director of national conduct. Even the ardent love of liberty will, after a time, give way to its dictates. The violent destruction of life and property incident to war, the continual effort and alarm attendant on a state of continual danger, will compel nations the most attached to liberty to resort for repose and security to institutions which have a tendency to destroy their civil and political rights. To be more safe, they at length become willing to run the risk of being less free.

Dismantling Our Layers of Internal Security

The long track record of subversive action by American Insiders makes it difficult not to *suspect* that at least *some deliberately* sought to encourage terrorist attacks against the United States.

In any event, the Conspiracy must be blamed for the evil that has occurred, because the Conspiracy created the Soviet Union and caused our government to keep it alive and even build the Soviet Union into an enemy. And American Insiders have actively covered up the Soviet role in creating terrorism.

But there is another part to the indictment — the decades-long campaign to strip America of her multiple layers of internal security so that she would be naked to terrorist attacks and then *using the resulting catastrophes to drive forward totalitarian measures*.

Until the early 1970s, America could boast of multiple layers of efficient and effective defense against terrorism and subversion. This layered protection also prevented the oppression that could come from heavily centralized police powers.

But this multi-layered security structure began to unravel in the 1970s. During that decade, radicals in Congress succeeded in abolishing the Subversive Activities Control Board, the Internal Security Division of the Justice Department, the House Internal Security Committee, and the Senate Subcommittee on Internal Security. Congress also killed the counter-intelligence units of the armed forces.

Soon to follow were the investigative committees of state legislatures and the intelligence units of state and local police organizations. In 1981, the Senate briefly reestablished the Subcommittee on Security and Terrorism. Constantly underfunded, the Subcommittee was scrapped again in 1987.

The FBI's counterintelligence activities and investigations were also crippled in 1976 by the guidelines issued by Attorney General Edward Levi. Levi served as attorney general under President Gerald Ford. Incredibly, Levi had been a member of the National Lawyers Guild, a notorious Communist front that represented Cuba in American courts.[30] Under pressure, subsequent attorneys general would revise the most restrictive of the disastrous Levi guidelines, a small step at restoring some sanity.

In the December 1984 *Reader's Digest*, Eugene Methvin described the pathetic condition of our internal security apparatus:

> While the terrorists were preparing a massive campaign of kidnapping, assassination, and bombing, the United States had virtually disbanded its domestic-intelligence apparatus. Civil-liberty lawsuits had vitiated or destroyed police-intelligence units across the country. In the five years before the Nyack attack, the FBI's informants in political-terrorist groups had been cut from 1,100 to fewer than 50. When a joint task force was set up to handle the Nyack case, neither the N.Y.P.D. nor the FBI had any worthwhile intelligence files to draw on.

Our congressional investigative committees represented a particularly great loss. An important responsibility of Congress is to hold the executive and judicial branches accountable for upholding our laws regarding internal security. In the past, congressional committees had been so successful in exposing top Soviet agents, such as Alger Hiss, Harry Dexter White, Virginius Frank Coe, Gregory Silvermaster, and many others, that the committees had been targeted for destruction by the Communist Party and its allies.

The committees and their chairmen were accused of "witch hunting," "McCarthyism," and "fascism." Tragically, this propaganda campaign was able to weaken needed support in Congress.

Although the campaign against our internal security apparatus was launched by the Communist Party USA as far back as the 1920s, the Establishment offered no effective resistance and often joined in the attacks, which eventually succeeded in the 1970s.

The campaign was clearly intended to blind law enforcement and intelligence agencies so the terrorists could operate freely. Much of the destruction can be traced to organizations, such as the ACLU, supported by Establishment foundations.

Following the September 11, 2001 terrorist attacks, a new, much more intrusive security apparatus was created to fill the vacuum. But it was a sad exchange. The multi-layered system that had been destroyed was *efficient and compatible with liberty.* It provided invaluable redundancy while dispersing power.

Unfortunately, under the post-9/11 system, a broad-based federalization of police powers concentrates the responsibility for America's security in the hands of one department. It will be very difficult to hold this system accountable for failure or abuse.

Where Are We Headed?

The excesses of government power in the previous century certainly confirm the warnings of Lord Acton and Patrick Henry.

It is frightening to imagine what might happen if such government were global. Could we expect to fare better than those who lost their liberty to Communist totalitarians or to their National Socialist cousins? Let's not forget that the Insiders of this new world order actually nurtured and sustained the Communist menace during the previous century.

Professor R.J. Rummel spent almost a decade studying the unspeakable tragedies of the last century — genocide and mass murder by government. Rummel defined a new term, "democide," as the systematic murder of human beings by governments. The death toll he estimated due to democide boggles the mind:

> In total, during the first eighty-eight years of this [20th] century, almost 170 million men, women, and children have been shot, beaten, tortured, knifed, burned, starved, frozen, crushed, or worked to death; buried alive, drowned, hung, bombed, or killed in any other of the myriad ways

governments have inflicted death on unarmed, helpless citizens and foreigners. The dead could conceivably be nearly 360 million people.[31]

Should we expect the death toll to be any less from unrestrained *world* government? Remember that the orchestrators of the world-government drive insist we must join with the perpetrators of these crimes in order to promote world peace.

More importantly, the perpetrators did not spring up independently. They were the natural offspring of the revolution promoted by the Conspiracy to achieve its world government. It is the Conspiracy, not just its bad children, who really turned the 20th Century into the bloodiest in recorded human history. And it would be that same Conspiracy that would dominate any totalitarian world rule in the 21st.

Nevertheless, the anticipated death toll isn't the only measure of the tragedy planned for us. We should also consider the impact of the Conspiracy's totalitarian rule on the survivors — on the human spirit, on our ability to pass on values and opportunity to our children, and even on our ability to provide succeeding generations with the opportunity to develop their religious faith.

21st Century totalitarian rule would allow nothing — not even the family — to compete for loyalty with the almighty State.

Consider for a moment the distorted "values" elevated by the Conspiracy's "modern" totalitarian societies and what happened when freedom of expression and dissent was suppressed. During the Stalin era, for example, 14-year-old Pavlik Morozov was made into a "Hero of the Soviet Union" for betraying his parents.

Pavlik had snitched to the KGB that his parents were sheltering victims of Stalin's collectivization program. As a result, the father was executed. Farmers, enraged over the betrayal, hanged Pavlik.

But the Soviet tyranny had the last word. A statue was erected to honor Pavlik, his house became a Communist shrine, and The Palace of Culture of the Red Pioneers in Moscow was named after him. In the 60s, author and researcher John Barron revealed that "Komsomol, the youth organization of the Communist Party, teaches Soviet youth that the life and deeds of Pavlik Morozov represent an ideal to which every worthy citizen should aspire."[32]

How about Nazi Germany, another offspring of the Conspiracy?[33] Hitler had his Hitler Youth. In a 1933 speech, Hitler declared: "When an opponent declares, 'I will not come over to your side,' I calmly say, 'Your child belongs to us already.... What are you? You will pass on. Your descendants, however, now stand in the new camp. In a short time they will know nothing else but this new community.'"[34]

In 1939, Hitler made membership in the Hitler Youth mandatory. Leftist historian William Shirer wrote: "Recalcitrant parents were warned that their children would be taken away from them and put into orphanages or other homes unless they enrolled" their children in the program.[35]

The Bottom Line

History shows it is always risky to trust *any* men with absolute power. But tyranny can virtually be guaranteed from *those who already have a track record of treachery and betrayal*. John Locke expressed it perfectly when he warned against the notion that "absolute power purifies men's blood."

Certainly, it can be difficult to imagine the worst of smiling leaders who sound so sincere. But we need to have "eyes that see" and "ears that hear" and realize what and whom these men represent. It is a grave mistake to trust those bent on gaining absolute power, particularly so, if they are unwilling to share their goals honestly with the American people.

Actually, most Insider politicians and leaders are little more than common con-men. Words of concern for the people's needs merely camouflage the basest of agendas. There is no sincere intent — only a lust for power and the people be damned!

We suggest the following corollary to Locke's warning and Lord Acton's dictum: "Expect the worst from those who are arrogantly determined by any means to strip the people of a voice in their own destiny."

ORGANIZE FOR VICTORY!

Section III

Our Positive and Permanent Purpose

Chapter 6

Foundations of Freedom

Although all men are born free, and all nations might be so, yet too true it is, that slavery has been the general lot of the human race.[1]
— James Madison, 1792

In February 1957, Robert Welch addressed an assembly of students and faculty at Dickinson College in Pennsylvania. In his extensive speech, carrying the title "The New Americanism," Mr. Welch chided conservatives for failing to champion something positive in the worldwide ideological struggle with the socialists and communists. And he outlined a different course:

> [W]e conservatives fight always on the defensive. The very name by which we identify ourselves defines our objective. It is to conserve as much as we can, out of all we have inherited that is worthwhile, from the encroachments and destructiveness of this advancing collectivism. We build no more icons to freedom; we merely try to fend off the iconoclast.
>
> Such has been the pattern during the whole first half of the twentieth century. From the bright plateaux of individual freedom and individual responsibility which man had precariously attained there has been a steady falling back towards the dark valleys of dependence and serfdom.... I for one, and many others like me, are no longer willing to consider only when to retreat and how far. There is a braver and wiser course....
>
> We have to be *for* something; we must know what that something is; and we must believe it is worth a fight to obtain. And a great deal of what we are for can be summarized as simply increasing freedom from the tentacles of government.
>
> There are many of us who want America and Americans to take the lead in this fight so rigorously, and to establish so

clearly as their goal those new heights of personal freedom never before reached, that the whole worldwide positive forward movement can be identified and will be identified as americanism, with a little "a," to come to mean not the jingoistic and provincial outlook of a certain geographical area, but a philosophy of freedom to which the courageous and the self-reliant everywhere can subscribe. We want "an americanist" to come to mean any man, no matter in what country he lives, who believes in and supports this philosophy....

There are many stages of welfarism, socialism, and collectivism in general, but communism is the ultimate stage of them all, and they all lead inevitably in that direction....

But there is an exactly opposite direction. It leads toward a society in which brotherhood and kindliness and tolerance and honesty and self-reliance and the integrity of the human personality are considered virtues; a society which venerates those traits exactly because they have helped the human animal to achieve some degree of humanitarian civilization, and are the common denominators of all our great religions. This direction leads towards a governmental environment for human life founded on the basis of long experience with government; on experience which shows government to be a necessary evil, but a continuous brake on all progress and the ultimate enemy of all freedom. It is the forward direction, the upward direction — and americanism, I hope, shall become its name.[2]

Within two years, Mr. Welch would found The John Birch Society — a body of members organized into chapters, providing leadership at the local level in the battle for freedom. His two-day talk at the founding meeting, the transcript of which was published as *The Blue Book*, would incorporate many of the thoughts from his earlier address at Dickinson College.

In addition to the thoughts expressed above, there are other reasons why it is imperative for *an organization*, such as Freedom First Society, to clearly identify what it is for. Any organization that wishes to provide leadership for a realistic program to disable the

Conspiracy must demonstrate a strong commitment to positive values worth championing if it expects to pull together, and hold, sufficient responsible support.

And while organizing that support into an effective force, the organization must articulate positive principles in order to avoid dangerous and tempting traps. Such traps are everywhere. In a battle with an enemy who thrives on sowing confusion, those who merely oppose, without a clear understanding of what is worth supporting, will inevitably end up laboring for something just as bad or wasting their energy pursuing one of the many non-solutions deceptively presented as opportunities.

A related lesson is that the enemy of your enemy is not necessarily your friend. As those in Latvia discovered during the last century, there was little to choose between Naziism and Communism. Even softer forms of collectivism still pave the way for slavery and harsher oppression. A better alternative is clearly the answer.

For This We Fight

We subscribe to Americanism. Americanism is the novel concept that guided the birth of our nation — the idea that government should be the servant of the people not their master, that individuals have God-given rights and "That to secure these rights, governments are instituted among men, deriving their just powers from the consent of the governed." (*The Declaration of Independence*)

According to this view, revolutionary in the 18th Century, governments are the creation of the people, and government, including those in government trusted with authority, should be subordinate to the people.

A republic is the form of government most suited to implementing and protecting this arrangement, whereby the people are ultimately in charge. A true republic is a government of laws, which even the rulers themselves must obey. A written constitution spells out the limits to, and authority for, the actions of those entrusted with authority.

The resulting republic contrasts starkly with the arbitrary rule of men (e.g., an oligarchy), the rule by majority (a democracy), and especially with the rule of the mob (anarchy). In a well designed republic, the law is developed through a process requiring long deliberation. We support the principles of a republic, and we enthusiastically proclaim the wisdom of our Founding Fathers who, with the U.S. Constitution, created the best, practical example of a republic to date.

Our Founding Fathers understood from their study of history and human nature that a carefully crafted republic offered great improvement in protection against the abuse of authority, regardless of its motivation, pretense, and source. Such a governmental system would be most able to secure the rights of individuals, even among minorities, and protect them against the whipped-up passions of the public at large (the mob). Even majorities must obey the law.

We're Not a Democracy

However, since the days of President Woodrow Wilson, who led us into war to "make the world safe for democracy," Americans have been told repeatedly and falsely that the United States *is* a democracy. Too few Americans today are aware that our nation was founded as a republic and that our Founders recognized democracy as one of the worst forms of government. Indeed, James Madison, justly called the Father of the Constitution, wisely observed:

> [Pure] democracies have ever been spectacles of turbulence and contention, have ever been found incompatible with personal security, or the rights of property, and have in general been as short in their lives as they have been violent in their deaths.[3]

Most Americans today think that we have always been a democracy and that our progress and strengths are evidence that democracy should be supported. They do not understand the flaws in democracy, and so, from this error alone, have been beguiled into accepting majority decisions, in contravention of our Constitution, as perfectly proper and legitimate.

Media spokesmen constantly retail the notion that the most important consideration in government is that our leaders can claim a mandate from the majority. Under this phony principle, the greater the number of uninformed citizens who can be induced to cast votes, the more sacred is the leader's resulting authority, as it then represents the "will of the majority." These widespread notions about our form of government provide a dangerous opportunity for any demagogue and especially for the Conspiracy.

Americans today would do well to heed the warning of Benjamin Franklin. As the story is told, upon completing their work in crafting a new Constitution, the delegates to the constitutional convention were leaving when a lady stepped up to Benjamin Franklin and asked him, "What have you given us, Sir?" To which, Franklin replied, "a Republic, Madam, if you can keep it."

Which should beg the question: How can we keep our Republic — preserve, nourish, and maintain it — if we don't even understand what has been entrusted to our care?

Heed the Lessons of History

The Founding Fathers did not invent a new government from scratch. They were great students of history. They were particularly familiar with the Greek and Roman experience with different forms of government and with the great thinkers of the past. Most of the founders were deeply religious. In the Constitution and Bill of Rights, they incorporated the wisdom of the ages.

More than a century ago, the American philosopher and essayist George Santayana observed perceptively: "Those who cannot remember the past are condemned to repeat it." We agree, and so we, too, seek to profit from the lessons of history.

In particular, we recognize that freedom has been a rare condition throughout history. As James Madison observed: "Although all men are born free, and all nations might be so, yet too true it is, that slavery has been the general lot of the human race."

Freedom continues to be rare in many parts of the world today, and its foundations under attack elsewhere. So, at a minimum, the principles that make freedom possible and promote its longevity need to be much better taught, understood, and respected.

Government has been the obvious proximate source of man's oppression. Governments have repeatedly misused their power to enslave their own people. However, the absence of government is not the answer. Government is necessary to establish the rule of law. As Robert Welch expressed the principle: "[I]t is only under the rule of law that civilized man can enjoy any freedom."[4]

The analogy attributed by some to George Washington summarizes well man's relation to government: "Government is not reason; it is not eloquence; it is force! Like fire, it is a dangerous servant and a fearful master."[5]

The lesson is that government must be empowered, but also suitably restrained. So the bigger question becomes, what is necessary to keep government as a servant of the people and prevent it from becoming their master? The answer is anything but straightforward.

In designing a Republic, our Founding Fathers were fully aware of the danger of entrusting men with power. Armed with a healthy skepticism, they built clever checks and balances into the Constitution designed to frustrate any who would seek to alter the balance and accumulate unrestrained, unchecked power. They hoped this would help.

But even a Constitution with clever checks and balances and a foundation of just laws will not by themselves produce a great nation or secure freedom. Far more is required for a nation to enjoy freedom than just the creation of a republic *in form*.

The Founding Fathers certainly did not expect any system of government to run smoothly by itself or to perpetuate itself according to plan merely because the plan was carefully spelled out on paper. They understood that the ultimate check on runaway government would have to be an informed, moral, and responsible people. The character and traditions of the people would determine whether any republic could succeed and freedom prosper.

And to preserve freedom over generations, patriots who heed the lessons of history, such as Robert Welch, must periodically step forward to warn of problems and provide leadership for the strengthening and repair of freedom's foundations.

Big Government — a Step Backwards
In a 1964 debate at Orchestra Hall in Chicago with the renowned socialist Norman Thomas, Robert Welch opened with these remarks:

> Ladies and Gentlemen, the increasing quantity of government, in all nations, has constituted the greatest tragedy of the Twentieth Century. This increasing seizure of

both the rights and responsibilities of individuals, and their absorption into the swollen complex of tyrannical government, is the disastrous trend from which almost all of our other sociological tragedies derive. For in a collectivized setting, and without freedom, man becomes a soulless robot, incapable of progress for himself and rapidly destitute of compassion for others.[6]

This view contrasts sharply with the "wisdom" of so many of today's politicians and their media supporters who suggest that entrusting a bigger role to government is the answer to almost every problem. Not surprisingly, that collective "wisdom" has been orchestrated and encouraged by the Conspiracy. But the Conspiracy is even more duplicitous. It actually breeds and fosters problems to justify the expansion of government authority at the federal and, if possible, even at the international level.

If Americans were familiar with the lessons of honest history, they would realize that our ostensible would-be saviors are advocating a return to what our forefathers fought to liberate us from — big, dominating, intrusive government. History shows clearly that big government, the opposite of freedom, is the enemy of human progress. Socialism, collectivism, and statism (the glorification of the State) are not the wave of the future. They do not represent progress, but, as Mr. Welch strongly insisted, a turning back of the clock.

We are convinced that the only reason these retrograde movements have any force at all today is that they serve the interests of a well organized Conspiracy. That Conspiracy actually seeks power for a few while it deceives the masses into thinking that its programs are intended for their benefit.

Of course, these statist movements are also fueled by ignorance and selfish ambition. But in the absence of the Conspiracy, ignorance and selfish ambition would cause comparatively little damage. Even the big-spending politicians who see the collectivist, statist course as the route to their reelection would not prosper, if they did not have a treasure chest from which to finance the expansion of government.

And, as author Gary Allen wrote in 1975, that treasure chest resulted from successes of the Conspiracy in the early part of the 20th Century:

> The name of the game, since 1913, has been so to alter the nature of our federal government as to make unlimited dictatorship possible. This has been done by arranging higher and then higher taxes, with larger and larger deficits run through the Federal Reserve to insure ever more massive inflation, billions in interest for the Insiders, and ever greater centralization of power in Washington. Of course this appealed to the politicians too. As F.D.R.'s assistant Harry Hopkins put it, the idea was "tax and tax, spend and spend, elect and elect."[7]

As discussed previously, the drive for more government is not limited to national government. The Conspiracy is also behind the drive for a new layer of government — international government — to which all nations and peoples would be forced to submit.

What's Wrong With World Government?

For decades, America's internationalist leaders have insisted, for public consumption, that world government is not in the cards, even as they take steps clearly intended to undermine national sovereignty and bring it about.

However, other organs of opinion molding take a different tack to defuse persistent concerns. They claim that world government should not be feared, since it is as American as apple pie. After all, they tell us, our country was itself formed as the union of independent sovereign states.

Unfortunately, such clever sophistry ignores several vital realities. The most vital reality is the nature and source of the momentum behind the drive for world government today. Americans are not faced with merely the idea of world government, but *a very particular implementation* of world government.

Of course, not all conceivable world governments would be the same, anymore than all forms of national government are the same. There is a big difference between a Nazi Germany, a Stalin's Russia, a banana republic, and the American Republic. So how about the world government that is being promoted, albeit semi-secretly?

Despite the internationalist lip service to "openness" and "transparency," the architects of world government have been anything but open about their aims. An explicit admission of their policy of concealment appeared in the 2002 "Special Davos Edition" of the international edition of *Newsweek* in an especially candid article by the managing editor. In "Death of a Founding Myth," CFR heavyweight Michael Hirsh explained the lengths to which the globalists go to conceal their intentions from the public:

> [T]he internationalists were always hard at work in quiet places making plans for a more perfect global community. In the end the internationalists have always dominated national policy. Even so, they haven't bragged about their globe-building for fear of reawakening the other half of the American psyche, our berserker nativism. And so they have always done it in the most out-of-the-way places and with little ado.

There are no foreseeable plans to have a public referendum on whether we should scrap American independence and subordinate ourselves to a specific world government — at least until the issue becomes merely a matter of ratifying a *fait accompli*. Instead, the internationalists are practicing the "Gulliver" strategy of gradualism. As the Lilliputians did with the giant Gulliver in Jonathan Swift's adventure satire, the internationalists are weaving thousands of threads around America's sovereignty.

The plan is that one day, when the American giant finally awakens, the individually fragile threads will collectively be so strong that America can no longer extricate itself from the clutches of world government.

What a difference in approach to the rights of the people from the way our nation was founded, when each part of the Constitution was fiercely debated prior to ratification by the states.

Our Founding Fathers were able to sell their plan to the people, because, in their understanding of human nature, they had gone to enormous lengths to put checks on the power of the proposed federal government to prevent the accumulation of unaccountable power in any one set of hands.

The restraints needed to safely bind the leaders of a world government would be massive, even if the architects were interested in putting limits on their power. But that is clearly not their intention.

Surely, it would be the height of folly to entrust the reins of such massive power to those power brokers who find it necessary to conceal those aims from the public. Moreover, as we demonstrated in the previous section, there is massive evidence that the architects of world government are totally without scruple. There is no way that they can be acting with the public's interest, even its long-term interest, in mind.

We simply must resist any union under the umbrella of such leadership. For the foreseeable future, Americans who value freedom must insist on national independence and work to extricate our nation from entanglements with international organizations that compromise our sovereignty. In particular, that means the United States must get out of the United Nations. The only safe course in today's world is for America to take charge of its own destiny.

The primary danger in the internationalist clichés is that they are cleverly designed to divert attention from reality — the *Conspiracy* is reality. As long as the Conspiracy has not been washed away, it would dominate *any* world government, and that simply means world tyranny.

World "Peace"

Nevertheless, we must rebut one further internationalist argument — that compulsory world government is the antidote to war between nations. Those who make this claim ignore the fact that there are things much worse than war, such as losing the war to a tyranny.

What should truly be feared is a tyranny so great and powerful that no war to challenge its authority is possible. Such an arrangement would offer peace — the peace of slavery and hopelessness.

There is a much wiser course. In the July 1978 *Bulletin*, Robert Welch explained why he believed that the increasing quantity of government in all nations contributed to the frequency and destructiveness of wars. And he referred to the *Blue Book* to argue for the opposite path:

Reduce all the governments of all the nations of the world to even one-third of their present size — not one-third of their power, please note, nor are we referring to their quality, but to just one-third of their bureaucratic numbers, their extensiveness, their meddling in the lives of their subjects — and you would immediately accomplish two things. You would reduce the likelihood of war between hostile nations to at most one-ninth of its present probability, and the destructiveness of any wars that did take place in the same proportion.

To summarize his point, Mr. Welch deferred to the 19th Century British political leader, Richard Cobden. With brilliantly expressed insight Cobden suggested:

Peace will come to this earth when her peoples have as much as possible to do with each other; their governments the least possible.

As you can see, what Cobden is extolling is not isolationism. But proponents of international *government* entanglements have disingenuously characterized opponents of these entanglements as isolationists, hoping that the epithet would stick.

Instead of allowing government officials to tie nations together through bigger government structures, we can best help the people of other nations improve their lot by setting an inspiring example of limited government and responsibility with our own nation, which others would wish to emulate. It happened once. It really should happen again. And with the help of inspired patriots following a sound plan, it will!

ORGANIZE FOR VICTORY!

Chapter 7

Economic Prosperity
— A Fruit of Freedom

Is life so dear, or peace so sweet, as to be purchased at the price of chains and slavery? Forbid it Almighty God! I know not what course others may take, but as for me, give me liberty or give me death.
— Patrick Henry, 1775

We hold these Truths to be self-evident, that all Men are created equal, that they are endowed by their Creator with certain unalienable Rights, that among these are Life, Liberty, and the Pursuit of Happiness.
— The Declaration of Independence

Religion and morality provide the primary imperative for man to be free. It is man's God-given right to be free. Some would say even his duty, for only as a free agent can man strive to fulfill God's purpose.

Although the primary justification for defending freedom is not economic, nevertheless a very visible fruit of a culture of responsibility and a political system supporting freedom *is* national prosperity.

Fertile Soil of Freedom

Man blossoms to his fullest in the fertile soil of freedom. If we look just at man's economic aspirations, we see that freedom has emboldened man to relieve drudgery, overcome poverty, and achieve unprecedented prosperity.

Henry Grady Weaver in his classic 1947 analysis, *The Mainspring of Human Progress*, examined the American experience in the light of world history and argued persuasively that the mainspring of human progress has been freedom. In leading up to his conclusion, Mr. Weaver asked, "Why did men walk and carry goods (and other men) on their straining backs for 6,000 years — then suddenly, on only a small part of the earth's surface, the forces of nature are harnessed to do the bidding of the humblest citizen?"[1]

Americans created more wealth than all of the other nations combined and were able to enjoy an unrivaled standard of living. "Three generations — grandfather to grandson," noted Weaver, "— have created these wonders which surpass the utmost imaginings of all previous time."[2] Weaver determined how all these wonders came about:

> It all comes back to the matter of individual freedom. We've been free to invent, free to try out new ideas and new methods, free to back up the other fellow's business or go in business on our own, free to take a chance on making a profit or going broke.[3]

Other factors — ideas, tools, natural resources — were also important, admitted Weaver. But the factor that has made the critical difference in raising our nation's standard of living has been freedom:

> ... new ideas are of little value in raising standards of living unless and until something is done about them. The plain fact is that we in America have outdistanced the world in extending the benefits of inventions and discoveries to the vast majority of people in all walks of life.[4]

Productivity stems from the effective use of human energy and better tools applied to natural resources. Freedom promotes the effective use of human energy, but *freedom also supports the constant improvement of tools*. (As a broad economic concept, the term "tools" includes items such as roads, trains and tracks, river delivery systems, electrical energy plants, transmission and distribution systems, and even factories.)

How so? Tools are the product of *investment*. And investment requires that some current consumption be deferred and/or extra effort expended. The motivation for voluntary *private* investment, potentially the greatest such resource, is the carrot of a better future.

That carrot works only when freedom is secure and one can expect to keep the fruits of one's labor and investment — private property.

Freedom simply allows the fundamental ambition to improve one's lot to flourish. In freedom, man is much more willing to sacrifice, work hard, and take risks for a dream.

So the critical factors that promote investment in tools and the use of human energy ever more wisely are simply a secure environment of freedom and respect for property rights. A culture that encourages individual initiative and responsibility is also essential.

Mushrooming Middle Class

Nowhere had these lessons regarding the foundation of prosperity been more dramatically demonstrated than in the new American nation. Americans enjoyed unprecedented freedom and opportunity, and the amazing result was a mushrooming middle class previously undreamt of in history. Writing in 1947, Mr. Weaver observed:

> In this republic, less than 7 percent of the earth's population has created more new wealth than all the other 2,010,000,000 people in the world; and the benefits of this great wealth have been more widely distributed here than in any other country — at any time.[5]

"It is a cardinal tenet of Americanism," insisted Robert Welch, "that a wide open middle class, into which any laborer can climb, and from which any millionaire can fall, must be the very basis and core of all the best civilizations."[6]

The opportunity for every individual to rise to join the middle class through his own efforts is certainly just. But the opportunity for upward mobility also provides a great motivator for the individual to help increase the nation's productivity.

A strong middle class also constitutes a formidable bulwark of resistance to any tyranny. The added independence of members of the middle class means they have greater means with which to organize resistance. This independence also means that they are more difficult for an emerging tyranny to blackmail into submission.

Accordingly, the present-day Conspiracy seeks to overcome that independence, and secure its control, by making the people dependent on government for employment, medical care, food, and survival. For these reasons, Mr. Welch explained, the destruction of

America's middle class is a fundamental objective of the Conspiracy.

Understanding that objective explains much of the economically destructive programs coming out of Washington. The architects of the assaults on the middle class are not stupid; they are clever traitors.

Barren Soil of Collectivism

An equally important lesson is that the opposite of freedom is barren soil *incapable* of supporting prosperity.

There are many ways that the improper exercise of government power can undermine economic prosperity. For example, Thomas Jefferson wisely observed: "Were we directed from Washington when to sow and when to reap, we should soon want bread."[7]

Although most Americans sense these truths, they are steadily being robbed of their unique inheritance by counterrevolutionaries who would turn back the clock and put man under the bridle and bit of the state.

Americans almost universally oppose socialism and communism by name. But too few realize that the two major political parties have advocated and implemented the socialist agenda for decades without identifying their proposals as such.

Socialists and communists seek to separate property rights from human rights. Particularly, they want to abolish rights in land. (For example, in 1935 Roger Baldwin, founder and veteran leader of the ACLU, wrote: "I seek social ownership of property, the abolition of the propertied class, and sole control by those who produce wealth. Communism is the goal."[8])

But property rights are among the most fundamental of human rights. And economic freedom is inseparable from political freedom. The assault on property rights is a backdoor assault on political freedom, prosperity, and the middle class.

Peruvian economist Hernando de Soto maintains that much of Latin America is mired in poverty primarily because property rights are non-existent.[9] In the absence of property rights, there is no upward mobility and no opportunity for a middle class to develop. Without ownership rights, the poor often seek shelter in huge squatter communities, sometimes growing to millions of people.

People live in shanties of cardboard and tin. They don't invest in building a house with a foundation when they might be evicted tomorrow.

The right to own property must not be abridged. In protecting this right, it is important to recognize that true ownership of property includes more than just title. It also includes the right to use and dispose of that property as the owner chooses. Otherwise, he really doesn't own the property.

Respect the Free Market

For reasons of both prosperity and of keeping potentially dangerous government power within constitutional restraints, government should also be prevented from interfering with and distorting the signals of the free market. Accordingly, government should not be allowed to control wages and prices. Nor should its Federal Reserve be allowed to manipulate the money supply or interest rates.

It is unconstitutional and improper for the federal government to tax one group to transfer its wealth to another. The necessary and legitimate purpose of taxation is to support government in its proper role as spelled out in the Constitution. Nowhere does the Constitution authorize the federal government to tax as an instrument of social policy or as a means of buying votes from a favored class (through deficit spending).

The preamble to the Constitution states the reasons for its enactment. The willfully misconstrued phrase "promote the general welfare" in the preamble does not authorize government welfare or unlimited government. It merely makes clear that the government was formed for the purpose of promoting the welfare of everyone, *within* the areas of activity specifically authorized in the Constitution as appropriate to government.

In summary, our support for human freedom, justice, and responsibility means that we oppose all forms of collectivism as dangerous steps backward in the evolution of civilized society. The previous century alone provides tragic evidence that a collectivist society is the enemy of freedom and stands in the way of responsibility to God. The collectivist state, as a false god, simply swallowed up individuals, making their lives and flagging energies completely subservient to its needs and purposes.

Tools of the Conspiracy

The persistence of socialist ideas today is not due to the fuzzy thinking of politicians and intellectuals unfamiliar with history. Instead, clever demagogues promote these "ideologies" because they find them very effective for advancing their agenda of concentrating more and more power in the hands of an all-powerful superstate.

The socialist and collectivist arguments have proven effective because they are the stuff of confidence games. The socialist arguments of "soak the rich" and "share the wealth" serve well as smokescreens to persuade a gullible public to give up their liberties and concentrate more authority in government.

The English philosopher Thomas Hobbes wisely observed: "Freedom is government divided into small fragments."[10] But Insiders (conspirators and opportunists) armed with socialist arguments have been able to amass power in nation after nation while pretending concern for the well-being of the masses. As this concentration of power progresses, the public is invariably impoverished under stifling government authority and taxation.

Undoubtedly, some advocates actually believe in socialist ideology. They accept that it is proper and effective to use the force of government to help the poor. And they may sincerely argue that government is more benevolent than, say, corporations.

But the driving force behind socialist thinking, ideas, and organization has been the Conspiracy. In fact, most socialists, who supposedly seek their revolution through patient gradualism and parliamentary means, have learned that socialism advances most successfully under false colors.

The Fabian socialists in Britain, for example, have from their inception followed a strategy of deception. They have practiced "penetration" and "permeation" to spread their influence through government, the press, universities, and even churches. The Fabian Society has large tentacles in the United States, but, as in Britain, its agents here seek revolution under false colors. Interestingly, two of the symbols for the Fabian Society are appropriately the tortoise and the wolf in sheep's clothing.

The late Gary Allen insightfully summarized the socialist scam in his brilliant 1971 bestseller, *None Dare Call It Conspiracy*:

If one understands that socialism is not a share-the-wealth program, but is in reality a method to *consolidate* and *control* the wealth, then the seeming paradox of super-rich men promoting socialism becomes no paradox at all.[11]

As we have noted, even absent the disingenuous motives of its proponents, the socialist program would be a fraud. Socialism would and does promote forced equality in poverty for all but the top echelon.

As the American experience overwhelmingly demonstrates, the route to prosperity for higher and higher percentages of people is not the forced equality of sheep managed by government. Instead, a widely shared prosperity results when there is a strong driving incentive for *individuals* to improve their lot. A prosperous society even benefits those unable or unwilling to struggle toward the top, because increasing wealth raises the value of *all* labor.

Progress and prosperity are best achieved in a society that does not restrict the opportunity to move up the economic ladder. Moreover, the principles of freedom and responsibility are consistent with Western ideals and religion.

Section IV

So What Is To Be Done?

Chapter 8

First, Correctly Define the Problem!

There are a thousand hacking at the branches of evil to one who is striking at the root.[1]

— Henry David Thoreau

Man's natural instinct, particularly in regard to current affairs, is to rush to address the symptoms of problems. But as any good doctor understands, adequate treatment requires an accurate diagnosis of the underlying disease. This is particularly important in our situation, because the causes are hidden and a rushed diagnosis will undoubtedly miss the mark.

In Sections I and II, we argued that the overwhelming reality in world affairs today is the influence of a generations-spanning Conspiracy seeking to build a tyrannical "new world order" dominating the entire planet. To accomplish that objective, this Conspiracy is deceiving the free people of many nations, Americans in particular, through a variety of pretexts, into allowing a steady accumulation and centralization of invasive government authority.

Some of these pretexts are even designed to facilitate the transfer of significant authority to essentially unaccountable *international* institutions. All the while, Americans are being kept in the dark as to the ultimate objective.

In planning an appropriate cure, we must recognize the influence of the Conspiracy on government, our institutions, and in particular on the means of getting information to Americans. But this recognition is only a starting point. We must also understand how that Conspiracy has been successful in gaining that influence and what has happened to derail the American dream.

Let's Look Deeper
Conspiracy and corruption are like opportunistic diseases. They are always lurking in the shadows, but their mere infection generally does not multiply to dangerous levels unless the body's immune system has first been weakened.

Today, an internationalist conspiracy is on the verge of consolidating the nations of the world into its long awaited new world order. However, this Conspiracy is in a position to threaten us with this unprecedented power grab only because America's natural, inherited defenses have been seriously weakened. These defenses have been eroded both through *predictable neglect* and through *insidious design.*

It has been wisely said that "Eternal vigilance is the price of liberty." As an example of *predictable neglect* consider that, following generations of unprecedented prosperity, the vigilance of Americans has waned, and they no longer even know what to look out for.

In particular, they no longer understand the principles of freedom embodied in their own unique Republic. And without an understanding of those principles, Americans lack a functional yardstick against which to judge the actions of their leaders. In view of such ignorance, it barely matters that they have become complacent and shallow in monitoring those whom they have allowed into government.

Early Warnings
Americans have dangerously and mistakenly come to regard freedom and its fruits as an American birthright. At the founding of our nation, early Americans had a natural fear of the power of government, particularly of remote government, and they had a strong, healthy desire somehow to limit government's potential for oppressing them. After all, only a few years earlier, Americans had fought a war for independence in the face of looming tyranny.

After the States gained their independence, their first attempt at a union proved to be too weak and, as a result, was fraught with problems. This early Confederation, for example, had a congress but no separate executive or courts of its own. As the problems with the Confederation mounted, the Congress suggested that the States send delegates to a convention in Philadelphia, for the purpose of recommending revisions to the Articles of Confederation. Instead, this 1787 convention proposed a constitution for a completely new government — the United States, which was sent to the States for ratification and implemented two years later.

106

The Founding Fathers had intensely reviewed the history of government and decided to give us a Republic. They carefully crafted this Republic to make it as difficult as possible for the new government to become a threat to our freedom. But early presidents, including several of the key participants at the Philadelphia convention, would warn their fellow Americans of the very serious challenges in keeping the new Republic on track.

Freedom and Ignorance
Several presidents warned forcefully of the incompatibility between freedom and ignorance. In 1816, Thomas Jefferson summarized this challenge well: "If a nation expects to be ignorant and free, in a state of civilization, it expects what never was and never will be."[2]

In his Farewell Address upon preparing to leave office, George Washington said:

> Promote, then, as an object of primary importance, institutions for the general diffusion of knowledge. In proportion as the structure of a government gives force to public opinion, it is essential that public opinion should be enlightened.

Perhaps the most eloquent warning of the danger of ignorance came from James Madison:

> Although all men are born free, and all nations might be so, yet too true it is, that slavery has been the general lot of the human race. Ignorant — they have been cheated; asleep — they have been surprised; divided — the yoke has been forced upon them.
> But what is the lesson? That because the people may betray themselves, they ought to give themselves up, blindfolded, to those who have an interest in betraying them? Rather conclude that the people ought to be enlightened, to be awakened, to be united, that after establishing a government they should watch over it, as well as obey it.[3]

Even though these men recognized that the people "ought to be enlightened," they did not generally propose more government as the means. And they undoubtedly would have opposed allowing the *federal* government to get into the political education business. Not only was no such role provided for in the Constitution, but any such program whereby the federal government can influence what young people are taught subverts the vital check on government of an *independent*, informed electorate.

Religion and Morality

In addition to warning of the danger of ignorance, our Founding Fathers also admonished their fellow Americans to recognize religion and morality as essential foundations. "Our Constitution," said John Adams, "was made only for a moral and religious people. It is wholly inadequate to the government of any other."[4]

In his Farewell Address, George Washington also expressed this conviction:

> Of all the dispositions and habits which lead to political prosperity, religion and morality are indispensable supports. In vain would that man claim the tribute of patriotism who should labor to subvert these great pillars of human happiness — these firmest props of the duties of men and citizens. The mere politician, equally with the pious man, ought to respect and cherish them....
>
> And let us with caution indulge the supposition that morality can be maintained without religion. Whatever may be conceded to the influence of refined education on minds of peculiar structure, reason and experience both forbid us to expect that national morality can prevail in exclusion of religious principle.

So our Founding Fathers were well aware that the American experiment in freedom would collapse if its underlying principles were not wisely and vigilantly protected. Unfortunately, most of these defenses against the subversion of our Republic have since been seriously weakened. Decades after our nation's founding, Abraham Lincoln would conclude:

At what point shall we expect the approach of danger? By what means shall we fortify against it? Shall we expect some transatlantic military giant to step the ocean, and crush us at a blow? Never!

All the armies of Europe, Asia, and Africa combined ... could not by force take a drink from the Ohio, or make a track on the Blue Ridge, in a trial of a thousand years.

At what point then is the approach of danger to be expected? I answer, if it ever reach us, it must spring up amongst us. It cannot come from abroad. If destruction be our lot, we must ourselves be its author and finisher. As a nation of freemen, we must live through all time, or die by suicide.[5]

Insidious Design

The Conspiracy has been at work in our nation, virtually from its inception. George Washington, John Adams, James Madison, and James Monroe all indicated some awareness of the Conspiracy.

The Conspiracy eventually recognized the futility of confronting our nation and its constitutional system directly, e.g., by fomenting open rebellion, as it had done in France. And so, it initiated a broad-based, long-term campaign to weaken our nation's immune system by subverting the institutions and culture necessary to support a free society.

In so doing, the Conspiracy has, in substance, pursued the strategy articulated by Communist theoretician Antonio Gramsci and his followers. In 1924, Gramsci became the leader of the Italian Communist Party and was imprisoned two years later by Italian authorities. Gramsci would devote much of the remaining years of his life writing his *Prison Notebooks*, in which he recorded his strategy for *quiet* revolution.

Gramsci argued that in the developed Western democracies, the quick seizure of state power was doomed to failure as it was a mistake to "count solely on the power and material force that are given by government."[6] Instead, he insisted that for a revolution to be successful the supporting culture first had to be changed. The altered culture would then prepare the people, intellectually and morally, to accept the revolution. In essence, the Gramscian battle cry became "capture the culture." The target also potentially included any supporting tradition.

So Gramsci urged his comrades to infiltrate and gain control of the institutions of civil society that shape and represent public opinion. Those institutions included the churches, political parties, trade unions, the mass media, and a variety of voluntary private organizations. Rudi Dutschke, one of Gramsci's disciples, described this strategy of culture war as conducting "the long march through the institutions."[7]

Gramsci was not proposing a completely new strategy unfamiliar to other branches of the Conspiracy. The Insiders had long ago laid the groundwork for their revolution by working to capture strategic positions in this country for the molding of public opinion.

Norman Dodd reported that Carnegie Foundation minutes revealed that in the aftermath of World War I the Foundation's trustees concluded that they "must control education in the United States." Working with other foundations they devised a plan to do so. Their plan included, as just one facet, building a stable of historians, which became the nucleus of the American Historical Association.[8]

Recall also that, according to Quigley, the Rhodes and Milner group had sought "the control of journalistic, educational, and propaganda agencies."[9] And the Fabian Socialists had long advocated a general scheme for social "permeation."

Nevertheless, Gramsci's influence has been significant. For example, one of Gramsci's apostles was Derek Shearer, a founder of the radical Campaign for Economic Democracy and adviser to Bill Clinton. And Gramsci was also a primary influence on Hillary Clinton's political guru, Michael Lerner.

Gramsci particularly targeted religion and morality. He wrote: "The conception of law will have to be freed from every remnant of transcendence and absoluteness, practically from all moralist fanaticism."[10]

There is little doubt that this strategy of organized cultural subversion has had its impact. In the Winter 1996 issue of the leftist intellectual journal *Dissent*, editor Michael Walzer listed some of the cultural victories won by the left since the 1960s:

- "The visible impact of feminism."

- "The effects of affirmative action."
- "The emergence of gay rights politics, and … the attention paid to it by the media."
- "The acceptance of cultural pluralism."
- "The transformation of family life," including "rising divorce rates, changing sexual mores, new household arrangements — and, again, the portrayal of all this in the media."
- "The progress of secularization, the fading of religion in general and Christianity in particular from the public sphere — classrooms, textbooks, legal codes, holidays, and so on."
- "The virtual abolition of capital punishment."
- "The legalization of abortion."
- "The first successes in the effort to regulate and limit the private ownership of guns."

There is ample evidence that the Conspiracy has helped to foster a climate of increasing ignorance, moral complacency, and religious fatalism. It has also taken advantage of that climate to further its ultimate objectives.

Accordingly, the Conspiracy has labored to neutralize obstacles to its power grab, such as the American middle class (by devastating it economically) and the U.S. Constitution (by entangling it with subversive precedent and international agreements). At the same time, it has steadily sought to centralize more power in the executive branch and in international institutions that it controls.

While working to overcome potential resistance, the Conspiracy has cleverly manipulated issues to enlist a public constituency supporting its agenda. For example, it has fostered the environmental movement and agitated environmental concerns (real, exaggerated, or completely phony).

Using the pretext of environmental crisis, the Conspiracy seeks to stampede unthinking support for proposals to centralize more authority in Washington, even create new, invasive international controls. Not surprisingly, there is a big gap between the advertised agenda and the real agenda of the leaders of this movement. The last thing the Conspiracy wants is to solve any of the problems it has served up as useful crises to further its revolution.

In a similar fashion, the Conspiracy has not merely worked to *weaken support* for existing religion and traditional morality. It has also sought to subvert and counterfeit established religion (e.g., the creation of liberation theology). And it has promoted its own "alternatives" to fill the vacuum in human values and loyalties.

The Conspiracy, through legal and judicial subversion, has helped pave the way for those who would promote a self-centered, whatever-feels-good immorality. And the Conspiracy has promoted non-theistic religions, such as humanism, or even the worship of the State or the UN as God, or at least as God's anointed agent protecting mother earth.

Widespread acceptance of such "theology" would allow a political leader to demand God-like loyalty, the fuehrer principle, much as did Hitler and so many other tyrants before and since. Unfortunately, the appeal of this act of subordination is strongly similar to the age-old demand for a King. Many, having lost the vision of freedom, willingly become sheep, abdicating responsibility for their future to a demagogue.

A Front-burner Campaign

The Conspiracy invests in many avenues to its objective of total power. A few of the most promising become front-burner campaigns. For example, as part of its campaign to undermine the middle class and the cultural traditions supporting our constitutional Republic, the Conspiracy has labored to saddle the United States with a huge immigration problem.

As part of that campaign, internationalist conspirators have helped to ensure that living conditions for many to the south are intolerable. Higher U.S. wage rates coupled with government-financed welfare (health, education, subsistence, etc.) prove to be an irresistible magnet. Much earlier, these welfare benefits were fastened on the U.S. through the influence of the Conspiracy. And now they have been extended through unpopular judicial decision to illegals (and their children).

In the process, the Conspiracy has managed to frustrate border enforcement, encouraged violations with massive amnesty programs, and greatly multiplied each amnesty's impact by permitting follow-up family chain migration. Unknown to most Americans, huge tax-exempt foundations have sponsored radical organizations that make it difficult to deport illegals and enforce the law.

Most immigrants, even illegal immigrants, do not present a serious national problem, individually. Most are good people merely seeking a better life. But their sheer numbers have overwhelmed America's ability to assimilate them readily into our culture. Adding to the difficulty in assimilation, revolutionaries sponsored by the Conspiracy have sought to prevent traditional assimilation by intimidating immigrants, while promoting "multiculturalism and cultural diversity."

Even worse, these revolutionaries are laboring to organize and radicalize new constituencies among the mass of immigrants who can be agitated to challenge the established order. They argue that several of our southwestern states rightfully belong to Mexico and should be reconquered through migration. In reality, these radicals cynically view massive immigration, legal or otherwise, not as a way to improve lives for Latinos, but as an opportunity to create the conditions for revolution through confrontation, division, and crisis.

Through its influence in the media and in radical immigration groups and with the aid of radical attorneys, the Conspiracy has been able to circumvent popular opinion. However, when the impact of out-of-control immigration grew to such proportions that in several geographic areas it couldn't be ignored, frustrated Americans demanded action.

But most of these outraged Americans are unaware of the conspiratorial agenda in which many of their own political leaders are involved. So they have been satisfied to engage in meaningless protests, deriving some satisfaction from sympathetic talk show hosts and politicians. They are easily manipulated, because they have no idea why the leaders they trust cannot or will not solve the problem. They also do not realize their opportunity and responsibility to force a solution.

"Natural" Cycles of History

From his own in-depth study of history, Robert Welch gave limited credence to theories of natural cycles of history, such as that advanced by Oswald Spengler. But he also believed that history recorded a long-term upward trend in civilization as a result of "a natural upward reach in the heart of man." In his optimistic view, the present conspiratorial inroads, even if successfully brought to completion, are only a temporary, albeit tragic, speed bump in that upward trend.

Moreover, Mr. Welch rejected the idea that any of the so-called natural cycles were inevitable. He firmly believed that history, for good or bad, was made by the dedicated few. Other leaders shared that view, among them a prominent industrialist from Massachusetts. In the middle 1950s, Robert W. Stoddard addressed the Worcester Sales Executive Club as follows:

> [W]e seem to be in the midst of an historic cycle, one that has repeated itself in nation after nation, almost from the beginning of history. It goes like this: "From bondage to spiritual faith; from spiritual faith to courage; from courage to freedom; from freedom to abundance; from abundance to selfishness; from selfishness to complacency; from complacency to apathy; from apathy to fear; from fear to dependency; and from dependency back again once more to bondage."

Mr. Stoddard went on to affirm that "whether this cycle will run its usual course or not will depend on the positive courageous action of enlightened citizens, of salesmen for freedom."[11]

Several years later, Bob Stoddard attended a two-day meeting where his good friend Robert Welch, already a "salesman for freedom," would launch a new organization — The John Birch Society — to develop and lead more "salesmen for freedom."

At that founding meeting, Mr. Welch concluded from his study of history that it was much too soon for America to die from "natural causes." America's decline was not due to natural forces — she was being pushed. Her ailments were imposed largely by the Conspiracy, and so she could be restored to good health by exposing and routing that Conspiracy.

In subsequent years, Mr. Welch would often refer to George Santayana's classic observation: "Those who will learn nothing from history are condemned to repeat it." In Mr. Welch's view, responsibility demanded that we learn those lessons and help enough of our fellow men (through opinion molders) to also learn those lessons, so that we could chart a better course.

That approach certainly worked for the men who founded our nation. "The simple truth," wrote Mr. Welch in 1980, "is that most of our outstanding civilizations of the past have been started on their early road to greatness by men with a pioneer spirit, who had indeed learned a great deal from history."[12]

In Summary

The Conspiracy has helped to accelerate the erosion of the foundations for freedom. In particular, it has sought to undermine morality and Christianity. It has also fostered widespread ignorance and misunderstanding of the principles of our Republic and of the wisdom of our Founding Fathers.

Taking advantage of predictable public complacency and a resulting climate of ignorance, the Conspiracy has succeeded over many years in amassing amazing, but disguised, influence both inside and out of government. With superior organization and influence, it is able daily to deceive Americans with respect to facts, principles, crises, the true intentions of our leaders, and many other things, in order to steal their heritage of freedom.

The great British statesman Edmund Burke wisely observed, "The people never give up their liberties but under some delusion."[13] As targets of orchestrated delusion, Americans, in their ignorance, are allowing the accumulation of enormous unchecked power in government, which history clearly shows is the midwife of tyranny.

But, as we demonstrated in Section II, the projected consequences of allowing this clique to achieve unrestrained power are far more than what *might* result from a mere *tendency* toward tyranny or from the *unintended* miscalculation by elites. From the track record of the Conspiracy and the writings of the conspirators, unprecedented global tyranny and destruction of all civilized values and the human spirit are clearly the objectives.

ORGANIZE FOR VICTORY!

Chapter 9

Next, Assess Our Strengths and Enemy Weaknesses

A man said unto his angel:
"My spirits are fallen thro'
And I cannot carry this battle;
O brother! what shall I do?"
— Louise Imogen Guiney (1861–1920)

Two reasons drive us to take stock here of our strengths and enemy weaknesses. First, it is an appropriate step in adopting a realistic plan of action. And second, the investigation provides a useful antidote to one of the most dangerous strategies practiced by the Conspiracy — break your opponent's will to resist.

The ancient Chinese strategist Sun Tzu preached that the highest art of warfare was to subdue your enemy without a fight. The attack on our culture and the many-pronged effort to demoralize our youth certainly support that strategy. And we know that the Communists are great students of Sun Tzu. Undoubtedly, top Insider strategists in this country are, as well.

In any event, one of the biggest challenges in the freedom fight, in the face of the Conspiracy's obvious momentum, is to give hope to prospective American patriots and help them see the opportunity to turn the tide in freedom's favor.

In fact, we *know* that our opportunities are much greater than they appear on the surface. A 1939 U.S. Army publication explains one generally overlooked principle:

> Resolute action by a few determined men is often decisive. Time and again, numbers have been overcome by courage and resolution. Sudden changes in a situation, so startling as to appear miraculous, have frequently been brought about by the action of small parties. There is an excellent reason for this. The trials of battle are severe; troops are strained to the

breaking point. At the crisis, any small incident may prove enough to turn the tide one way or the other. The enemy has invariably difficulties of which we are ignorant. To us his position may appear favorable, while to him it may seem desperate. Only a slight extra effort on our part may be decisive.[1]

Even though we are not in a shooting war, the lesson in the Army publication still applies, particularly as intelligence regarding the struggles in the enemy's inner circles is sparse at best. And since God expects us to stand up for right, without any guarantee of immediate success, we should be willing to act resolutely with the knowledge that such action by a few may very well make the difference. And with the corresponding understanding that to omit such action may allow the enemy his victory.

Nevertheless, it is not unusual for some who discover the Conspiracy to immediately accept defeat, even before they fully explore the possibilities and understand the hurdles the enemy still has to overcome. This is not a new reaction. Indeed, Robert Welch's comments in the April 1973 *Bulletin* demonstrate the theme's persistence:

> We are told that it is too late. Usually by people who a year ago did not know and would not believe that there was even a Conspiracy. Then all of a sudden they see the picture, and in no time are shouting that the Conspiracy is too powerful and too far advanced for anybody to be able to stop it. To these unrealistic pessimists we would have volumes to say, if there were room....
>
> Of course it's too late, unless we do enough about it. The hour was already too late, when the Society was founded. This was made clear to us by both a Congressman and a Senator, who were voluntarily retiring in 1960 because the Conspiracy was already so powerful that nothing could stop it.

Individuals make a big mistake, if they quickly conclude that our situation is hopeless, just because they themselves don't see any opportunity for a solution. Clearly, adopting the attitude that it is too late plays directly into the hands of the enemy.

It's Not *Too* Late

How do we *know* that it is not too late? A short answer is because the Conspiracy still goes to enormous efforts to deceive the American people. As long as the Conspiracy has to conceal its aims under a smokescreen of pretense, then the opportunity exists to expose those aims to a force that can stop it. Don Fotheringham addressed that topic with great insight in the August 1992 *Bulletin*:

> When all pretense and play-acting [by the Conspiracy] ends, then we know that the war of words is over and that liberty must again be purchased at the price of blood. [But] anyone who gives up while education is still possible, and while truth is still available, will forfeit a priceless opportunity to save lives and to secure liberty.

In 1958 at the meeting he organized to found The John Birch Society, Mr. Welch summarized his conviction that we do not have to lose the fight:

> We have *many layers of strength not yet rotted* by all of the infiltration and political sabotage to which we have been subjected. Our danger is both immense and imminent; but it is not beyond the possibility of being overcome by the resistance that is still available.[2] [Emphasis added.]

In the decades since Mr. Welch spoke those words, the Conspiracy has made great gains in centralizing power, eroding individual freedom and the middle class, creating revolutionary organization, ensnaring the U.S. in international institutions, and in circumventing the Constitution, to cite a few of its major advances.

But many layers of strength are not so easily eradicated. They are the cumulative contribution of countless individuals over centuries. In fact, Mr. Welch's assessment still applies: We *still* have many layers of strength not yet rotted by all of the infiltration and political sabotage, and by the culture war, to which we have been subjected.

The enemy generally recognizes those layers of strength much better than do freedom's defenders. Antonio Gramsci recognized those strengths, but too late. Initially, he underestimated them and his miscalculation landed him in a prison cell.

Power of Informed Public Opinion

Public opinion is stronger than the legislature, and nearly as strong as the ten commandments.[3]

— Charles Dudley Warner (1829-1900)

The American people have aptly been described as a sleeping giant. Once informed and aroused, they still have the power to reverse the gains of the Conspiracy that would enslave them.

The Insiders greatly respect the force of informed public opinion. A major part of Insider strategy regularly targets public opinion with pretexts and smokescreens to prevent us from taking alarm and offering any substantial resistance. The Insiders also find it valuable to misrepresent public opinion by orchestrating the appearance of widespread support for their schemes.

Given the strategic importance of public opinion, it is not surprising that a sizeable portion of the CFR's membership consists of "journalists, correspondents, and communication executives." (The CFR's 2000 *Annual Report* stated that 386 of its members, about 10 percent, fell in that category.)

In the February 1966 *Bulletin*, Mr. Welch examined this constraint on the Conspiracy's strategy:

> [A]s a general rule, until freedom of expression is too severely limited by the tightening shackles and pressures of a police state ... neither political candidates nor even legislatures dare go *too far* beyond what public opinion is willing to accept. A patient gradualism, therefore, in leading the public along, coupled with a massive deception as to the real reason for various governmental policies and extensions of governmental tyranny — these parallel concessions to the power of public opinion are vitally necessary components of Communist strategy for the subversion of our country.

The power of public opinion is supported by many of our layers of strength.

Our Strengths

Few Americans fully appreciate how America's unique layers of strength support a free society. In the nearby table (p. 123), we have identified quite a number of those strengths. As an aid to the reader, we have attempted to introduce a little pattern to an otherwise long list by grouping these concepts into four somewhat arbitrary, often overlapping categories.

Much could be written about each layer of strength. But we can afford to comment on only a very few here to illustrate what is so often underappreciated by the *defenders* of freedom.

More good people than bad.

Despite the ravages of the culture war and other negative social pressures, Hollywood and MTV do not reflect our society as it is. Instead, these change agents depict American lifestyles and attitudes as the Insiders want them to become. And surveys have shown that Americans, outside of elite social and "leadership" circles, have generally been slow to imitate what they see in entertainment.

These conclusions were echoed a decade ago during the height of the Clinton scandals by acclaimed British journalist Ambrose Evans-Pritchard. In his 1997 book on Clinton malfeasance and corruption, *The Secret Life of Bill Clinton*, Evans-Pritchard wrote: "The American elite, I am afraid to say, is almost beyond redemption. Moral relativism has set in so deeply that the gilded classes have become incapable of discerning right from wrong."

Yet Evans-Pritchard claims, "The ordinary citizens, thank goodness, still adhere to absolutes," still recognize that "a lie is an abomination," that "a vow is sacred," and that "injustice cannot be excused."

"A lesser nation," he notes, "would have succumbed to Clintonism, a little at a time, from complacency and servile nature." But "Americans are too high-spirited. They have shown that it is impossible to graft the practices of a banana republic onto their political culture. It makes me feel almost proud to witness such defiance."

Evans-Pritchard continued: "While credentialed officials looked the other way or colluded at the edges, it was the construction worker, the paramedic, the man-in-the-white-van who refused to change their testimony in the [Vince] Foster case. The well-connected, privately-educated prosecutors on the staff of the Independent Counsel went along quietly with the coverup; the Hispanic son of migrant farm workers resigned on principle."[4]

Responsibility.

Volunteerism among Americans is still strong, especially when the need is clear. Yet the Conspiracy would have us believe that Americans have become so degenerate and so preoccupied with personal concerns as to be unwilling to make the sacrifices necessary to preserve freedom. The response of Americans to the terrorist attacks on September 11, 2001 suggests otherwise.

Recall the heroic actions of Jeremy Glick and the other brave passengers aboard United Flight 73. And who can forget the hundreds of police and firemen who gave their lives attempting to rescue the wounded when the Trade Center towers collapsed upon them? In the days following the attack, thousands of Americans traveled to New York to serve as volunteers and millions donated blood or money to relief efforts.

Local and locally controlled police.

Our *local* police constitute a vital bulwark against the police state. Local police obtain their funding (mostly) from local citizens, and they naturally identify with the people among whom they live and often grew up. Their charter is to protect the local citizens and their property, not to sustain a national government in power.

Of great concern, the independence of local police is progressively being compromised. In the past several decades, a long row of deceptive initiatives have been launched with the aim of eventually nationalizing our local police. Some of these initiatives have failed miserably, as a result of strong organized opposition. But other steps have made serious inroads on police independence. The Conspiracy is persistent.

A Sample of Our Layers of Strength

Character Traits
- A self-reliant, adventuresome spirit.
- A strong desire to help others and improve the world.
- Responsibility.
- Patriotism (strong, although today generally shallow).
- Religious faith.
- No tolerance for perceived injustice.
- Respect for the law.
- Summary: Still more good people than bad.

Traditions of Independence & Responsibility
- Free enterprise and the free market.
- Widespread private gun ownership.
- Home schooling and private education.
- A vibrant civil society (proliferation of non-governmental organizations).
- Independent news sources and media of communication.
- Independent book publishing.
- Proliferation of churches.
- The family.
- Local and locally controlled police.

Republican Government
- Rule of law — a republic.
- Property rights and the American middle class.
- Basic freedoms, Bill of Rights.
- Federalism (delegation of authority bottom up, not top down).
- Constitutional system, though damaged, still intact.
- Congress (particularly the House).
- The secret ballot.

Some Timely Leadership
- Robert Welch's legacy.

Vital bulwark: The above list illustrates our nation's many layers of strength. All are under attack. Though many have been greatly weakened, combined they still represent a formidable hurdle for the Conspiracy to overcome. And they provide a solid and sufficient foundation for a counterattack.

Federalism (delegation of authority bottom up, not top down).
The particular organization of government responsibility known as federalism is a uniquely American arrangement. Federalism developed because the original 13 states came first and, with the approval of the people, were the *creators* of the federal government. As totally sovereign entities the states decided to work together to create a new layer of government, possessing only a limited number of appropriately national functions, which were specifically defined in our Constitution.

The accountability of city, county, state, and federal government is generally and ultimately to the people (prior to the 17th amendment, the U.S. Senate was accountable directly to the state legislatures). The delegation of government authority is *bottom up*, not top down. State and local governments are *not* (yet) part of an administrative system for control of the population by a centralized authority in Washington.

This independence of the many layers of government is under attack by a power hungry central government, and increasingly the states are being transformed into mere provinces, with their state governments more and more subservient to Washington.

Constitutional system, though damaged, still intact.
Over more than two centuries, our constitutional order has been engrained in the habits and thinking of Americans. Our Constitution is by far the oldest such written system of fundamental laws currently in operation. It has weathered the storms of change amazingly well.

But not without damage. The strength of our Constitution has been greatly weakened, as many of its provisions have been disregarded or distorted and some unwise barnacles appended. Nevertheless, our Constitution still provides an immense limitation on the Conspiracy's advance. And it is an invaluable asset for any reasonable effort to rout the Conspiracy and return fully to republican government.

Also, consider that regular elections are still held on schedule, the outcome of which is respected. Americans must not sacrifice these advantages by giving up on the system our Founding Fathers designed with such foresight.

Robert Welch's legacy.
During the 1950s, Robert Welch stood almost alone in his understanding of the Conspiracy's attack on our nation. And he did stand alone in his determination to offer a realistic solution commensurate with the problem.

Mr. Welch's books and publications are still accessible. But his much greater legacy is to be found in the people he influenced — the people whose eyes he opened and whose minds he informed — and in the fruits of the battles in which they were involved.

Few outsiders can appreciate that impact, since it rarely made the nightly news. But that legacy has contributed immeasurably to the understanding of many of today's opinion molders and to the resistance the Conspiracy still faces.

During the past two centuries, peoples of many nations have had brief opportunities to secure their freedom. But too often those opportunities evaporated for lack of adequate leadership, a realistic plan, or the cultural support to make such a plan work. Robert Welch's legacy simply offers the solution that American patriots of courage and character seek and need.

Enemy Weaknesses

On the flip side of our "advantages coin" are enemy weaknesses. Fortunately, the Conspiracy has several truly major vulnerabilities, and it still faces substantial difficulties in achieving its goal of unrestrained global power.

Just a Conspiracy
Perhaps the most surprising vulnerability is the good news that we are faced with *just* a conspiracy. In the July 1964 *Bulletin*, Mr. Welch explained this apparent contradiction:

> What we face *is* a conspiracy. In fact, it is extremely important for all of our members to realize that this is just a conspiracy. If I could be pardoned for putting it so bluntly, I should like to say: Get it through your heads!! *This is just a conspiracy*. There is no ideological wave supporting these criminals, except what they have artificially created as a

pretense and a weapon. There is no superpower behind all of this frightening front which they present. There is no solid substance inside the thin and glittering shell of power with which they dazzle and demoralize the opposition....

It is true that the conspirators now constitute a numerous and very influential clique all over the world, that they are long experienced, powerfully entrenched, irrevocably determined, and brutally ruthless, in their ambitious drive for total power. But this clique — no matter how suave their manners, high their positions, striped their pants, plush their offices, or fat their bank accounts — this clique is still nothing more nor less than a gang of utterly amoral criminals engaged in a *conspiracy* to rule the world.

And all you have to do to defeat *any conspiracy* is simply to expose it. The fact that its members have to carry on their operations *as a conspiracy* shows that it cannot stand the light of day.

Opposed to Man's Natural Desires

A major hurdle the Conspiracy has to overcome is the fact that its objectives are counter to man's natural desires. Robert Welch identified this weakness very clearly at the founding of his organization (at that time Mr. Welch referred to the entire Conspiracy as Communist):

> But — there is one basic consideration of tremendous importance which we must keep always in mind. This is that Communism has been imposed and must always *be* imposed, from the top down, by trickery and terror; and that it must then be maintained by terror. In other words, at least ninety-five percent of all human beings, on *both* sides of the Iron Curtain, *do not want Communism.* The job is not to unsell a majority from something they want or think is good for them, but to enable a *preponderant* majority to resist and refuse something they do not want.[5]

Other Constraints

The Conspiracy seeks to centralize government control (of police, of education, etc.), because its own influence and control are necessarily greatest at the top. However, the longer its lines of influence become, the less it is able to protect its policies from local influences. It simply doesn't have the means to influence the massive number of local opinion molders directly, and so it can't compete with personal contacts at this level.

The Conspiracy's influence spreads out in concentric circles. Those in the outer circles constitute the largest number, but their commitment to the Conspiracy's goals is the weakest. Many of these would switch sides if the Conspiracy were under serious attack. Nevertheless, all of these agents, however strategically placed in positions of great influence, are still numerically small compared to the population at large.

This numerical inferiority is one reason why all would-be-tyrants seek to keep their potential opposition confused and divided (divide and conquer), even fighting among itself.

The Conspiracy Can Be Stopped — Here!

History, for good or evil, is regularly forged by the dedicated few. In the April 1969 *Bulletin*, Mr. Welch observed:

> The pages of history are rich with the stories of men, and women, who have banded together against overwhelming odds, and who have, through persistence and unified efforts coupled with rock hard spiritual dedication and unwaning courage, conquered the impossible.

Paralleling our current challenge is the amazing but little-known story of British army Captain William Henry Sleeman (1788-1856). During the 1820s and 30s, a well entrenched conspiracy that had plagued India for centuries was successfully routed through the determined leadership of this one man.

When Sleeman arrived in India, the cult of the Thugs was operating as an immensely powerful, vicious criminal conspiracy. Its membership extended into and had corrupted the top levels of politics, the military, banking, commerce, and religion. Remarkably, given its long history and extensive activity, the Thugs had managed successfully to conceal their very existence from public view.

The Thugs had acquired substantial wealth through unimaginably vicious murder and robbery. Gangs of Thugs would often pose their members as traveling merchants in order to infiltrate commercial caravans transiting India. Then in absolutely ruthless and remorseless attacks, they would strangle their victims, loot their possessions, and dispose of the bodies. Incredibly, an estimated 30 to 40 thousand travelers each year would simply disappear from the face of the earth.

When the young army captain initially discovered the conspiracy and attempted to expose it, he encountered a wall of disbelief and ridicule from his superiors. For the British had been in India for more than 200 years and yet were unaware of the Conspiracy's existence. However, Captain Sleeman continued to gather evidence until the Conspiracy's deeds, scope, and methods were fully exposed.[6] Thanks to the courage and persistence of this one man, an all-out "war" by the British colonial government was launched that wiped out this generations-old conspiracy.

William Sleeman's campaign, like our challenge today, was no cakewalk. Fortunately, America has many layers of strength, upon which Sleeman could not rely for support.

In their wisdom, our Founding Fathers gave us a system that provided significant protection against the imperfections and ambitions of men. And it worked — it really worked! As recently as the opening of the previous century, Congress acted in accordance with the public's then-prevailing attitudes *to protect* America from significant internationalist subversion.

We are fortunate that the key battle in the freedom fight is here. America is the principal stumbling block to the new world order and to the realization of the Conspiracy's plans. We don't have to sit on the sidelines cheering the people of some other nation on to success.

In summary, we have plenty and adequate resources at our disposal. It is still not too late to change the course of history if a minority of Americans will dedicate themselves to enlisting still others in pursuit of a sound plan of action. We just need to realize that it can be done and do it now!

Chapter 10

Set Reasonable
and Sufficient Objectives

The people never give up their liberties but under some delusion.[1]
— Edmund Burke

It's time to establish reasonable and sufficient objectives — the foundation for a realistic plan of action. So let's summarize what we have learned in the previous chapters that will be helpful. We suggest these six points:

1. There is a Conspiracy working to deceive the world into slavery. It has major influence over key institutions as well as the government of the United States, and it is perilously close to accomplishing its objective of unrestrained global power.

2. Our inherited, natural defenses against such a threat have been damaged and continue to be under serious attack.

3. Those damaged defenses are nevertheless sufficiently intact to provide Americans with powerful means to resist, and those defenses still represent a formidable obstacle to the completion of the Conspiracy's plans.

4. An aroused, well informed American public, with good leadership, relying on those strengths has the power to rout the Conspiracy and repair America's foundations.

5. The American public currently lacks that good leadership and is not sufficiently informed to confront either the Conspiracy or the damage wrought to our foundations. Moreover, thanks to the enemy's influence and ability to sow confusion, the public lacks the understanding to find and recognize better leadership — it desperately needs help. That is the essence of the challenge.

6. It required many decades of neglect and even centuries of conspiratorial effort to get our nation to this point. It is unrealistic to expect a quick fix or an easy solution.

Further, we believe that America was once on the right course, setting a positive example of Americanism for the rest of the world. Our chosen task is not some frustratingly impossible objective, but merely to help put America back on its upward course and help secure it on that course for future generations.

Admittedly, that task alone is tremendously ambitious, but taking on the challenge is unavoidable if we are to act responsibly to avert disaster and protect our heritage.

Based on the above premises, we believe that our objectives must be, in brief, to "Rout the Rats and Rebuild." In the rest of this chapter, we will explain why we believe those are the essential objectives, we will state them in more detail, and we will contrast them with popular "non-solutions." We will also examine some principles of strategy.

Rout the Conspiracy ("the Rats")

How can we rout the Conspiracy? Mr. Welch summarized the general answer in the July 1964 *Bulletin*:

> [A]ll you have to do to defeat *any conspiracy* is simply to expose it. The fact that its members have to carry on their operations *as a conspiracy* shows that it cannot stand the light of day…. It is why the Comsymps have gone to such incredible lengths to smother or try to smother several hundred revealing books…. The one and only thing they cannot stand is *exposure*; or any "sufficient understanding" of what they are doing and how they are doing it.

If we can expose *the essentials* of the Conspiracy widely enough, then we rob it of its energy and influence. Such exposure would *alone* deny the Conspiracy much of its strength.

Certainly, to seal the Conspiracy's doom, the proper authorities, armed with subpoena powers and the threat of prosecution or impeachment, would have to act to uncover relationships and the culpability of individuals. However, such intervention by government authorities will follow naturally once there is sufficient public understanding of what has been going on and public pressure is brought to bear. So the key to routing the Conspiracy is simply to build *and use* that public understanding.

Essential Understanding

What widespread knowledge of the Conspiracy will stop it? Certainly, much of the detail is unimportant. And it is not necessary (or possible) that everyone be enlightened. A *large segment* of independent opinion molders proclaiming certain essentials would be sufficient. In the May 1970 *Bulletin*, Robert Welch provided a pretty good summary of what must be understood:

> What the public — or a sufficient fraction thereof — must be shown conclusively is: (1) That there is a powerful Conspiracy now imminently threatening to make all of us slaves in a one-world Communist empire; (2) that almost all of the destructive forces at work around us are activated and controlled by that Conspiracy; (3) that massive deception, as to both personnel and purposes, is at the very core of the strategy, as well as of the tactics, of this Conspiracy; (4) that a sufficient understanding of the methods, purposes, and progress of the Conspiracy is the only thing that can head it off; and (5), that stopping, exposing, and routing this Conspiracy is worth whatever it may cost, in labor and money and sacrifice and courage.

Why are these five points the important ones, and why are they sufficient? Essentially they describe the *seriousness*, the *nature*, and the *extent* of the threat. It is important to create understanding of the seriousness and extent of the threat in order for sufficient numbers of Americans to become appropriately serious about heading it off.

And understanding the *nature* of the threat — the Conspiracy's methods and its reach for creating deception as well as what it is trying to accomplish — will enable individual Americans to become streetwise and avoid succumbing to the Conspiracy's deceptions. If we accept Burke's statement that "[t]he people never give up their liberties except under some delusion," then this understanding alone, if widespread, should hold the Conspiracy at bay for a time.

For example, moves to nationalize local police or give government new authority to "protect the environment" immediately become suspect when you realize that the Conspiracy must centralize power in order to exercise total control. And when you understand the reach and influence of the Conspiracy, you are not about to accept the glib assurances of politicians that they will look out for our interests.

Consider the problem of uncontrolled immigration, for example. At the dawn of the 21st Century, every politician was well aware that the public had been clamoring for the U.S. to regain control of its borders and limit immigration. In response, most politicians would feign concern and promise action.

But the borders remained open. Even authorized fences were not built.[2] Why? Because the Conspiracy, for many subversive reasons, wanted open borders. And the naive, uninformed public, unable to imagine that such an agenda would reach into the highest levels of government, allowed itself to be satisfied with empty promises. Similar disconnects between public opinion and government action are evident in such areas as the attack on the right to keep and bear arms and U.S. subordination to the United Nations. To paraphrase a former senator from Pennsylvania, "The people get the rhetoric, the Conspiracy gets the action."[3]

The many politicians who do not understand the conspiratorial agenda are themselves vulnerable to being conned. Time and again, we have seen politicians downplay the concerns of informed constituents only to express amazement later when damaging legislation was "unexpectedly" jammed through Congress. Only when constituents understand the influence and agenda of the Conspiracy will they develop sufficient counter pressure to prevent such betrayals.

The Right Primary Focus
We agree with Mr. Welch's assessment in the December 1964 *Bulletin*: "The eventual outcome of this battle hinges on just one thing: Our ability to convince enough of the American people, soon enough, that this enemy is a criminal conspiracy."

In the next sections, we will discuss the methods, the campaigns, and the organization needed to reach more Americans and convince them that they are facing "a criminal conspiracy." But the first, and sometimes the biggest, hurdle to overcome is merely to recognize the need to focus on this objective.

Following Mr. Welch's lead, we contend that any sound plan to put our nation back on track must have exposing the Conspiracy as its primary focus. Which of course means that the authors of any such plan must recognize and be willing to proclaim that there is a Conspiracy. They cannot wince at the "C" word.

We regard this emphasis on exposing the Conspiracy as a fundamental principle of strategy. Unfortunately, it is a tough principle for many to accept. So it's worth taking some space here to explain our position.

Many concerned Americans, even when they are aware of compelling evidence pointing to the Conspiracy's influence, would still prefer to just argue the issues on their merits or demerits. They cave in to an understandable desire to avoid the controversy and the resistance our claims sometimes generate.

The Conspiracy has certainly made it awkward in many circles to present evidence that a Conspiracy is at the root of our problems. So the response of potential helpers in the freedom battle may be to question whether it is really necessary to go to the trouble and risk rejection. After all, they could correctly point out, as private citizens, we can't investigate the Conspiracy directly anyway.

But this attitude ignores a crucial reality: The Conspiracy has enormous resources at its disposal to lobby for its plans and to confuse, confound, and mislead potential resistance. Were that not the case, then reasoned arguments might well be sufficient to inspire opinion leaders to put America back on the right track.

Unfortunately, the nature of the battle we are in is duplicitous. It is also much more serious in both scope and consequences than those unfamiliar with the organization, methods, and reach of this Conspiracy could imagine. *Unless the public is aware of how the debate is being rigged, the public will fare no better than the victims of a crooked card game.*

History also teaches that it is dangerous to ignore a conspiracy. Cicero, the ancient Roman scholar and statesman, who lived during the turbulence that destroyed the Roman Republic, reportedly gave this assessment of the danger of the traitor (working in secret concert with foreign interests):

> A nation can survive its fools, and even the ambitious. But it cannot survive treason from within. An enemy at the gates is less formidable, for he is known and he carries his banners openly against the city. But the traitor moves among those within the gates freely, his sly whispers rustling through all the alleys, heard in the very halls of government itself.
>
> For the traitor appears not a traitor; he speaks in the accents familiar to his victims, and he wears their face and their garments, and he appeals to the baseness that lies deep in the hearts of all men. He rots the soul of a nation; he works secretly and unknown in the night to undermine the pillars of a city; he infects the body politic so that it can no longer resist. A murderer is less to be feared.[4]

A *conspiracy* of domestic traitors must be even more dangerous.

Hiding the Big Picture

But there is another difficulty in merely confronting the Conspiracy's arguments at face value, as though the debate were fair. Looking at issues individually in isolation rarely reveals the big picture of what is being constructed. For example, few Europeans could discern back in 1951 when the treaty establishing the Coal and Steel Community was signed, that, in fact, the subversive treaty was intended by its architects to start a decades-long process leading to a new supranational government — the European Union.[5]

The Conspiracy is very adept at this type of salami slicing — breaking down its agenda into thin slices that don't seem particularly dangerous, individually. And, unfortunately, few busy Americans today have the background to appreciate this invaluable lesson stated by James Madison:

> [I]t is proper to take alarm at the first experiment on our liberties. We hold this prudent jealously to be the first duty of citizens, and one of [the] noblest characteristics of the late

Revolution. The freemen of America did not wait till usurped power had strengthened itself by exercise and entangled the question in precedents. They saw all the consequences in the principle, and they avoided the consequences by denying the principle. We revere this lesson too much soon to forget it.[6]

Recall Richard Gardner's 1974 admonition in *Foreign Affairs* that the path to "world order ... will look like a great 'booming, buzzing, confusion'...." Unfortunately, few Americans, when faced with the dizzying array of alphabet-soup international organizations, treaties, understandings, and agreements, will recognize the design and take alarm. They need help to avoid being conned.

The Conspiracy is also adept at disguising its intentions through the use of code words, such as "harmonization," "integration and convergence," and "world order." What busy American could take alarm at such fuzzy, innocent sounding concepts? But activist supporters understand very well what these buzzwords represent and that their use helps disguise very specific, revolutionary objectives, such as the destruction of national sovereignty and independence (as is the case with the code words mentioned).

"It's Only Ideology"
Another variation of the misguided insistence on debating the issues at face value is the argument that we are fighting primarily an ideological battle. To be sure, branches of the Conspiracy make heavy use of ideology — Marxism, for example. But these branches also rely on conspiratorial organization to achieve their objectives.

The false claim that we are only involved in a battle of ideas serves the Conspiracy well. In fact, the Insiders have sometimes found it advantageous to subsidize opposition to their own program, provided that opposition confines itself to the ideological plane and omits any mention of the Conspiracy. By bolstering such opposition, the Conspiracy can better entice other potential opposition into supporting a completely ineffective method of resistance.

The Conspiracy is perfectly happy to let conservatives win debates in the purely ideological, academic realm. Intellectual arguments over whether balanced budgets are superior to deficits or the free-market to socialism do not threaten the Conspiracy. Despite regular ideological "victories," conservatives lose badly where it counts — in the real world. And they will continue to do so until the spotlight is turned on the conspiratorial organization and agenda.

In the March 1969 *Bulletin*, Robert Welch argued forcefully against the "it's only ideology trap":

> The philosophies of Collectivism and Conservatism are supposed to be battling against each other on the academic and political levels, for the intellectual acceptance that will bring victory to either side. The whole show is an enormous fraud. For under cover of this superficial debate the Communists are using every conceivable form of diplomacy, deception, pressure, bribery, treason, and terror for seizures of power. They then claim that these acquisitions of power are the result of ideological conquests.

Expose the Arsonists

In the March 1962 *Bulletin*, Mr. Welch discussed a very useful analogy that summarizes our strategic concerns. The analogy: How best to deal with a rash of fires caused by an arsonist (today, one might substitute "by a terrorist").

At the time, Mr. Welch had been criticized by a prominent citizen who actually argued that we must "forget about the arsonist and put out the fires." Mr. Welch chose that opportunity to strengthen the understanding and resolve of his members:

> [W]e certainly admit there is disagreement here. For, to use his own figure of speech, suppose an arsonist is setting fires in a community, and you and your neighbors have all rushed to try to put out the fire in the case of two or three houses that are already visibly aflame. But much faster than you can subdue those fires the same arsonist is setting fire to other houses on other widely scattered streets. And you are told: "Never mind catching the arsonist, we haven't got time for that. Let's put out these fires."
>
> Frankly, it doesn't make sense to me — and I do think the analogy is a reasonably good one. Forgetting about the

arsonist and simply working like heck to put out the fires has been the policy of most of the organizations fighting the advance of the Communists in America for the past thirty years. And neither the policy, nor all of the efforts and expenditures of these hundreds of groups and — in the aggregate — millions of supporters, have stopped the Communists any more than the same policy would stop the arsonist or save the homes of a community. This is why the Communists have never particularly disturbed, or been disturbed by, any of these groups. Fighting fires is an eminently respectable and praiseworthy endeavor (which salves a lot of consciences), which even the Communists hesitate to criticize. But trying to expose the arsonist who set the fires is likely to be a dirty business, especially if the arsonist, although a vicious criminal, is himself garbed in the garments of respectability and is posing as one of the most industrious firefighters.

The same reasoning applies to the culture war. Any strategy that concentrates exclusively on the fires fueled by the Gramscian attack — crime, drug abuse, abortion, broken families, weakened religious faith — while ignoring the arsonist, is merely a holding action ultimately doomed to fail. Yet uninformed Americans universally accept that the way to address our national decline is to attack only the symptoms — i.e., to fight the fires.

The Insiders are undoubtedly content to see Americans focused on putting out fires. They know they can always set more fires.

The Deceptions Are Deadly

The Gramscian attack on our culture has succeeded, not because there aren't plenty of Americans who hate evil and value goodness, but because too few Americans can see through the deceptions the Conspiracy uses.

When most Americans see, for example, a panel of "experts" commenting on policy issues, they have no idea that several of the authorities are CFR members and that the pedigrees for the others include a long list of affiliation with subversive organizations.

And when most Americans hear "major" policy issues debated,

they do not realize that the alternatives have been restricted to favor the Conspiracy's agenda of centralizing more and more power in Washington. They do not miss what is not discussed: the alternative of forcing government to operate within constitutional constraints.

When surveys, interviews, panels, and articles show individual after individual expressing the same attitudes and opinions, most Americans do not recognize that the apparent consensus may have been orchestrated for revolutionary purposes. They do not understand that a primary goal of the revolutionary is to portray radical schemes as "the will of the people" and to isolate traditionalists by making them feel out of step.

When most Americans view television coverage of outrageous, violent demonstrations outside international conferences, they don't realize that the protests are phony. They don't realize that the protests have been designed to repel viewers into emotionally accepting the internationalist agenda and to provide internationalists with the pretext for broadening their agenda, supposedly to address all concerns.

When most Americans hear the same line from multiple sources and in multiple media (e.g., the alleged threat of man-made global warming) and accordingly accept it as fact, they do not suspect that they may be the victims of an orchestrated multi-media propaganda campaign.

And when they hear politicians offer more government to solve crises, they don't realize that the Conspiracy has very calculatingly invented or exploited these crises precisely to provide the emotional pretext for the people to "give up their liberties" and grant government revolutionary new powers.

Most Americans relying on "normal" media for information and opinion on national and world events have no idea that they are the victims of managed news. For how can that be? They see a huge variety of news sources from magazines to radio stations to cable channels offering apparently both "mainstream" and "alternative" perspectives. But they fail to appreciate the common ownerships and Establishment influences that dominate most sources and even constrain their favorite "maverick" broadcaster.

Helping Americans to see through these deceptions is the path to victory. The Conspiracy must be able to operate covertly to succeed.

Which is why Mr. Welch would maintain: "All we must find and build and use, to win, is sufficient understanding."

And Rebuild

Fortunately, the tasks of exposing the Conspiracy and rebuilding our subverted foundations overlap. Effective action to repair those foundations must start with leadership that recognizes the work of the Conspiracy.

One of the best ways to motivate that repair is to help other potential opinion leaders understand why and how the Conspiracy has succeeded in subverting those foundations. That story forcefully drives home the importance of repair while shocking many out of their complacency.

Politically active Americans especially need to grasp the subversion. For much more is needed to restore good government and preserve our freedoms than just naively electing politicians or campaigning on policy issues at the federal, or even state, level.

The Conspiracy's "long march" through our institutions to change the political and cultural environment is what has enabled it to achieve a steady string of victories in Washington. The balance in Washington will not be tilted in freedom's favor until a sound plan is implemented to counter that subversion and a favorable environment is built back home.

We cannot expect success, for example, when the enemy monopolizes the channels of communication with the American public. The long work of rebuilding subverted foundations and developing "sufficient understanding" among the public simply cannot be avoided.

In addition, any serious effort to rebuild must seek to prevent further destruction as a top priority. That means exposing the Conspiracy's continuing influence and agenda, which will also help deny the Conspiracy its power to confound the efforts to rebuild.

The Battle for Public Opinion

Many issue-oriented conservatives focus their attention exclusively on Washington. They have not discovered that public opinion must be changed as the only sure rout to political victories. Or they simply do not have the organization to tackle that task.

Molding public opinion has been at the heart of the Conspiracy's strategy. Its agents of influence and subordinate organizations diligently pursue that strategy. Consider the following example.

The Establishment media have characterized former President Bill Clinton as perhaps the most charismatic of U.S. presidents. But where does Bill Clinton direct that charisma? At Congress? No. He addresses influential opinion molders across the nation.

On September 17, 2007, Clinton spoke to a crowd of 2,000 at the Colorado Convention Center as the keynote speaker for the Aurora Economic Council's third annual A-List luncheon. His principal topics: global warming, the global economy, and the war on terrorism. Mr. Clinton sought to convince the audience that these global problems required international solutions (meaning that sovereign nations must subordinate themselves to internationalist organizations, paving the way for world government).

Clinton's message was also preventative — to denounce "isolationism," once again. It was calculated to prevent the reawakening of America's "berserker nativism" (to use the words of CFR heavyweight Michael Hirsh). The *Rocky Mountain News* reported on Clinton's speech under the headline: "For U.S., 'divorce not an option' — Nation can't isolate itself from the world, ex-president says."

Ever since the Establishment used World War II to entangle the U.S. in the United Nations, it has repeatedly sought to kill an alleged isolationist impulse so that no potential political leader would think of ever again advocating that America act independently. Both Democrats and Republicans, including current President George W. Bush, have joined in the chorus denouncing "isolationism."

But our point here is that President Clinton knew to take his message where it would count. He understood that public opinion had to be prepared in order to make it easier for Washington to implement the internationalist agenda.

Our side needs to grasp that lesson and follow it with as much dedication as does the Left. And that means our campaigns must also battle for public opinion.

We will continue with the challenge of rebuilding America's foundations in the next chapter.

Chapter 11

To Restore Constitutional Government

Confidence is everywhere the parent of despotism.... In questions of power, then, let no more be heard of confidence in man, but bind him down from mischief by the chains of the Constitution.[1]
— Thomas Jefferson, *Kentucky Resolutions*

Any realistic effort to put America back on course must include leadership to restore constitutional government. For freedom to survive and prosper in America, our Republic must be repaired and restored to full effect.

Restoring constitutional government would alone solve many of our problems. For example, if the Constitution were fully enforced, the U.S. would have to withdraw from the UN and from the World Trade Organization (WTO). We would no longer send our men off to war unless Congress voted to declare war. Foreign aid would end and balanced budgets would return. We would quit financing socialism abroad and at home.

The size of the federal government would be cut dramatically, perhaps as much as three-fourths, since many of the contemporary departments and agencies have no constitutionally authorized function.

Few Americans can imagine the incredible boost to *national prosperity* that would result from such a reduction in the overhead of government. As it stands now, for example, government increasingly confiscates through taxes and inflation the greater part of the private earnings that would otherwise go into savings and investment.

In addition, taxpayer dollars would no longer flow to thousands of left-wing organizations. Most of these non-governmental organizations, which have been subverting our culture and institutions, would find it increasingly difficult to be accepted under false colors, and the funding to continue operations would dry up. And loyal, concerned Americans would no longer have to defend against tax-supported subversion with their voluntary after-tax dollars.

One could cite many other benefits that would flow from forcing government to operate within the Constitution.

So how can government be put back on the right course? Ultimately, it is the people, as the superior party in their contract with government, who must enforce that contract — the Constitution.

Congress Is *Part* of the Key

The route to restoring constitutional government (and even breaking the Conspiracy's grip on Washington) runs through the House of Representatives. Individual representatives, to be sure, do not enjoy the prestige and power of a president, but collectively the House of Representatives is arguably the most powerful branch of government.

Although not widely recognized, the Constitution gives the House sufficient power to curtail unconstitutional government spending all by itself. And the House even has the investigative and impeachment power to force the other branches to clean up their act.

The House currently lacks the will to take these steps. But fortunately, the House is the branch most susceptible to public influence.

Moreover, the Founders certainly *intended* that the House would be accountable to the people. To assure that connection, they provided for relatively frequent (every two years) *direct* election of representatives from relatively small districts.

Today, all three branches of the federal government have been corrupted by the same Conspiracy, thus undermining constitutional checks and balances. Of the three, the executive and judicial branches are the most solidly under the Conspiracy's control.

It is the House that provides the greatest natural opportunity to break the Conspiracy's grip on the federal government. Few members of Congress are firmly in that grip — there are just too many representatives, and the territories too small, for a centralized Conspiracy to dominate the local politics. Yet almost all congressmen are quickly, even while candidates, hobbled to the influence of party, which at the national level (for the two major parties) is solidly controlled by the Conspiracy.

Fortunately, the party's heavy corruption of legislator

independence can be overcome. All that is needed is to inform *and organize* an influential segment of a representative's constituents.

Why is that sufficient? Because, the primary motivation for most congressmen still is the desire to be reelected. And parties hold sway over congressmen generally only so long as candidates and incumbents view maintaining the support of the party leadership as the easiest, if not the essential, path to their successful election and reelection.

Those voters who imagine they can, as individuals, reason with their nice congressman to get him to vote properly are greatly deceiving themselves. Real influence with *almost all* congressmen on *significant*, closely contested issues requires clout — the clout to influence their voting constituents.

How much clout? Enough so that the incumbent congressman begins to suspect that he won't be reelected, term after term, if he ignores that clout.

Illusion of Political Gains

One reason why conservative Americans regularly end up with the short end of the stick is that they look to partisan politics for an easy solution. They are fond of supporting a candidate who talks a good game but all too often finds a reason to vote with the internationalists and socialists. They have difficulty accepting the fact that their own smiling, friendly politician may betray them.

Although supporting political candidates is as American as apple pie, such efforts rarely make much of a difference because of the enormous pressures felt by every representative when he gets to Washington. Americans generally don't understand what they are up against, and that is why they are easily persuaded to waste their time and resources in wheel-spinning activities. (See, also, Chapter 17: Presidential Politics.)

Unfortunately, experience proves that just sneaking a "good guy" in the door in Congress for a quick "electoral gain" does little good. The new representative, if he survives a few years, almost always turns out to be a disappointment.

Even the best representatives will rationalize "going along to get along" with their corrupted party leadership, unless their constituents provide them with regular wake-up calls. And invariably the party leadership will argue that "smart" representatives must bend to the pressure of the Conspiracy's orchestrated policy "consensus."

Admiral Ward explained what an individual constituent must often overcome to win the support of his representative: "Once the ruling members of CFR have decided that the U.S. government should adopt a particular policy, the very substantial research facilities of CFR are put to work to develop arguments, intellectual and emotional, to support the new policy, and to confound and discredit, intellectually and politically, any opposition."[2] No representative wants to appear foolish opposing a policy that seems to have no credible opposition.

In his 1966 *Tragedy and Hope*, Carroll Quigley argued that "the two parties should be almost identical, so that the American people can 'throw the rascals out' at any election without leading to any profound or extensive shifts in policy." When the electorate grows weary of one of the Establishment parties, continued Quigley, "it should be able to replace it, every four years if necessary, by the other party, which ... will still pursue, with new vigor, approximately the same basic policies."[3]

Unfortunately, few, even well intentioned, rookie representatives are able to see through the charade of partisan politics. They don't understand that Quigley's "admonition" reflects reality, and so even the idealists among them will invariably rationalize bowing to party pressures.

The reality, however, is that when the party with the more "conservative" image (the Republican Party) dominates, the Conspiracy advances in areas where it can posture its programs as conservative. And when the Democrats are in charge, they sell their programs for centralizing power in Washington as needed social reforms.

The opposition Republicans invariably take a dive against the Conspiracy's "Democrat" agenda by mounting ineffective, pragmatic opposition rather than challenging the underlying premises. The campaign for socialized medicine provides a prime example: The dispute between the parties quickly degenerated into an argument over which form of government control of medicine is most able to address the crises (crises manufactured by prior legislation, the leftists, and the media).

A switch in party domination just substitutes one flavor of socialism for another.

The Action Is *Not* in "Political Action"

Partisan *political* action directed properly at the House of Representatives — the people's House — is surprisingly *ineffective* if a representative's constituents are not first informed, organized, and activated.

Former conservative Congressman Lawrence P. McDonald was a rare political leader. He argued that building an educational base must precede real political gains. "Larry" enjoyed that base in Georgia's 7th district. As a result, he was able to maintain a hard-line position in Congress and still get reelected despite a hostile local press and the infusion of Establishment money to fund opposition candidates from both major parties.

As Larry's popularity grew among conservatives, he was often contacted for advice by would-be imitators in other parts of the country who had visions of quickly getting elected to Congress and taking on the Establishment. Invariably, Larry would counsel them that conservative political victories were difficult and temporary without the grass-roots education that a strong, well informed activist organization would provide.

We would go even further to argue that with such a strong organization providing issue leadership and education locally, political change will materialize naturally — representatives cannot long remain out of step with an informed constituency.

Beyond Elections

Even so, such political change will not necessarily come via the ballot box. Many representatives are very astute at determining which way the political winds are blowing and then quickly adapting to any change in direction. That's to be expected. Though not admirable, such opportunism is certainly tolerable — if we are doing our job to create the right political weather.

Although it's nice to have some true statesmen elected to Congress, good government *can* be obtained and *must* be obtained by pressuring a majority of *incumbents* to vote properly. The greatest value of changing a few seats at election time is not in purging the

House of genuine socialists but in *gaining the attention* of the political pragmatists in office by reminding them who is in charge — the voters, not their party leadership.

To overcome collectivist pressures, particularly pressure from a representative's own party, the bulk of informed constituent pressure must be applied *between* elections.

Yet Americans are being sold a totally false idea that *the ballot box* is the exclusive means by which we can affect how we are governed. Today, it is not even the primary one!

Elections themselves have much too little impact on what our elected representatives think they are accountable for (such as upholding the Constitution) or what they believe they can get away with. Consider the following analogy.

An employer hires several employees because they talk a good line during the job interview. Then he turns them loose without any training or clear explanation of what is expected of them.

Two years go by and the busy employer has paid little attention to what his employees were actually doing or whose agenda was driving them. His principal source of information on their performance has been a newspaper controlled by his competition and dedicated to his destruction. And occasionally, he would also get thank-you notes from his employees, who would invariably reassure him that they were doing a great job on his behalf.

Much later, to his dismay, he discovers that these employees haven't lived up to his expectations — they have created new problems or failed to solve old ones and haven't added sufficient value to his business. *So he fires the lot and starts over.*

The flaws in that approach are obvious, yet that's how many people view the election of their representatives. It is an open invitation to get swindled, and the only surprise should be accountable performance. The more sensible management approach, of course, is for the businessman who pays the salaries to also call the tune to which his employees march. But that means he must give regular direction (signal approval or correction) based on reliable information.

With respect to government, Americans today are generally misinformed, without their realizing it, by the information sources upon which they rely. Unless that is changed, any real course correction through improved constituent supervision or revolt at the ballot box becomes impossible.

The Work Back Home
To gain control of their government, Americans need not only reliable information, but also *an understanding of the principles of freedom* (including constitutional principles) and *an understanding of the Conspiracy*. All that is part of *the educational base* that Congressman McDonald said must be built.

In fact, *exposing the Conspiracy and restoring constitutional government are not either-or options*. The Conspiracy must be exposed to remove its grip from Congress and the other branches. Unless the public, through its opinion molders, is sufficiently enlightened regarding the influence, objectives, strategy, and tactics of the Conspiracy, any well intended constituent pressure on government will be deflected.

Only when there is sufficient pressure from an enlightened and committed public, can we expect any of the three branches of government to develop a proper respect for the Constitution and resist pressures to implement conspiratorial agendas.

Politicians, as a group, will always reflect the pressures that are put upon them. If the Conspiracy succeeds in confusing an apathetic and uninformed public, the politicians will perceive only the internationalist, socialist pressure, with predictable consequences.

However, when the public is properly informed, the political contest moves in the direction of protecting freedom. "Constitutional" Republicans will compete with "constitutional" Democrats and "constitutional" Independents to represent a district.

Real and lasting political results come only from doing the hard work to change the environment that elects, guides, and reelects politicians to public office.

Ultimately, politicians march to the tune of those who mold the political environment. The revolutionary discovered this principle long ago, which explains, in part, why this unpopular minority has been so successful.

And Deeper Still!
The Conspiracy's plans for revolution will not be stopped by

targeting the federal government alone — even the House — because, as we have explained, the Conspiracy's strategy for revolution goes much deeper. The Insiders constantly work to mold public opinion. And they are in a position to do so, because of their "long march" through our opinion-forming institutions.

Through the culture war, the Insiders are attempting to change the values of the people, so that radical changes in the direction and authority of government can be sustained. The Conspiracy has worked to undermine morality, dumb down the public regarding the principles of freedom, eradicate the middle class, alter the culture through massive immigration, and condition Americans to depend on government for the necessities of life.

So even though there is a great opportunity for informed, organized Americans to influence Congress, particularly the House, influencing Congress can be *only one part* of a successful strategy to preserve freedom.

Organized influence is needed to prevail on the American people to overcome the entire Gramscian agenda — to recognize the orchestrated duplicity, champion proper values, and recapture our institutions. Providing this influence in our communities is a major reason why a nationwide Americanist membership organization is essential.

Veteran followers of the great patriot Robert Welch will certainly be familiar with the circles of (direct and indirect) influence concept and the influence projected for a thousand active members in a congressional district (see the next two chapters).

Active, informed members necessarily have influence in many arenas. Thank goodness. For we cannot succeed in preserving freedom if our institutions and the environment surrounding the American people remain permanently in the hands of the enemy. An activist minority will not even be able to hold Congress on track without the support of the public and our other institutions.

The Right Idea
In the middle 1950s, Robert Welch gave up on purely political action and especially on political leadership as a solution to America's problems. He then spent several years searching for the answer — a membership organization under strong leadership. Three years after

founding that organization, Mr. Welch explained in its November 1961 *Bulletin* how public support for needed measures would have to be developed:

> Putting the whole matter as simply as possible, the truth can be stated by political leaders, and the public exhorted by them to accept and follow that truth. But for the truth to be made convincing, to enough key people with enough influence, against all of the deliberate obfuscation practiced so long by the enemy, a far more thorough job of education and exposition must be carried out than the politicians can even initiate. It is a massive undertaking for any group, or for hundreds of patriotic groups all together, but it simply must be done *outside* of the field of direct political action. [Emphasis added.]

At that time, Mr. Welch saw freedom's defenders as underdogs facing an arduous, uphill struggle. He argued that, as in any serious war, responsibility could not be delegated. Meeting the challenge would demand the attention and involvement of all who could be reached in pursuit of *an appropriately realistic plan.*

We will only succeed, maintained Mr. Welch, if we work together to organize and enlist many other pullers at the oars under sound leadership. If we do that, then, and only then, are we on the road to victory.

For a realistic plan to build such an organization, please see the next chapter and section.

ORGANIZE FOR VICTORY!

Section V

And *Organize* for Victory!

Chapter 12

A Realistic Plan of Action

All we must find and build and use, to win, is sufficient understanding.[1]

— Robert Welch, 1958, *The Blue Book*

As developed in the previous section, here, in brief, is what we need to accomplish:

- As our top priority, the conspiratorial forces threatening freedom and our nation must be exposed and routed.

- Simultaneously, we seek to motivate and influence the repair of our institutions and foundations of freedom.

What remains is to present a realistic plan for accomplishing those ambitious objectives.

Our plan is fundamentally the same as was Robert Welch's: Freedom First Society will offer freedom-loving patriots a unique opportunity to work together under principle-driven leadership to make a difference. Collectively, that body of individuals will strive to inform, organize, and give leadership to a sufficient segment of the American people to wake the sleeping giant and change the course of history.

Fortunately, as members and leaders of Freedom First Society, we don't have to do all the work ourselves to accomplish either of the two objectives. But we do have a critical role. Our job must be to fill the pervasive leadership vacuum and provide the initial and decisive leadership to the process.

A New Layer of Strength

Actually, Mr. Welch's plan is to build a new layer of strength that has been sorely lacking since the founding of our nation — a voluntary force of informed and determined patriots, outside of government, whose sole mission is to act as freedom's champion.

That force will not only expose freedom's enemies but also articulate and give leadership to freedom's principles, while reminding us of history's vital lessons.

Although such a plan would have merit in any age, it is an absolutely vital step today. For the Conspiracy has gone to enormous lengths to undermine, capture, and replace the leadership structure within American society. And from that strategic position, the Conspiracy has been able to persuade the public to accept the steady assault on our constitutional order.

As part of any realistic solution, a new grassroots leadership force is essential to counter that subversion. In the past, the Conspiracy had never been confronted by an educational army specifically organized to expose it. Mr. Welch would often argue that this new approach was the one form of opposition that could succeed:

> A sufficiently large organized force which is determined to expose the whole Conspiracy. It is all that will be required. [May 1969 *Bulletin*]

> The Communists and their bosses, the Insiders, have no fear whatsoever of old-fashioned political hostility, or military resistance, or an anti-Communist religious movement, for the reasons we have given above and many others. They have learned from generations of experience how to handle each such problem. The one form of opposition they have never faced before is a sizable, organized, permanent educational force dedicated to the task of exposing their Conspiracy. [April 1973 *Bulletin*]

> Only when a counterattack is based, not on political smartness, but on the solid foundation of information and understanding such as we supply — and the patriotic determination which we try to inspire — do the *Insiders* tremble over the possibilities. [September 1972 *Bulletin*]

The track record compiled by Mr. Welch's infant organization amply confirmed his assessment of this strategy (see next chapter for more details).

Expanding Circles of Influence

A primary mission of members of Freedom First Society is to expand their influence by informing a larger independent circle of opinion molders in the communities of America.

The objective is to help responsible individuals within this circle to understand what the Conspiracy has done and is doing to America as well as to understand the principles of freedom.

Our members will want to focus particular attention on those individuals who, once they have the knowledge, demonstrate the courage, integrity, and determination to speak out and inform others.

Of course, it will be desirable to recruit many of these newly awakened opinion molders into Freedom First Society. These individuals can be most effective if they are plugged into our concerted action campaigns as members, so they can help recruit others. For the plan to work, the organized core of members radiating the leadership simply must grow.

But we would also expect to influence some opinion molders directly, and many indirectly, who might never become members. This ripple influence is also important.

Building this circle of influence is precisely the reverse of the Gramscian long walk through our institutions that has captured or subverted so many of them for socialist, statist objectives. Some of our institutions can and must be recaptured for Americanism and fixed. As the tide of battle shifts, it is likely that more institutions will "discover" better leadership. But still others will have to be exposed and left to die when their support withers.

As a result of our influence, we would also expect leaders to come forward and launch new institutions (such as Robert Welch University) that incorporate Americanist values and set high standards for others to follow.

Because of our immediate heavy organizational focus on exposing the Conspiracy, much of our initial contribution to rebuilding will likely be limited to inspiring and influencing the repair process. We would expect our educational materials and the reach of our members to influence the direction of much of the rebuilding.

A New Channel of Communications

Because of the Conspiracy's dominant influence over the media, particularly as it affects our culture and national and international reporting, a new channel of communications is needed to reach the American people with the truth and leadership.

We are not talking about a technology alternative to the Internet. In fact, the Internet provides exceptional opportunities for improved communication, of great advantage to the freedom fight (see below).

Instead, we are talking here about *organizing* a core of Americans (members) to use their time and personal influence to form *an open, direct line* of communications from new leadership to a growing segment of the American public. This segment needs to be heavily weighted with opinion molders and even include some established opinion *leaders*. The reach of this channel will then extend to even larger numbers of the public *indirectly*.

It is our active educational army, with its expanding circles of influence as described above, that can and must provide this communication channel. One of the powerful benefits of a strong network, with reliable information and leadership at its core, is that it serves to deny the Conspiracy an effective monopoly on information reaching the public. Such a communication channel is essentially immune to Establishment control.

The effectiveness of this new channel will depend to a huge extent on member *activity and influence*.

The *kind* of activity is also important. In our fast-paced world, personal contact is the best route for penetrating the information glut and gaining the attention of responsible Americans at *a sufficiently deep level* to inspire commitment and action. One of the greatest potential strengths of a grassroots organization is this ability of its members to direct personal attention at specific individuals, particularly those they know.

Education Alone Is Not Enough
At this point, it is well to clarify the objective of those communications. Although Mr. Welch selected, for very good reason, the motto, "Education is our total strategy and truth is our only weapon," we should not understand this to mean that we can be satisfied to merely educate ourselves and quietly educate those we can reach.

We must also build on that education and offer leadership for a sound program of action (much of which, of course, starts with more education). Let's remember that Mr. Welch also said, "All we must find and build and use, to win, is sufficient understanding."

We *use* that understanding, for example, by enlisting others in campaigns with specific objectives that resist, reverse, or rout the Conspiracy's plans. So, for example, we would provide leadership to organize informed pressure on Congress to get the United States out of the United Nations. This leadership is far more than just education. It supplies tactics, direction, and organizational support for specific objectives.

Why isn't education alone sufficient? After all, one could point correctly to the Conspiracy's obvious concern about what the American people, *as a whole*, know and think. Otherwise, it wouldn't go to such lengths to deceive. With widespread understanding of the principles of freedom and of the Conspiracy's agenda, the Conspiracy's deceptions would no longer work, would they?

With such an informed public, couldn't we confidently expect that some leaders and resistance would spring up to attack the Conspiracy's influence and roll back its accomplishments? Wouldn't such a result follow as automatically as political victories flow from an informed electorate?

The Flaw in Just Knowing

The rub is that such an informed public *does not exist* — that is the essence of our problem and our challenge. The scenario described above is *pure fantasy* and totally implausible. With the major media in the hands of the enemy, such an informed public *cannot suddenly spring up* anymore that a 10-division army could spring up out of nowhere.

Realistically, knowledge and understanding starts with a few. To impact the general public significantly those few must have a mechanism to gain the public's attention and keep growing. The Conspiracy really doesn't care what these individuals know, even if they should number in the many tens of thousands, if they hold that understanding silently or if their activities fall below the radar of public attention.

The Conspiracy only fears effective resistance, and knowledgeable individuals threaten the Conspiracy's plans only if they use their understanding to:

1. Engage in *visible* activity that challenges the Conspiracy's fiction of a popular consensus;

2. Put pressure on policy decisions; and

3. Support a program to enlighten, organize, and offer leadership to an uncapped growing number of others.

This is the only realistic way that sufficient understanding can be *built and used* to derail the Conspiracy's plans and even threaten the Conspiracy itself. And for those three actions to take place with any significant focus and volume, the activity must be organized.

Opportunity Through the Internet
When Robert Welch started The John Birch Society, he used the most up-to-date methods of communication and outreach available at the time. If he were starting over today, he would be eager to exploit the amazing opportunity provided by the Internet.

Only a couple of decades ago, few could have imagined the extent to which the American people would adopt the home computer, the laptop, and the Internet as an essential part of their lives. Our youth, working professionals, and even many older Americans are now regularly online. With proper Internet technique, broader audiences can be reached more quickly and with less effort than ever before.

And with modest investment, impressive multi-media impact is very realistic. In addition to traditional text communication, members, prospective members, and visitors to Freedom First Society's website will find persuasive video and audio clips to share within their circle of influence.

The world wide web also provides an opportunity to archive forgotten information damaging to the Conspiracy, such as important books long out of print, where it is only a click away for visitors and serious researchers.

The storage capacity and accessibility of the Internet can also make other brief communications very effective by adding depth.

For example, a high-visibility flyer, a short pamphlet, a radio or TV ad, and even a billboard or bumper sticker can create interest and refer the interested individual to a website for more information and recommended action.

As with other websites, our website becomes, in effect, a 24-7 information booth, which the initially curious can visit to determine their level of interest without fear of getting on a mailing list or receiving sales pressure.

The Internet will also serve our organization itself by permitting faster communications and even more personal communications between leadership, volunteer leaders, and members. Live chats and discussion forums are already popular. Action committees will enjoy the improved ability to communicate.

And as more and more Americans take advantage of the latest technology advances on the Internet, even chapters may wish to meet online (e.g., via video conferencing).

Clearly, the rise in popularity of this new medium of free and open communications provides a tremendous opportunity for the freedom fight. The Internet has, at least temporarily, undermined the monopoly on information the Insiders need to advance their plans. And fortunately, steps to regulate the Internet have thus far encountered great resistance. An important agenda item for Freedom First Society will be to help ensure that communication freedom is held inviolate.

Although visitors may be drawn to our website because of its growing reputation for explosive, reliable information, the website will necessarily be focused on involving a portion of these visitors in effective action. With this resource, the Internet becomes a fantastic tool for locating and activating patriots eager to make a difference.

In particular, a website and the Internet are ideally suited to find and enlist new patriots in national concerted action campaigns. We just need to tap the talents of a few young techies who have the same kind of vision that has driven the phenomenal growth of this technology.

National Concerted Action Campaigns

Well constructed national concerted action campaigns challenge the Conspiracy's plans and even the Conspiracy itself. That means they promote the three categories of activity identified above — activity that exposes the fiction of a consensus, puts pressure on policy decisions, and helps build a growing, organized, informed resistance.

For example, the Conspiracy's orchestrated consensus isn't disturbed until busy Americans have a reason to question that consensus. That's where campaigns come in.

What happens when our friends and neighbors see bumper stickers and billboards promoting an alternative message? And newspaper articles and speeches at service clubs do the same? And another friend is seen passing literature around challenging the supposed consensus? Or when Congress begins to hear from concerned citizens who are not regular letter writers and obvious members of an activist minority?

Our answer: Such *visible* activity cannot be ignored. The new alternatives, particularly if they enjoy responsible and authoritative backing, will be recognized as having support and become accepted as challengers in the public debate. Other Americans and especially opinion molders will begin to consider the new information and ideas and become emboldened to question the Establishment's "wisdom."

Keep in mind, however, that we can't afford for these campaigns to just address "issues" and problems without also exposing the arsonists. We must be the "one who is striking at the root," to draw on Henry David Thoreau again.

Although the organization's leadership designs these campaigns, all of their impact, including especially the three impacts listed above, must be accomplished through the activity of members.

The "Impeach Earl Warren" sidebar at the end of this chapter examines a highly successful campaign from the past that illustrates the ripple influence a relatively small *organized* group can achieve when following good leadership.

There are several standards for measuring the success of concerted action campaigns, but a primary standard should be whether the campaign helped the organization to grow stronger for the next battle (the third impact).

It is certainly advantageous, when possible, to *win* significant early battles that slow down the Conspiracy's agenda. However, in virtually any extended war, success is achieved primarily by efforts that strengthen, modernize, and equip your forces for *future decisive* battles.

National concerted action campaigns are just part of the formula for success. Exposing the Conspiracy successfully requires that a growing segment of the American public step up to the plate and become involved in a new leadership force. Since our nation's leadership hierarchy has been corrupted, the cleansing must be forced from the bottom up.

As we shall see in the next chapter, leadership for a program to build that core force (the active, educational army) to an *adequate size* must be a part of any plan with victory as its goal.

"Impeach Earl Warren"

In January 1961, The John Birch Society launched a nationwide concerted action campaign calling for the impeachment of Chief Justice of the Supreme Court Earl Warren. But the campaign did far more that just popularize the symbolic "Impeach Earl Warren" slogan, and it was concerned about much more than the transgressions of the chief justice.

At the time, very few Americans had any awareness of the judicial activism then permeating the Supreme Court or of its numerous subversive, even pro-Communist decisions. Most Americans were simply accustomed to regarding the Court and its decisions as sacrosanct.

The Establishment media generally dismissed the campaign with ridicule. But the very fact that the campaign was mentioned at all was an indication that the Establishment, worried about the impact, was trying to do damage control.

Previously, a number of speeches, reports, and newspaper and magazine articles attacking subversive decisions of the Supreme Court had appeared in print. But collectively they had not achieved much circulation or impact.

That changed after the Society launched its campaign and its members began "putting legs under literature" and *urging support for a plan of action*. Their activities succeeded in getting the shocking revelations about the decisions of the Court heard widely and taken seriously. As a result, Congress began to hear from a growing number of well informed concerned citizens.

The campaign had impact, because Society members dealt in facts and specifics. They made good use of a stirring, well documented exposé of the Supreme Court entitled *Nine Men Against America — The Supreme Court and Its Attack on American Liberties*. Published initially by Devin Adair as a hardback, it was soon republished in less expensive formats and perhaps as many as a hundred thousand copies were distributed personally by Society members.

Although Earl Warren was not impeached, the impact of the Society's educational campaign continues to this day. Other opinion leaders were emboldened to turn the spotlight of public criticism or applause on the Court. Supreme Court decisions and nominees became regular political campaign issues.

Abe Fortas

The nomination of Associate Justice Abe Fortas to succeed a retiring Earl Warren as chief justice became an immediate target of that new scrutiny. In a sane world, the leftist credentials and communist affiliations of Fortas should have quickly disqualified him from consideration. But this was the world of Conspiracy-managed politics, and the Senate had long acted as a rubber stamp for the most outrageous of presidential nominations.

This time, however, thanks to the Society's earlier work to expose the subversive actions of the Court, a follow-up grassroots letter-writing campaign was able to persuade the Senate to refuse to confirm Fortas. This was the first time since 1795 that a presidential nominee for chief justice had been rejected.

Chapter 13

The Principal Challenge: Building Organization

Our objective, however, is victory, not martyrdom. And we are very realistic about the chances of a battalion armed only with rifles against a division equipped with field artillery.
— Robert Welch, August 1969 *Bulletin*

If we can get just one thousand members in every Congressional District, before it is too late, we can win the war. The solution is that simple, and the task is that important.
— Robert Welch, July 1971 *Bulletin*

When a powerful conspiracy dominates our major institutions of influence and is skillfully employing the strategy of divide, confuse, and conquer, there is no easy, instant remedy. But the smart response, and likely the only viable one, is to inform *and organize* the intended victims whose liberties are at stake. What the architects of world government fear most is an aroused and informed American public, receiving organized leadership they don't control.

Although exposing the Conspiracy's plans in all their implications to the general public would undoubtedly derail those plans, building a force equal to the task is easier said than done. In the process, several major obstacles to waking and leading the sleeping giant must be overcome.

After a decade of experience developing and leading a quality organization under fire, Robert Welch was convinced his organization could do the job — if only it could grow substantially larger.

Mr. Welch had mapped out the path. The whole challenge became a race to gain sufficient members in time. In the May 1970 *Bulletin*, he wrote:

Just one Coordinator, and one thousand members, of the

same caliber and dedication as those we now have, in every one of 435 Congressional Districts in this country, could do the job. They would supply the base of information and understanding which would enable Conservative anti-Communists, of any and all parties, to use successfully the mechanics of political action that would halt the whole approaching horror.

Organization Works

By 1970, Mr. Welch had plenty of experience upon which to base such a statement. He had seen the impressive impact that a relatively few active members had achieved on many fronts.

For example, in 1966 inspired area members organized the defeat of a dangerously subversive proposal put forth by the popular liberal New York City Mayor John Lindsay. The proposal supported a nationwide campaign to hamstring local police with civilian review boards — a campaign actually orchestrated by the Communists. New York City was to be the prototype. But the overwhelming defeat of the civilian review board proposal in *the liberals' own backyard* effectively killed this dangerous initiative nationwide.

Mr. Welch's assessment of The John Birch Society's impact was echoed many times in the liberal press.

Numbers Matter

The impact of a thousand members in a congressional district can perhaps best be understood by realizing the influence that opinion molders have in general and how much greater is the impact of an *activist* opinion molder.

Rough estimates have been frequently given that one active member of Mr. Welch's organization would exercise substantial influence on at least 10 others directly over the course of a year. And these 10 would become to some extent opinion molders themselves influencing 10 others to a lesser degree. In combination, 1,000 *activist* members could be seen to influence, with some overlap, roughly 100,000 directly and indirectly.

For 2004, the national voting-age population was estimated at 221,257,000 or approximately 509,000 per congressional district. Of these, on average 402,000 were registered. 220,000 (per district) actually turned out to vote in the general election. Two years earlier, in a non-presidential election year with a slightly smaller registration, an average of only 184,000 voted in each district.

Undoubtedly, the number voting in the primaries was even smaller. Clearly, 100,000 relatively informed voters would have a decisive impact on the outcome of any congressional election. And that is just *one* of the impacts of a thousand-member activist educational force.

The formula works and has worked. It doesn't require organizing an impossible percentage of the public, but it does require that the force be tenacious and focus on principle above party and personality. And the members need sufficient understanding so that they will refrain from sacrificing principle on the altar of partisan politics.

In a few areas of the country, with heavy investment in organizing, active membership approached the target density. While that membership level was maintained, the impact was impressive.

By 1980, for example, thanks to member educational efforts, Idaho voters had become sufficiently aware of the very left-wing record of their veteran senator Frank Church that they elected a conservative congressman to replace him. Constituents continued to hold their new senator's feet to the fire through several terms during which he became a strong dissenting voice, supporting the Constitution and taking the lead to challenge key liberal initiatives, such as O.S.H.A.

Hitting the Growth Wall
The initial growth of Mr. Welch's organization, which really got underway in 1959, was spectacular. At the time, there was a leadership vacuum in the conservative, anti-Communist movement with thousands of small organizations and efforts going in many directions, but collectively accomplishing very little. To many patriotic Americans, Mr. Welch's plan and leadership seemed to be the answer, and organizational growth skyrocketed.

But it was unreasonable to expect that the Conspiracy would sit idly while Mr. Welch built an organization that could derail its plans. So, in fact, the Conspiracy orchestrated a major campaign to smear The John Birch Society, which began in February of 1961.

Surprisingly, this smear helped as much as it hurt because of the free publicity and credibility it gave the organization. Some of the weaker members went by the wayside, but Mr. Welch had invested a great deal in helping members to understand what they were up against. He explained convincingly that any group that seriously intended to be effective had to expect to be attacked. In fact, the way to avoid being smeared was not to avoid making mistakes, but simply to be ineffective.

The outrageous smear campaign incensed most members and helped motivate them to greater efforts and dedication. The high-profile attention particularly gave them an added sense of being at the center of something truly effective.

The smear's negative impact was that it took more time to recruit individual members, i.e., to convince prospects that Mr. Welch was providing outstanding leadership. But because of all the attention the Society was receiving, more prospects were interested and willing to spend that time.

Even so, the organization was eventually forced to change tactics and emphasize the growth of ad hoc committees such as Support Your Local Police and MOTOREDE — the Movement to Restore Decency. By participating in the Society's ad hoc committees, skittish individuals could support specific projects of the organization without becoming "official" members of The John Birch Society and appearing to endorse all its ideas, particularly those distorted by a hostile media.

Then the Conspiracy, likely recognizing its error, changed tactics. In the ensuing decades the Establishment media gave The John Birch Society the silent treatment or treated it as though it were an artifact of the past and no longer a viable force.

That treatment undoubtedly made recruiting more difficult because of its impact on member morale and the organization's image. It was no longer so easy to convince members and prospects that Mr. Welch's organization was really where the action was and that it was having an impact.

More Difficult, Still Achievable

Other concurrent trends in society made it more difficult to compete for the interest and time of progressively overcommitted and uninformed Americans. Volunteer recruiters were themselves experiencing increasing demands on their time. Nevertheless, growth was still very achievable, particularly if tactics were adjusted to take advantage of new methods and technologies such as the Internet.

But recruitment requires focus, and achieving that focus became perhaps the biggest challenge of all. Too many members, and even staff, had lost the vision of growth and had become complacent or wedded to easier, but inadequate objectives.

And many field staff responded to the pressure for growth by focusing on immediate recruitment opportunities rather than providing leadership for the often more time-consuming investment in recruiting future potential leaders. The absolutely essential growth could not explode, or even be sustained, without a focus on recruiting men and women with demonstrated influence and developing a quality leadership structure.

Clearly, adjustments were necessary, but they were extremely difficult to implement within the framework that had evolved over many years. That is why the opportunity to relaunch Mr. Welch's strategy with a brand new organization having the proper focus is exciting. Although it is a daunting task in today's climate to attract the needed resources, this time around we have the advantage of decades of experience.

Traps for the Unrealistic

Building organization under sound leadership is still the path to an informed electorate that can defend itself against the Conspiracy. But we must avoid some traps by learning from the past.

In the more challenging recruiting climate of recent decades, many veterans of the freedom fight succumbed to the temptation to take the easier but ineffective path of immersing themselves in projects and campaigns, while ignoring the necessity to recruit and build. They would even ignore the improved recruiting opportunities through the campaigns and the fact that successful recruiting adds muscle to future campaigns.

Yet in doing so they became totally *unrealistic*, repeating Mr. Welch's words, "about the chances of a battalion armed only with rifles against a division equipped with field artillery."

Even dedicated veterans fell victim to variations of ineffective strategy. Some, for example, would immerse themselves in an issue and just try to *educate* the public at large — an absolutely losing strategy for a small force.

Of course, many members listened to leadership and started down the right path. They would work diligently to make a breakthrough in understanding with some individual or group. But through lack of local leadership, too many would often stop short of the follow-up steps to interest a potential prospect in becoming a member. Unfortunately, as every farmer understands, sowing without reaping is quite unproductive.

What Thomas N. Hill, Mr. Welch's right hand man for more than 25 years, wrote in 1973 is still on target: "[S]imply to reach and inform the uninformed is not enough at this stage of the battle. The plain simple truth is that, in order to win, we need more steady 'pullers at the oars.'"[1]

Even involving non-members in our campaigns, a very worthwhile step, does not go far enough to tap the full power of building organization. To tap that power, the practice of inviting and persuading some to join must be added.

Incredibly, other veterans who had lost the vision of building were satisfied to confine their influence to communicating with their congressman, attempting to inform and reason with him. Unfortunately, this imagined shortcut expects too much of a politician and can only lead to disappointment.

We are not suggesting that the organization can succeed without projects and campaigns. *Using* the organization *while building* it is essential. But merely using it *without building it* is a strategic blunder.

Success requires both activities — *building* and *using* the organization. Fortunately, the two activities reinforce each other. Campaigns (using) provide the appeal, the urgency, and the excitement for joining. But building organization provides the realistic hope of victory (of an organization big enough to wage victorious campaigns).

Let's Go for the Gold

The only reason Mr. Welch founded a membership organization was to provide the best leadership he could *to win*. His goal was not just to be heard, to publish a successful magazine, or to earn an income from the fight (he used up virtually all his personal assets in the battle). His responsible objective instead was to provide leadership for a difficult, but ultimately effective, strategy to save his beloved America.

And we seek to carry on that responsibility. So we are enthusiastic over the opportunity to start fresh and build a new organization with new habits and disciplines.

One thousand members in a congressional district is a difficult, but not unreasonable, target for recruitment. It represents only two-tenths of one percent of the adult population. Moreover, with further experience, Mr. Welch lowered his estimate of the number required by half.

In the July 1969 *Bulletin*, Mr. Welch provided this admonition to his members:

> There is a familiar adage that the worth of every accomplishment is directly proportional to the labor and cost that it requires. There may be exceptions, we suppose. But in the struggle that engages us we cannot run the risk of counting on any lucky breaks.

The outcome of this battle surely hinges on what we do with what we know. We have a tried and tested formula that works. But will we dedicate ourselves to applying it? That is the question.

The enemy has tried to poison the well to make it more difficult to alert our fellow citizens. And its burden on the economy has diminished the free time for many. But we are still free to talk to our neighbors, and we have the advantage of being able to make personal contact to gain our neighbors' attention. Moreover, time *is* running out, and we cannot expect the opportunities for successful action to improve.

Becoming a part of an organizational body, such as Freedom First Society, is the most powerful investment an individual can make in the freedom fight. And it is a necessary investment. Anything else by way of individual efforts will be meaningless against the Conspiracy's investment in organization.

But building a *big* organization is not the *total* answer. It must also be the *right kind* of organization with the *right kind* of leadership.

For more on that issue, please refer to Appendix C: Not Just *Any* Organization.

In our next chapter, we hope to seal the issue that organizing is the essential path to victory.

Chapter 14

Organize, You Say?

When bad men combine, the good must associate; else they will fall one by one, an unpitied sacrifice in a contemptible struggle.[1]
— Edmund Burke, 1770

The importance the Conspiracy has placed on organization provides perhaps the most compelling reason for its prospective victims to organize. Anyone who appreciates the extent to which the Conspiracy is able to manipulate world and national events to advance its goals has to be impressed with its supporting organization.

We are referring not only to the hidden conspiratorial structure, but also to the numerous front groups (such as the Council on Foreign Relations) that the Conspiracy has created and directly controls, as well as to the network of influence, in some cases outright domination, it has achieved over many other independently established organizations, institutions, and even governments.

That supporting organization enables the Conspiracy to implement audacious strategy, to practice deception on a grand scale, to engage in intricate, long-range, and patient planning, and to support a mind-boggling array of subversive programs. The capacity of this conspiratorial organization to create problems, grab or divert public attention, and lobby effectively for dangerous solutions is immense.

There have always been men who lusted for power. But never have they been so well organized. From his study of history, Robert Welch was convinced that improvements in organization of the enemy were at the root of the immense danger we now face:

> There has, nevertheless, been a tremendous increase during the past two centuries in the efficacy, the unceasing impact, and the deadliness of the collectivist weapons. It is the basic reason for this huge difference that is the chief theme of our concern tonight. And that difference can be expressed quite simply in just one word: *organization*.[2]

Individuals working alone cannot adequately do battle with this force. They have to organize. Such a step is the necessary antidote to the age-old "divide and conquer" strategy of the ambitious few who seek power over the complacent many. Would-be tyrants can only succeed if they can keep their prospective victims confused and disorganized.

Sale Not Automatic

Despite the increasing urgency to organize in self-defense under sound leadership, busy, often overcommitted, individuals naturally resist committing to organization, until they clearly understand the need.

With insufficient understanding, many are easily tempted to follow those who promise an easier "solution" — one that doesn't make many new demands. (For example, the line of so many Washington, D.C. beltway organization fundraisers can be summarized as: "Just send money, and we'll fight the battles for you.")

A great many Americans recognize that something is seriously wrong in our nation. But too many conclude, perhaps uncomfortably, that America is simply beset by a series of unrelated or politically motivated problems. Those who do not yet appreciate the magnitude of conspiratorial influence, and the looming disaster, undoubtedly find it tempting to rationalize that half-way measures can save the American dream.

In that state of mind, many individuals would understandably prefer to act alone without making any significant commitment to others. How much easier to just take up a single-issue challenge when one feels like it, write a few letters from time to time, share some books, email a few links, carry some pamphlets, and educate our friends.

In this section, we explain at length what should perhaps be obvious — that organization is absolutely essential to defend against and defeat a well organized, influential, experienced, successful enemy. We devote so much space to this topic precisely because this is arguably the most difficult hurdle to overcome in stopping the Conspiracy — helping a sufficient number of fine Americans to recognize both the need for organization and the imperative to focus their energies on building it.

A Closer Look
Several attributes of organization help explain why building organization is the only responsible reaction to the well organized attack on our freedoms:

• Organizations provide the **opportunity to pool resources**, information, experience, and manpower for greater effectiveness or for tasks simply beyond the capability of an individual acting alone. Accomplishing anything of major magnitude, such as rebuilding our layers of strength, requires organization.

• Organizations benefit similarly from the **power of specialization** of function. For example, the person whom you recruit into an organization can be quickly passed on to others for training, development, and activation.

• Another benefit is that participating in a small group within the organization helps **overcome the weakness of good intentions**. Everyone faces pressures on his time. But as members, individuals are much more likely to keep working in the fight, because they constantly receive leadership and because they associate with other committed volunteers.

If we wake up an individual to the threat of some internationalist initiative, such as the North American Union, he may offer resistance for a time. But there is little likelihood he will remain involved beyond a few weeks or months unless he is committed to a permanent, organized program.

Although each member's participation is completely voluntary, implied commitments are nevertheless forged that make it easier for many to set aside time for the freedom fight and maintain long-term involvement.

Impact of Concerted Action
A primary reason why organization is needed for defense against a powerful aggressor is the opportunity organization provides for **concerted action** — the coordinating of sizeable forces at carefully selected targets.

Following the Japanese attack on Pearl Harbor, many young men enlisted in America's *organized* effort to fight a war. They understood the need for concerted action following a sound plan. Few would have considered grabbing a rifle and going off to fight the Japanese as individuals.

Mr. Welch discussed the advantage of concerted action in the August 1968 *Bulletin*:

> In the preceding pages we have borne down on the value of *organization*, and of organized activity, in this struggle with the Communists — or in any struggle. We can put the whole theme in its simplest form as follows: Ten men, doing the same thing at the same time, in support of some strategically sensible effort, are worth more in any battle or to any cause than a hundred men, each of whom is fighting for the same purpose, but in whatever way, and at whatever time or place, may best suit his own fancy. Real wars are won by armies, not by sniping stragglers, no matter how patriotic and determined each straggler may be. This is why army draft boards ... pay no attention to a man's claim that he "can accomplish more on the outside."

For successfully opposing an organized force, an organized movement is greatly superior to even strong leadership that lacks an organized following. In the July 1977 *Bulletin*, Mr. Welch offered a prime example:

> To some extent our activities have constituted primarily a continuation of the effort begun by Joe McCarthy. But with one vital difference. McCarthy had no grassroots organization for implementing his arguments or extending his reach. And without such permanently organized popular support he and his whole effort could be, and were, completely destroyed in the six years of 1951 through 1956.

Leverage through Enlisting Others

So you want your influence to make a difference, a big difference? If so, consider that organization provides the means to enlist others to join with you in effective action. Moreover, it is far easier to persuade others to join an organization when you yourself are a member. As a member, you also gain the opportunity to extend your influence through your colleagues in the organization. No one individual can do it all. But one individual can inspire many others to commit to an organizational vision that can move mountains.

By contrast, the non-joiner is unable to recruit others to follow in his footsteps with his energy, judgment, and commitment. Surprisingly, we have encountered many individuals who do not seem bothered by this dilemma.

Some of these committed non-joiners work diligently to share all kinds of information with others. A few notable individuals have been aptly described as the "fastest pamphleteer in the West." They always seemed to have a hard-hitting pamphlet to share with everyone they met. You certainly had to admire their dedication and enthusiasm — some kept at their self-appointed task for decades.

In the past, the "weapon of choice" was the pamphlet. Now it is more likely to be an email of a link to a story or website. Irrespective of the tactic, however, there are serious weaknesses with the "we don't need to organize, let's just get the word out" approach.

The primary weakness is that these loners are following a program that, by itself, can't win. They are not developing anyone to stand shoulder to shoulder with them or even follow in their footsteps. They have no ongoing action program to offer those they might briefly influence. And, as confirmed non-joiners, they cannot credibly connect others to a reliable source for such direction.

As lone soldiers, they are, in effect, trying to overcome the combined negative influences constantly bombarding their communities all by themselves. It's not a strategy that works in the military, and it won't enable America to defeat its enemies.

This example of the non-joiner activist illustrates one of the great illusions gripping even many *joiners* — the idea that a sufficient objective in the freedom fight is to "just get the word out." That strategy is about as effective as fighting poverty by tossing money from the windows of a skyscraper. Or as effective as a farmer trying to feed his family by tossing seed out the window as he drives down a country road.

Forward thinkers seek ways to leverage or multiply the impact of their efforts. They invest in tractors to replace the horse-pulled plow or in factories and organizations that enlist many hands. Enlisting others in an organized defense of freedom is a powerful way to leverage your influence.

Opportunity to Perpetuate One's Impact

Perhaps the most powerful leverage comes from building an organization founded for a continuing purpose. That is particularly so if building the organization to a specific size equates with success. As with investing at compound interest, your investment in organization continues to grow, even when you stop adding to the principal.

As an example, an individual's investment in building a chapter often continues for generations and gives birth to or inspires other functioning units. By contrast, when acting alone your influence pretty much stops when you stop. Even ripples of education get weaker and weaker and need to be renewed.

A comparison of the lives of two of the most influential preachers of the 18th Century illustrates this principle. Each of these preachers followed a quite different course for spreading the Gospel.

George Whitefield was famous for his exceptional speaking talents. His open air-preaching to crowds, often numbering 10,000 or more, contributed significantly to the Christian revival movement in America known as the Great Awakening. It has been estimated that, throughout his life, Whitefield preached more than 18,000 formal sermons in America and England, sometimes averaging 10 a week. However, he often left his converts without any organization so that much of his work had only short-term impact. Very few Christians would even recognize his name, today.

Not so with Whitefield's contemporary — John Wesley. One influential Christian author offered this explanation for the contrast: "Wesley was an itinerant preacher just like Whitefield, engaging in large, outdoor evangelistic meetings. But Wesley was also an organizer. He created an organizational structure to fulfill his purpose that far outdated his lifetime. That organization is called the Methodist Church!"[3]

Perhaps another example of contrasting approaches will drive home the principle. During the middle of the last century, Haroldson Lafayette (H.L.) Hunt became one of the wealthiest oilmen in

America. Concerned about our nation's future, Hunt invested heavily in several Christian and conservative causes.

One of the big projects H. L. Hunt supported was a nationally syndicated radio program, *Life Line*, headquartered in Dallas, Texas. *Life Line* consisted of a series of daily 15-minute commentaries, powerfully narrated by Melvin Munn. So powerful were many of these "wake-up calls" that transcripts were made available as pamphlets. Enthusiastic listeners could and would buy and share these pamphlets widely.

But again, no organization was offered. Listeners could applaud the personality-driven radio program and encourage others to tune in, but the program's leadership pretty much stopped there.

H.L. Hunt's son, Nelson Bunker Hunt, followed in his dad's footsteps. He was also very generous with several Christian and conservative causes. But Bunker Hunt became a very good friend of Robert Welch, whom he greatly respected. And for many years, Bunker was a major benefactor of The John Birch Society and even sat on its Council.

Although aging veterans of the freedom fight may still recall the radio program supported by the father, the organization Mr. Welch founded not only became a household word, but, more importantly, the generations of members of that organization had a major impact on building resistance to the Conspiracy and slowing its timetable by decades.

Conspiracy Vulnerable to Organized Counterattack

Although the enemies of freedom are well organized and very influential, with tremendous resources at their disposal, they are still only a small minority. That small minority can enslave the greater population only if it can keep the public disorganized, confused, and divided while it consolidates its power.

The Conspiracy's attack cannot stand up to a sizeable force of dedicated patriots organized under sound leadership to simply bring out the truth. Building that force is our challenge.

Fortunately, the potential supply of members is virtually unlimited: The Freedom First Society can and must be built from those members of the uncorrupted public who have the sense of responsibility, the means, the motivation, and the courage to step forward and accept leadership for a plan of action to influence others.

In addition, Freedom First Society must be built according to sound principles that are actually *applied* throughout the organization. This book has been written as a first step to ensure that those principles are both understood *and* applied.

Section VI

Members in Action

Chapter 15

Member Opportunity
and Responsibility

It is not the speeches that we sponsor, nor the articles we print, nor the films we produce, nor the books we publish, which will bring the American people to their senses before it is too late. It is the work which you thousands and then more thousands of patriotic members do, to get these messages more widely heard and seen and read, that really counts on this field of battle.
— Robert Welch, February 1973 *Bulletin*

Freedom First Society offers members the opportunity to change the course of history by working with other patriots under sound organizational leadership.

As its first priority, Freedom First Society will provide members with the organization, programs, campaigns, and educational tools to build an active force of sufficient size to expose and rout the Conspiracy. And we must do this building, exposing, and routing before the Conspiracy can completely subvert our freedoms and establish its tyrannical new world order.

Members have special opportunities not available to non-members. Those opportunities stem principally from the fact that only the right kind of organization, built to sufficient size, can stop the Conspiracy (see Appendix C: Not Just *Any* Organization). Not surprisingly, patriots can support that solution much more effectively by working on the inside of that body, as members. Here are some examples of the unique opportunities members have to make a difference:

- Participate at a level where many pullers at the oars can turn the tide of battle.
- Help bring others into the organization.
- Work with others in planning and executing campaigns.
- Serve in volunteer leadership positions.

- Inspire others through one's own participation.
- Get plugged in. Receive regular organizational communications.
- Get to know and work with others who are part of an organization and a strategy to change the course of history.

Opportunity often comes in disguise. As the year 1995 opened, one of your authors (as JBS CEO at the time) shared this lesson with JBS members about recognizing and seizing opportunity:

> With an enemy completely surrounding us, opportunity abounds. But there are no gifts in this battle. Only by strength of vision and determined effort can we turn opportunity into accomplishment. Our situation is not unlike that described by the poet Edward R. Sill:
>
> This I beheld, or dreamed it in a dream: —
> There spread a cloud of dust along a plain;
> And underneath the cloud, or in it, raged
> A furious battle, and men yelled, and swords
> Shocked upon swords and shields. A prince's banner
> Wavered, then staggered backward, hemmed by foes.
>
> A craven hung along the battle's edge,
> And thought, "Had I a sword of keener steel —
> That blue blade that the king's son bears — but this
> Blunt thing!" — he snapped and flung it from his hand
> And lowering crept away and left the field.
>
> Then came the king's son, wounded, sore bestead,
> And weaponless, and saw the broken sword,
> Hilt-buried in the dry and trodden sand,
> And ran and snatched it, and with battle-shout
> Lifted afresh he hewed his enemy down,
> And saved a great cause that heroic day.[1]

Indeed, much can be accomplished with meager means provided there is determination and a clear vision of the objective. The resistance of the Mujahideen to the Soviet invasion of Afghanistan in December 1979 provided a stirring example. Initially, the Moslem freedom fighters were forced to meet that unwanted challenge with little more than pre-WWI Lee Enfield rifles. Yet during a decade of persistence they were able to prevent the Soviet occupation forces from completing their conquest.

With respect to *our* challenge, prime examples of opportunity in disguise are those created using scarce organizational resources, such as locally hosted public educational programs (e.g., seminars, speeches, and video presentations). These programs have been developed for outreach — to offer members an unusually effective vehicle for bringing others into the fight.

Please don't take these fleeting, hard-earned opportunities for granted. Members with vision and determination will seek to take advantage of these events by interesting qualified guests in attending.

Prospective members will certainly want to know what else they can do and need to do to make a difference. So let's look at some of the key responsibilities of *volunteer members* of Freedom First Society.

Responsibilities

The activity of volunteers is our organization's lifeblood.

Freedom First Society is an organization of volunteers. It must be *built* by volunteers for *the use* of volunteers. Organized members are, in effect, the lifeblood of our organization.

Of course, leaders — staff and volunteer — provide direction to the total effort. But our entire meaningful influence and impact comes from the activity of volunteer members. If our campaigns are taken seriously in Washington, it is because members have worked to inform and mobilize the local non-member community.

Member outreach activity also generates interest in Freedom First Society locally, and even nationally, so that recruiting becomes easier. As a bonus, sufficiently inspired prospects may contact local leadership or national headquarters, perhaps through our website. By contrast, any stand-alone PR undertaken by headquarters to enhance Society's national presence should be viewed as an occasional welcome dessert, not the main course.

Headquarters staff exist to provide members in the field with the tools, strategies, and recommended action plans to be effective in influencing others. Staff and staff projects count only as they enable members to use their influence effectively.

Although volunteers will differ in their abilities, opportunities, and even commitment to participate, each member should understand that preserving America is his responsibility. By joining Freedom First Society, a volunteer does not pass along or delegate this responsibility to volunteer leaders or staff. Through his membership in the organization, a member is simply able to carry out his own responsibility with much greater impact.

And that points to **the ultimate responsibility** of any member who seriously wants to make a difference — **to be effective**. To be effective, a member needs to observe several principles:

Effective action means action *focused* on the *current* agenda.
Scattered activity cannot succeed in exposing and routing the Conspiracy and restoring a healthy constitutional republic. For Freedom First Society to achieve these goals, its volunteer members must act as a body with specific ends in mind.

Perhaps a favorite analogy will clarify our point. After Pearl Harbor, America's forces set out to accomplish very specific strategic objectives in the war with Japan. The infantry did not just go out in all directions and kill the enemy wherever it could be found. Instead, the branches of the military, acting as a body, sought to capture very specific islands that would help set the stage to force Japan's capitulation.

Sound battle strategy (military, marketing, or activist) dictates concentrating your forces for a noticeable or break-through impact at a strategic point. It is particularly important for smaller forces to follow that rule. For if a relatively smaller force fragments its efforts to work on many fronts, then the resulting unimpressive impacts go largely unnoticed. This is not the way to gain attention and support to build your forces.

It is leadership's responsibility to select the targets and campaigns. In so doing, leadership must carefully weigh the various opportunities, our own limited resources, the time required for build-up of our campaign vs. the need for timeliness, and past experience.

It is then the responsibility of members to support these campaigns, absent any disagreement on principle, so that our body can act in unison for maximum effect. In fact, the opportunity to participate effectively in quality concerted action campaigns is a principle reason why prospects should consider membership in Freedom First Society.

Effective action means action with the *end in mind*.
To be effective one must execute any activity with the end in mind. In the Pacific branch of World War II, capturing strategic islands was never an end in itself. The military didn't stop because it won one of these battles. Nor did it get caught up with capturing every island while forgetting why these very costly battles were necessary. Indeed, General Douglas MacArthur would bypass many Japanese-held islands, because he properly viewed the island campaign as only a means to an end.

It is a similar situation with Freedom First Society. In the remainder of this chapter we are going to list a number of responsibilities of volunteer members. But most of these responsibilities are mere steppingstones to building a body of sufficient strength (health and size) that can roll back the Conspiracy's gains and defeat it.

And even though some members will need to specialize, from time to time, in their responsibilities, such as in hosting speeches, those activities must never become ends in themselves. So when we discuss specific responsibilities in what follows, realize that many are merely intermediate steps supporting the building process.

Effective action means *following through* to the objective.
Effective action means following a good strategy that leads to the right objective. But it also means following the strategy to completion.

Consider the farmer planting his crops. Planting is certainly a necessary step if the farmer hopes to be able to harvest down the road. However, it would be silly for the farmer to forever plant and never harvest. Yet, strangely, many in the freedom fight forever plant seeds without following up to reap what they have sown.

Effectiveness requires *a balance* between education and (organized) action.

It has been aptly observed: "Education without action leads to frustration, whereas action without education generates fanaticism." But there are other reasons why a balance between education and action is necessary.

Self-education is important, but only as a means to an end. Although a primary responsibility of members is to develop their own understanding of the principles of freedom and to inform themselves of the threats to it, the primary *purpose* for informing oneself must be as a means for taking effective action — of becoming educating fire-fighters. We simply have no need for the educated who will do nothing with what they know.

As we shall see, a similar consideration applies to educating others. Little is accomplished by informing those who will do nothing with what they learn. Or by informing others without going to the next step of recommending effective action and asking for their involvement.

Effective action means *informing others*.

During his two-day presentation at the JBS founding, Robert Welch introduced his ambitious solution with these thoughts:

> Truth, reality, human instinct, and the overwhelming weight of human desire are on our side. We have these points in our favor, against a conspiracy which must depend on falsehood, cunning, and terror, utilized by less than five percent of the total population. To feel that we cannot win that struggle is a form of pessimism to which I, for one, shall never yield.[2]

And Mr. Welch did not yield to any such pessimism. "The difficulty," as one of your authors would later point out, "is that those truths must be conveyed to individuals who have sufficient character to act upon them. Our message cannot deliver itself. You and I must take responsibility to spread it. Just as we have been warned, we *must* warn our neighbors."[3]

Often, members of Freedom First Society need to act like the little boy in the fable about the emperor's new clothes. The boy provided a much needed "reality check" by simply blurting out the truth.

Effective action means *involving others*.
As we noted in our discussion of the Impeach Earl Warren campaign (see the sidebar following Chapter 12), several excellent reports exposing the subversive actions of the Supreme Court had previously been published. A powerful transcript of a Senate subcommittee hearing was even available from the Government Printing Office.[4] But few Americans took notice of this information, and very little happened until Mr. Welch launched his campaign.

Moreover, this campaign would never have earned media attention and achieved the impact that it did — on the public and on Congress — if Mr. Welch's members had confined their efforts to contacting Congress directly. Instead, *members created a movement!* They posted billboards, wrote letters to newspapers, inspired other organizations to pass resolutions, circulated petitions, and *enlisted the support of others*, who contacted Congress.

And many of those non-members who became involved in the campaign would also become members.

Members need to recognize that when it comes to controversial issues most public officials and political leaders only respond to clout. Yet many activists naively expect to move political leaders to tough action simply by reasoning with them *directly*. The shortcut approach simply doesn't work.

Effective concerted action campaigns are those designed to mobilize *new* and *growing pressure* by informing and activating *non-members* to use their influence. That is the kind of member activity politicians and the media notice.

Effective action *measures success by* the bottom line — *growth*.
Growth is not the ultimate objective of our efforts. Our ultimate objective is to preserve our freedoms by routing the Conspiracy and restoring our Republic. But logic and experience both demonstrate that *the essential path* to that accomplishment is to build a *healthy* organizational body of *sufficient size*. Growth is both the primary *obstacle* and the *key* to our success.

So we should focus our serious educational work on persuading *specific* individuals to *do something* with their knowledge to influence others. And then we must *further focus* on helping to inspire the best of these contacts to *join* our organization for more permanent and constructive activism.

In the past, JBS members would frequently work diligently to make a breakthrough in understanding with some individual or group but too often stop short of the next step of creating interest in joining. But, as we have discussed, such sowing without attempting to reap is quite unproductive. In fact, if the habit becomes widespread, it can be catastrophic.

To prevent this kind of shortsightedness from taking root in Freedom First Society, all of us — volunteer members, volunteer leaders, and staff — must measure the success of our campaigns, projects, and activities almost entirely based on the responsible individuals we *help* bring into the organization.

Note that by "*help* bring into the organization" we don't mean doing the whole job necessarily by oneself and certainly not in isolation. In fact, a primary function of the organization is to help members use their influence productively and relatively painlessly to interest others in membership. And every member, regardless of his or her talents and current influence, can play a part (see Recruitment 101, the sidebar following this chapter).

Since our activities must keep the end in mind, we cannot be satisfied with placing ads in newspapers, distributing pamphlets, obtaining signatures on petitions, erecting billboards in prominent locations, or hosting speeches. Those activities are great, but only if they are part of a program to increase our numbers.

Perhaps a little more bluntly, we insist that educating a few other busy Americans from time to time accomplishes little, if anything, of lasting value — by itself. The only way to attain sufficient influence to change the course of history is for our members to pursue *high-leverage objectives* rather than *no-leverage activity*.

The powerful way for members to *multiply* their impact is to help give birth to self-perpetuating organization that can effectively mold public opinion.

Effective action means *steady* action.
Many of those in the freedom fight have witnessed individuals who

behave like roman candles. They suddenly catch fire, devoting seemingly all of their time to the fight, only to burn out shortly thereafter and disappear from sight. We certainly don't want to disparage enthusiasm, but we would point out that those who pace themselves and are able to stay in the fight for the long haul end up making by far the greatest contribution.

Moreover, steady participation and support are the glue that makes local organization possible.

Effective action means *reporting*.

In order for those at the top to give good leadership and make good decisions, they have to have quick and reliable feedback on the progress and effectiveness of our campaigns. If something is working spectacularly, our leaders will want to let others know right away. If something isn't working well, headquarters needs the timely opportunity to fix it. Accordingly, members, volunteer leaders, and paid field staff need to respond to the organization's requests for reports on activity.

We recognize that this responsibility can be a source of frustration for some of our most active members. They hate paperwork, and any requirement to take time out of the battle to report simply smells to them like wasteful bureaucracy.

We can sympathize. Certainly, soldiers and their commanders on the front lines would understandably be irritated if right in the midst of heated battles they were constantly being bugged by headquarters for status reports that served no immediate need and brought no apparent relief. But leaders at headquarters can't possibly plan or even continue to obtain support if they have no intelligence on how already deployed troops are faring.

Our headquarters staff will strive to make reporting systems as convenient as possible. But they won't always hit the mark, and improvements will be needed. Nevertheless, members, volunteer leaders, and field staff need to understand that without quality and timely feedback, long-term success is simply impossible.

Effective action means *associating*.

All members are urged to participate at some level in local activities. Keep in mind that your participation encourages others.

Moreover, it is much easier for members to direct prospects to the local organization if they themselves are involved with it. And new members generally need and are looking for that association, particularly to help them get off the ground. Those who start out as lone wolves seldom truly get involved with the organization or maintain their membership.

We realize that working with others can *often* be frustrating; trying to communicate the truth to non-members can *sometimes* be frustrating; and viewing the progress of the Conspiracy is *always* frustrating. But we need to make a special effort to overcome our frustrations, maintain a positive can-do attitude, and not pass our frustrations on to others.

In the January 1963 *Bulletin*, Mr. Welch wrote:

> The aim [of much of Communist strategy] is to create such overwhelming confusion, frustration, and despair as to cause even the ablest individual anti-Communists to throw up their hands in a feeling of hopeless inadequacy to the struggle.

It is well to take to heart the words of Henry Austin: "There is no failure save in giving up."[5] Of course, we hand the enemy just what he seeks if we give up.

The best antidote to frustration with the Conspiracy's advances is simply to immerse oneself in constructive action.

A Related Caution

When associating with other members at Freedom First Society activities and events, we should focus on the purposes for which we have come together. No matter how passionate you may be about some other cause, don't mix in another agenda.

A sample, non-exhaustive list of intrusive agendas would include: selling insurance, gold and silver, or vitamins; promoting multi-level network marketing schemes; or recruiting for political activism or a religion. Introducing such agendas is an abuse of membership.

Long experience shows that attempts to use our programs, organization, and associations to promote other agendas inevitably diverts much needed focus, can lead to hurt feelings and damaged pocket books, can cause division and confusion about our purposes, and may even raise doubts about the real motivation behind the advocate's membership.

Mixing in other agendas can be even more damaging when contacting prospects or meeting them at Freedom First Society events. It is particularly important for the growth and health of our organization that prospects not be misled or confused as to our real program and positions.

Recruitment 101

A primary responsibility of every member is to seek out, inform, and recruit like-minded patriots into Freedom First Society. This is not a responsibility that can be delegated to the few paid field staff or even the more numerous volunteer leaders. The hard reality is simply that members either recruit and we grow or we lose our freedom!

But please don't misunderstand us. We are not suggesting that members must behave like salesmen, especially not like the popular image of salesmen.

In fact, members are generally the most effective with their recruiting responsibility when they merely *guide* prospects to good information, make a few suggestions and let *the information* do the selling. They then follow up to ask for comments and reactions and supply additional information tailored to each prospect's concerns. They let the prospect's interest catch fire so that the prospect is *eager* to join. Membership is simply not something you would want to force.

Moreover, the most effective recruiters do not act in isolation, but instead they make full use of the organization's resources — the campaigns, the events, as well as other members and volunteer leaders. Recruitment is best accomplished as a team effort also because a serious prospect will want to meet the other individuals with whom he would be participating, before making a decision about membership.

Properly understood, the recruitment process does not have to be intimidating. But it does require persistent work.

Below is a list of concepts that support successful recruiting. These concepts will be communicated many times by the Society's staff and volunteer leaders. They are presented here primarily to give prospective and new members a better appreciation for the task. But they can also serve as a reminder for veterans:

- Realize that the recruitment of most great members involves a journey. Don't expect instant results. The reason: For many, membership means a big commitment and a realignment of personal priorities.

  Perhaps it's a little bit like a marriage decision. You don't expect such a decision on the first date. It takes time and shared experiences for a couple to really appreciate each other. And so it is with Freedom First Society. The decision to join an organization working to defeat the Conspiracy often requires some thought, experience, reassurance, and the building of desire before anxieties over the prospective commitment can be overcome.

- So be patient. Responsible individuals shouldn't be crossed off your list merely because they aren't ready to commit, even after a great deal of contact. Perhaps move them to the bottom of your list for less frequent contact, if you feel your time is better invested with more promising prospects.

- On the other hand, don't assume that a new desirable prospect is not ready to join. Be sure to let the prospect know he is welcome to join and wanted as a member.

  At an early stage in the process — once the value of Freedom First Society has been presented —invite the prospect to fill out an application. You may not get an immediate yes, but that's okay. And sometimes you will be pleasantly surprised.

- Look at recruitment as a process: First gain attention, then create interest, and then reinforce the prospect's interest until the prospect is ready to join.

- There is no one perfect process or model leading to membership. One possibility is simply to help the prospect follow the process that *you* went through in deciding to join. The process does not even have to be structured to work. But more success will usually come when you commit to a plan.

- Rely on the organization (national and local) for help. No member should want to recruit entirely in isolation, anymore than a soldier would take off on his own to fight the enemy. Freedom First Society exists to support such efforts.

- Particularly, make use of local public Freedom First Society events — speeches, video showings, etc. — to further develop your prospect's interest and understanding. Many of these activities are designed to help prospects decide to join. Prospects are much more willing to join a group they have met and seen in action.

  Events where members and prospects meet in significant numbers to consider serious problems and actions help build the confidence of a prospect in the organization. And sometimes a prospect just needs to hear another voice before he is ready to take the next step.

- Make use of the Society's campaigns to open doors and create interest in and respect for what we are doing. Good prospects are attracted by the dedicated people they see in action, dealing with real problems.

- If your prospect is comfortable online, introduce him to the Society's website. In particular, point him to information for which he is likely to have a special interest.

- Focus your attention on a few good prospects until they feel the urgent need to join or until you discover that they are not good candidates. By concentrating your attention on a *half-dozen* or so prospects with *regular follow-up* you will accomplish far more toward recruitment than by targeting dozens with scattered contacts where you have no possibility of personal follow-up.

- Prospects are everywhere. They just need to be identified. And campaigns can help you do that.

- Start with your friends, relatives, neighbors, and associates. Also consider merchants and service providers (e.g. doctors and dentists) with whom you have rapport. People you know generally make the best prospects and are the most likely to fit productively with you into a local chapter.

- Be persistent in looking for good prospects. Realize that not everyone is cut out to be a good member. It may take a lot of sifting of sand before you find the nuggets of gold. But keep sifting and have confidence that your persistence will pay off.

• Give your prospects personal attention. Be a good listener and tailor your follow-up to their interests and concerns.

• In one-on-one contacts, don't try to hold yourself up as an expert. It really is better to act as a guide in such exchanges. Remember the saying: "A man convinced against his will is of the same opinion still."

• If you are asked a question and aren't sure of the answer, don't hesitate to admit you don't know. Your honesty and humility will often impress your prospect more than any extensive knowledge you might be able to demonstrate. But express your willingness to find out. Other members and staff of Freedom First Society can help with most questions.

• Don't just be the bearer of bad news. Also share Freedom First Society solutions and positive accomplishments.

• Understand that objections are generally *not* what they may seem to be — a rejection. In essence, many objections are merely indirect requests for more information. When a prospect raises an objection it often means that he is really interested but wants to be convinced.

And a final piece of recruitment advice: Look forward to the satisfaction you will receive from enlisting another patriot in this great battle. Then grow in your determination to recruit. You will amaze yourself at how effective you can become by following good procedure.

Chapter 16

Destructive and Neutralizing Tangents

It is no wonder that the Communists count so heavily on the unceasing and inevitable tendency of Conservatives and anti-Communists to weaken concerted action by going off on tangents of their own.

—Robert Welch, July 1967 *Bulletin*

There has been plenty of energy and enthusiasm and money expended by patriotic Americans, even since 1945, to have stopped half a dozen Communist conspiracies. Most of it, however, has actually and cleverly been shunted off course, or guided into support of the very things that the Communists wanted to accomplish.

—Robert Welch, June 1970 *Bulletin*

For an ambitious clique to gain absolute power over a nation's population, it must employ clever and deceptive strategy. One strategy that has often enabled the unscrupulous to rise to the top is to "divide and conquer." A corollary to that strategy is to make sure that whatever resistance does develop is fragmented, isolated, and ineffective.

When Robert Welch decided to launch The John Birch Society, there were already thousands of conservative, anti-Communist organizations, collectively accomplishing very little. In general, their leadership failed to grasp the extent of conspiratorial influence, was content to dabble with small pieces of the problem, and certainly was unable or unwilling to offer a sufficiently ambitious and appropriate solution.

Although most of the names have changed, that still pretty much sums up the situation today. New proposals and new organizations appear constantly. But almost all offer solutions that do little for, or even undermine, the cause of liberty.

These tangents come in a variety of stripes. Some are merely wasteful, misdirecting and consuming valuable effort and resources. Others alienate potential patriots, discouraging them from seeking realistic, responsible solutions. And still others actually provide the Conspiracy with a welcome pretext to seize new powers and authority. But none significantly challenge the Conspiracy's grip on our nation.

Of course, true leaders will always differ in their judgments as to what are the best opportunities. Those are not the differences that concern us here. Instead, we are talking about programs based on seriously flawed assumptions or equally false objectives.

There are many examples of tangents. Some are easier to recognize as such than others.

The following table lists tangents that Don Fotheringham analyzed in a highly insightful booklet, last updated in 2002.[1] These chapter titles provide a quick feel for what we are talking about. However, the specific nature of the objection often cannot be discerned from the titles alone. For example, we obviously do not object to religion or political action in general.

Fotheringham's Tangents

• The Income Tax Rebellion	• The Modern Militia
• Religious Neutralism	• Jury Nullification
• Anti-Semitism	• Single-Issue "Friends"
• Information Junkies	• Partisan Politics
• False Leadership on the Right	• Wild Speculation
• The Masonic Implication	• Local Battles
• Why Not Disband and Start Over?	• Public Protest
• Civil Disobedience	• Divide and Destroy
• Militant Revolt	• The Posse Comitatus
• The "State Citizen" or "Sovereign Citizen"	

Off track: These tangents were examined by Don Fotheringham in his April 2002 booklet *Tangents: Neutralizing movements that undermine the work of patriotic Americans to preserve freedom.*

In the introduction to his booklet, Mr. Fotheringham also provided some important clarification: "Not all tangents are hatched by the enemy. Many ideas for patriotic action come from individuals who feel certain there is a better or easier way to restore freedom and limit government. So, in addition to deceitful programs, we will also describe certain innocently devised activities that still take good Americans off course."

As Mr. Fotheringham pointed out, new proposals for action emerge almost daily, and many qualify as tangents. So it is very difficult to address in a timely manner even those that attract a significant following. Fortunately, many tangents are built on common errors. One of Mr. Fotheringham's greatest contributions to the subject was a list of key questions that informed patriots could use to determine whether any proposed program was a tangent:

- Does this movement or activity help identify and expose the enemy?
- Does this proposal take into consideration the existence, cunning, tactics, and power of the Conspiracy?
- Would this undertaking lead to a reduction — or to an increase — in the size, power, and scope of government?
- Is it legal, honorable, and constitutional?
- Is the objective to be accomplished by building informed pressure for an act of Congress, or does the plan presume favorable rulings in the courts?
- Can it be accomplished without help from the Establishment news media?
- Does this organization work at the grass roots educating the people or in the hallowed halls of leadership lobbying the famous?
- Does this group strike at the root of the problem or slap only at the tentacles?
- Do the organizers work at what they say, or do they mely raise funds and employ public relations to win people to their banner?
- Do they enlist, inform, and challenge patriotic Americans to work in an organized program to alert their neighbors, or do they offer a "program" that does it all for you?

Mr. Fotheringham went on to write:

The importance of these questions is almost self-evident. America will not be saved in a court of law. The nation will not be saved by a multiplicity of new laws, but by the repeal of many measures that corrupt the simple, proper role of government. An idea that relies on favorable media coverage cannot get off the ground at present. America cannot be saved without God's help, and no act of Providence can be expected unless perfectly honorable and legal means are employed. Anyone or any group professing to save America, but refusing to identify the enemy, can never accomplish its purpose.

The old saying "An ounce of prevention is worth a pound of cure" certainly applies to tangents. It is much easier to inoculate individuals against these tangents than it is to talk them off the ledge once they have emotionally committed to one of these courses.

With respect to the more destructive tangents, we hope they do not apply to any of our members. Our main reason for presenting them here is not as counsel for existing members, but as a notice to those who might consider applying for membership that such attitudes and activities are not welcome in Freedom First Society.

We take space here to highlight a couple of the unwelcome attitudes and activities that we regard as particularly destructive.

Civil Disobedience

Freedom First Society values and enthusiastically supports the great Roman accomplishment in protecting our rights — the rule of law. The concept of a body of laws that even those in government had to obey was a magnificent contribution to civilization over the arbitrary and capricious rule of men.

Robert Bolt's drama *A Man for All Seasons*, portraying the tragedy that befell Sir Thomas Moore, includes a pertinent exchange. In the story, a friend ridiculed Moore for refusing to ignore the law to get at an evildoer. To which criticism Moore replied, "I'd give the Devil benefit of law, for my own safety's sake."

Otherwise responsible citizens weaken the rule of law, and so its protective shield, when they put themselves above the law by deciding which laws they will obey and which they will ignore. The rule of law is such an important asset in any civilization that even a significant corruption of the law does not justify either civil disobedience or treating the law with contempt.

Respecting the law does not mean that we should regard all laws as just and accept them as such. Certainly many official acts are not legal or even constitutional. However, when there are problems within the legal system, rather than promoting cynicism, the responsible approach is to observe the law and work to make it more worthy of respect.

In fact, we do not strengthen the rule of law when we tolerate unjust laws. Unjust laws must be purged, but purged within the law, as long as we have the freedom to do so.

Legal systems are major social accomplishments. They are not put together during periods of chaos and confusion. We can preserve the umbrella of safety the law provides only by helping to see that the law is respected.

As a strategy, civil disobedience is not only wrong, it is also dangerous and counterproductive. Its widespread practice leads to anarchy, while providing an easy path to tyranny. In fact, lawlessness paves the way for a police state.

The Conspiracy would profit from any breakdown of law and order or even a tendency in that direction. Indeed, the Insiders provide many provocations, undoubtedly hoping for just such impulsive, ill-considered reaction. We must do the opposite and refuse to step into their trap.

To make change, we must tap our nation's strengths. And our principal potential strength is still the power of informed, aroused public opinion.

Right now we are confronted with widespread public ignorance of both principles and the Conspiracy at work. We can best fix that condition in a stable, peaceful environment suitable for education, not in a chaotic environment in which only demagogues can prosper.

Moreover, irresponsible or improper conduct would jeopardize our access to the responsible Americans we must inform and persuade. The bottom line is that we will not allow individuals to organize agendas of civil disobedience within our ranks.

Racism, Anti-Semitism, Bigotry

We subscribe to the principle, as stated in the Declaration of Independence, "that all Men are created equal, that they are endowed by their Creator with certain unalienable Rights." Thus we vigorously oppose racism and anti-Semitism.

Moreover, we believe that men are endowed with free will and are thus accountable for their acts. It would therefore be a contradiction to judge individuals by any class to which they might belong by condition of birth.

We also recognize hatred and bigotry as destructive forces and motivations. Not only are these attitudes wrong in principle, but they are repugnant to responsible Americans. It is impossible for those consumed with these attitudes to positively influence the people we must reach and organize into a body that can save America. And so we cannot accept them into our ranks.

Of course, the Conspiracy, following past performance, will likely seek to attach these labels to any organization that seriously threatens it. Our job is to make it is as difficult as possible for the Conspiracy to achieve any credibility for such accusations.

One way we do so is by stating as clearly as possible what our true positions are and repeating those positions regularly. In most cases that will be enough to discourage prospects with such proclivities from seeking membership. But if we should discover that one of our members is caught up with such ideas, then we will refund the prorated part of his dues paid in advance and ask him to take his energies elsewhere.

A related problem is that some groups and individuals irresponsibly identify the Conspiracy with a public group. Years ago, for example, some would claim that Communism was a Jewish Conspiracy. They struggled to explain the heritage of Mao Tse-tung.

Of course, as Mr. Welch pointed out, the Conspiracy infiltrates its agents into all of the major religions. But these agents are not believers. If any force deserves the description satanic, the Conspiracy does. It abhors all the great religions and their values. The Conspiracy routinely seeks to infiltrate, undermine, neutralize, and subvert all significant institutions, including religious institutions.

Moreover, the Conspiracy would never permit its core membership to be readily identifiable as a public group. So it is wrong and even a destructive tangent to refer to the Conspiracy as, for example, Jewish, or Catholic, or Masonic, and we separate ourselves from those who do. Even the Conspiracy's most useful public fronts contain non-conspirators, and, conversely, these front groups undoubtedly exclude many among the Conspiracy's ruling elite.

In the next chapter, we examine a major neutralizing tangent: presidential politics.

Chapter 17

Presidential Politics

Patriotism means to stand by the country. It does not mean to stand by the President or any other public official save exactly to the degree in which he himself stands by the country. It is patriotic to support him insofar as he efficiently serves the country. It is unpatriotic not to oppose him to the exact extent that by inefficiency or otherwise he fails in his duty to stand by the country.[1]

—Theodore Roosevelt, 1899

The Great Myth: "In our enlightened democracy, electing a president every four years is the primary opportunity Americans have to ensure the best possible direction for our nation."

The "Great Myth" is insidious because it is so appealing, and yet, as we shall see, the consequences of its general acceptance are disastrous.

A Seductive Appeal

The great myth appeals to the natural human desire for a quick fix and for a leader on a white horse to come forward to solve all our problems. It's so easy just to vote every four years for a presidential candidate, and then — voila — we can, supposedly, all enjoy the "blessings of democracy."

Americans have long feasted on the fruits of a culture of freedom. But rarely are they told that they have any further obligation toward maintaining that culture than to watch the nightly news and trek regularly to the polls.

It would undoubtedly surprise many to learn that the Founding Fathers never intended for the public to choose a president directly. And certainly not for the public to choose a president based on what could be learned about candidates from partisan political campaigns. Sadly, few Americans today have any acquaintance with the wisdom of the Founders on choosing a president, the logic behind the Electoral College, or even the College's existence.

Similarly, most Americans fail to recognize *the very real*

opportunity that the Constitution gives them to exercise control over the federal government through the House of Representatives.

The Great Myth is not a new development. Samuel Pettengill, a statesman who served in Congress during most of the 1930s, expressed his dismay over the misdirection of Americans in his 1940 book *Smoke-Screen*:

> At the present time the attention of the nation is largely and somewhat hysterically centered upon the question of who will be nominated and elected President of the United States.... But the nomination and election of a President is not going to pay the national debt. It is not automatically going to cure unemployment.... It is not going to balance the budget....
>
> Any man who is President of the United States by virtue of his commanding position may greatly aid in these matters, but he cannot accomplish them. If legislation is wise there is a good chance it will be wisely administered, but if the legislation is bad, even the best administration cannot cure the evil.
>
> With a strong Congress an ambitious President can do little harm, and with a weak Congress a strong President can do little good.[2]

Rigged for Lose-Lose

Today, the situation is far worse than what Pettengill described. For, unknown to most Americans, a Conspiracy has long since consolidated its effective control over the process by which a president is elected, and *all* the serious contenders are now *securely* in its grip.

Americans get the same internationalist policies regardless of which of the front-runners is elected. The reason there is not "a dime's worth of difference" between the candidates is because both the national Democratic Party and the national Republican Party are beholden to the same power elite, which also uses its control of the mass media to make or break presidential candidates. With this evolution, the Great Myth has become the Great American Swindle.

Revelations from the "inside" bolster the overwhelming evidence of the Conspiracy's control. Recall that the Council on Foreign Relations (CFR) was established in 1921 as a front group for the international bankers, especially J.P. Morgan and Company. Former veteran CFR member, then CFR critic, Admiral Chester Ward (see Chapter 2) stated:

> [The] CFR, *as such*, does not write the platforms of both political parties or select their respective presidential candidates, or control U.S. defense and foreign policies. But CFR members, as individuals, acting in concert with other individual CFR members, do.[3]

In fact, the Conspiracy's efforts to control the political parties reaches back much earlier. For example, Professor Carroll Quigley claimed: "To [J.P.] Morgan all political parties were simply organizations to be used, and the firm always was careful to keep a foot in all camps." Indeed, Quigley observed that one Morgan colleague allied with the Democrats, Morgan himself and other partners supported the Republicans, and still other Morgan associates had connections with the "extreme Right" and the Left.[4]

Nor do third party candidates for president in any way threaten the Conspiracy's effective control of the presidency. But they do generally serve to misdirect attention and resources away from serious solutions, while helping to reinforce the Great Myth that presidential elections are where the action is. And these candidacies encourage many frustrated Americans to be satisfied with spitting in the wind.

Serious-minded Americans who understand the looming danger the Conspiracy poses to our freedoms should think twice before supporting and promoting such misleading third-party non-solutions. The Conspirators will certainly sleep soundly if they know their potential opposition is focused on mounting a meaningless, unnoticed protest vote.

Just consider for a moment what it would take for a third party to grow to sufficient size and influence to win a national election in the face of the Conspiracy's dominant influence in the media and *still stay true* to principle. Recognize, too, that any political party, because of its structure is easily infiltrated, tied up with controversy, and split into factions. As a third party grew in size, there would be mounting pressures for it to compromise to become popular, and the third party would soon look little different from the other two — because the underlying problem had not been addressed.

The bottom line is that third party presidential efforts completely put the cart before the horse. Before the office of President can be put in good hands, the Conspiracy must be exposed, its grip on the major media broken, and the public generally enlightened regarding proper principles of government.

Without these changes, any good candidate fortunate enough to become president would be impotent to stand up to the Conspiracy's influence and set a proper course for our nation. At this point in the battle, electing a man on a white horse who will rescue America is the stuff of movies and comic books.

Why Perpetuate the Illusion

Although the quadrennial presidential contest is now a sham, the Conspiracy strives to maintain the illusion that something substantial is being decided demanding the attention and involvement of every American. And it certainly wants as many citizens as possible to join a cheering section for one of its candidates and get caught up in the frenzy of its staged wrestling match.

The illusion that the good guys can win this "important" contest provides the Conspiracy with multiple benefits:

• It conceals the Conspiracy's domination of the executive branch and the leadership of the major parties.

• It entices American conservatives eager for immediate results to do battle where the advantages all favor the enemy.

• It provides an enticing, safe (for the Conspiracy) outlet for frustrated Americans, thus neutralizing potentially serious opposition. Attention and resources are thus drawn away from opportunities to fight genuine battles where astute opposition could threaten the Conspiracy's agenda.

• If an overt liberal should win, the election demoralizes Americans concerned over the consolidation of power in Washington and the erosion of traditional values.

- And should an ostensible conservative get the nod, the election puts these same Americans to sleep with the comforting feeling that the occupant of the White House is championing their concerns.

So the Conspiracy has an *interest* in promoting exciting presidential contests. Now, let's examine a few of the principal tactics for creating that excitement and reinforcing the illusion of genuineness.

Promotion 101

Any good promoter knows that conflict helps to build an audience. The promoters of the presidential election wrestling match are very effective at creating drama, so that even many of the most informed conservatives can't resist getting caught up in the *apparent* contest.

One often used tactic is to create a heavy — a monster — counterbalanced by a "good guy." In his 1972 reelection campaign, Richard Nixon faced "liberal, left-winger" George McGovern. McGovern provided the ideal foil to get Nixon reelected. The media images of both candidates were so cast that McGovern had no serious chance of being elected.

Yet conservative voters, bombarded with McGovern's leftist credentials and his clear support from the anti-war, beatnik, peacenik, hippy movement, greatly feared the prospect of McGovern in the White House. With this threat in mind, few conservatives would tolerate any criticism of Nixon. The common retort was: "You don't want McGovern to get elected do you?"

Notice, however, that had the "liberal" McGovern become president, he could never have gotten away with opening up Red China to the Insider-sponsored investment now devastating our nation's manufacturing base. But few Americans registered any alarm when Nixon, supported by his *image* as a tough anti-Communist, did exactly that.

Does Nixon vs. McGovern sound like shades of George W. Bush vs. John Kerry in 2004? Now, imagine how passionately conservatives will support the Republican presidential candidate should "Hillary Clinton" get the democratic nod in 2008. They will argue vehemently that "we just have to stop Hillary." And the

Insiders will laugh all the way to the bank.

One way to ascertain whether the Insiders endorse a candidate is to see how the media treats that candidate. A "liberal" candidate acceptable to the Insiders will be insulated against devastating criticism. An example was Bill Clinton. By the time Clinton got the Democratic nod in 1992, he had plenty of skeletons in his closet. A hostile media could easily have quashed Clinton's ambitions.

By contrast, a phony conservative with Insider backing will be criticized by the media, but in such a way (e.g., from an obvious liberal perspective) that he is endeared to those with conservative instincts. That's generally how the Establishment press treated Ronald Reagan and Newt Gingrich.

Contrast that with the vitriolic campaign launched against Barry Goldwater in 1964. It became really tough to support Goldwater after all that was said about him by the press.

We should keep in mind that if any candidate for president seriously threatens the Establishment, the Establishment media will effectively ridicule and discredit the candidate as a threat to world order or national prosperity, as outside serious civilized debate, or as carrying embarrassing baggage. Or the Insiders can reuse the clever tactic they employed to keep Robert Taft from getting the Republican nomination in 1952. The line went that Taft was good but not electable — "I like Taft, but he can't win."

Another companion illusion, greatly fostered by the Establishment media, is the notion that a president is actually the leader in his administration. Perpetuating this illusion is necessary so that the American people will continue to believe that they are the actual decision makers in the process. If Americans thought that their presidential candidates were mere front men and that the real leadership decisions were made elsewhere, then the glamour of the contest would disappear.

With few exceptions in recent history, the leadership and authority of the president is pure fiction. Many presidents, such as George W. Bush, exercise very little authority and generally have their cabinets selected for them. Their primary role is to provide a confident image for the cameras. The real working decisions are made by cabinet officials and other "advisors" loyal to the Insiders and their goals.

Such was certainly the case with the "Great Communicator,"

Ronald Wilson Reagan. President Reagan undoubtedly wielded little authority and provided little leadership in "his" administrations. Yet here is how the Establishment's *Time* memorialized him in 1998: "Ronald Reagan knew, going in, the sentence he wanted [to be remembered by], and he got it. He guided the American victory in the cold war. Under his leadership, a conflict that had absorbed a half-century of Western blood and treasure was ended — and the good guys finally won."[5] Unfortunately, we cannot devote the space here to correct the many fictions in *Time's* assessment.

Another ruse to involve citizens in backing a presidential candidate is the hoopla over the prospect that a conservative president will be able to influence the direction of the Supreme Court through appointment of replacement judges. The unfortunate reality is that many of the worst Supreme Court decisions were supported by appointees of so-called conservative presidents.

Certainly, the Insiders would like to bolster the image that a qualitative difference exists in "conservative" judicial appointees. But that need has not prevented the Supreme Court from "rewriting" the Constitution.

Betrayal of "Conservatives"
Conservatives readily fall victim to the Great American Swindle, since, as a group, they are busy with their careers and particularly prone to wishful thinking. And they are regularly betrayed by popular conservative media hosts who reinforce many of the fictions discussed here.

The Conspiracy constantly seeks to channel conservative opinion because conservatives represent a powerful bloc of resistance to be overcome. That is why the Conspiracy often casts one of its politicians as a conservative.

Not that the Insiders necessarily prefer that their "conservative" always win. Both the Conspiracy's agenda and the effectiveness of the Great American Swindle benefit from hard-fought battles where the party "leadership" sometimes changes and from allowing the American people occasionally to, as Quigley advocated, "throw the rascals out." Moreover, there are undoubtedly many tradeoffs to what each respective party candidate could accomplish for the Conspiracy as president.

But if the outcome really mattered to the Conspiracy, the race would not even be close. For otherwise informed activists to think that they can positively influence the outcome of a national presidential contest is absurd. The votes of even a hundred thousand activists spread across the nation would have miniscule impact at the polls. Yet the year-round work of these same individuals, if directed at building organization, can make a very significant difference in Congress and in the nation.

Political action is as American as apple pie. But political action as a remedy for the inroads of the Conspiracy is a tangent. Without first building a membership base of sufficient size to inform the electorate, political action, even directed at Congress, can accomplish little. And with that membership base established, effective political action will spring forth naturally.

As members of Freedom First Society, we seek to be informed, thoughtful, passionate patriots, defending our country, its independence, and the principles that made it great. As individual citizens, our members may choose to support political candidates. However, to remain true to our chosen mission, Freedom First Society, including its chapters, committees, programs, and publications, will never support or oppose candidates for elective office.

[Note: Most of the material in this chapter was adapted from an August 2007 article, "The Great American Swindle," by Tom Gow.]

Section VII

"And So, Let's Act" — Now!

Chapter 18

With God's Help

Let us not be weary in well-doing: for in due season we shall reap, if we faint not.

— Galatians 6:9

Freedom First Society has been founded on the premise that men and women have responsibilities in the world — responsibilities to God, family, and country — and in particular, responsibility to oppose evil. Although we do not offer theological leadership, what we are doing is consistent with the religious view that God *could* heal our nation *for us*, but *He has chosen to let us do it* — at least to take the first steps.

In this view, God didn't put us here to be spectators and watch Him work to make our lives more comfortable. He expects us to earn our bread and participate and struggle in the world. When we truly do our best, while sincerely recognizing His authority, we can have confidence that God will bless our efforts.

Since we strive as much as possible to avoid even the appearance of offering religious leadership, we are at a disadvantage in arguing with those who claim a theological basis for shirking responsibility to oppose evil. Fortunately, those who espouse such views are in the minority. Most Americans realize that we must do our part, pray for God's blessings, and be as careful as possible in our motives and actions to deserve those blessings.

No Religious Test

There is no religious test for membership in Freedom First Society. We invite, encourage, and want the support of responsible men and women of different religious faiths who recognize a common purpose and will work together to preserve freedom. Without compromising our individual faiths in any way, we join together in a common struggle based on values we all share.

We believe that for success in this desperate struggle, we must seek to enlist all good men and women of character. In the

213

September 1961 *Bulletin*, Mr. Welch enunciated the same organizing principle:

> For we are pulling together into one body the devout Catholics, the sincere Protestants, the spiritually faithful Jews, the truly good men and women of all creeds and color and racial origins, to work together for a mighty purpose that is common to us all....
>
> We seek no doctrinal union, which inevitably means a sacrifice of some parts of each personal faith, but exactly the opposite. Simple cooperation and mutual support, between men and women of good will and good conscience, in forwarding those moral purposes which are held in common by them all, and which joint purposes are made stronger and more resolute by the very depth of their respective faiths. We begin our cooperation with a belief in absolutes, and an eschewal of relativity, as the foundation for morality. There is a right for man, and a wrong, in connection with every course. And our troubles do not arise from the slight differences, as between our separate faiths, in determining what is morally right or morally wrong — but in our failures to stand up for the right, at all costs and against all odds.

It is easy to recognize a common religious and moral purpose in what we are doing since the enemy we oppose seeks to eliminate all worship of a deity and substitute a satanic worship of the State. In the April 1966 *Bulletin*, Mr. Welch summarized the appropriate moral challenge that unites our members:

> We must oppose secrecy with openhandedness. We must publish to the world our beliefs, our purposes, and our methods as fully as the collectivists conceal and disguise their own. We must oppose conspiracy, not with counter conspiracy, but with exposure, justice, and education. We must oppose falsehoods with truth; blasphemy with reverence; foul means with good means; immorality and amorality with more spiritual faith and dedication; rootlessness and chaos with tradition and stability; relativity

with absolutes; pragmatism with deeper purposes; hedonism with a more responsible pursuit of happiness; cruelty with compassion; and hatred with love.

As an aside, Freedom First Society regularly opens its meetings in prayer, as a standard practice. Despite the absence of a religious test for membership, we fully expect that most members will recognize that we need God's help or at least God's blessing for success in this great struggle. And we regularly follow an opening prayer with the Pledge of Allegiance.

A Vital, Uniquely Different Mission

Freedom First Society is also founded on the assumption that God may choose to bless a nonsectarian undertaking seeking to preserve Judeo-Christian values. And that it is acceptable in God's eyes for men and women of strong religious faiths to band with others to accomplish some of life's objectives.

In order to pull together good men and women of character, regardless of their particular religious faith, into *one* effective body, we cannot organize separate units along sectarian lines. Such division would be inappropriate for our mission, for much the same reason that the U.S. military is not organized along sectarian lines. Of course, there are no Catholic divisions or Baptist divisions in the U.S. military.

Moreover, it is certainly a normal occurrence in America for men and women of different faiths to work for a common, non-sectarian employer. In fact, our nation itself was founded on the principle that diverse faiths would cooperate on some level. And America appears to have been singularly blessed for many years.

Alexis de Tocqueville, disillusioned with the political instability in France, traveled to America to study our nation, its institutions, and its people in search of what made us great. In 1840, he wrote:

> I sought for the key to the greatness and genius of America in her harbors...; in her fertile fields and boundless forests; in her rich mines and vast world commerce; in her public school system and institutions of learning. I sought for it in her democratic Congress and in her matchless Constitution.

215

> Not until I went into the churches of America and heard her pulpits flame with righteousness did I understand the secret of her genius and power. America is great because America is good, and if America ever ceases to be good, America will cease to be great.[1]

Freedom First Society doesn't claim that its mission is all that needs to be done to protect and heal our land. We just claim that we are the right tool, at the right time, for the right job. In the face of a powerful Conspiracy working to destroy freedom, America desperately needs an organization with the specific, narrow focus of stopping that Conspiracy and, with God's help, preserving freedom.

Freedom First Society fills an obvious vacuum in leadership for a reasonable strategy to address that specific and immediate danger. Partisan politics can no longer effect a solution. Those seeking remedy in political action simply underestimate the depth of our problem while emphasizing the quick fix to the wrong problem.

On the other hand, we do not have to allow a Conspiracy to destroy that heritage, simply because there are unsettled religious differences. Freedom First Society believes that there is sufficient religious capital and more than enough good people still available to open eyes and turn back the clock on the Conspiracy's advance. And if we don't target and slow the Conspiracy now, there will be insufficient time to repair America's religious foundations.

We do not overlook what religious movements have and might still accomplish for America. Actually, the religious and moral standards of millions of Americans form the bedrock on which our hope for America is founded. And we agree with George Washington's comments in his Farewell Address regarding the importance of religion as the necessary foundation of morality (see Chapter 8).

As the reader can see, we are not in competition with religious undertakings. In fact, our work will naturally cause many to become more involved with their church. When new members get their first deep appreciation for the organized evil at work in the world today, they often become more conscientious about their religion and sensitive to all their responsibilities.

But we don't believe that the Conspiracy can be stopped and

freedom preserved through religiously organized undertakings alone. More needs to be done in teaching the principles of freedom and communicating the agendas of those who would destroy freedom than our churches can be expected to accomplish.

As individuals, we all have multiple responsibilities. For example, no church would expect a farmer to neglect his crops and still expect to feed his family.

Our Active Defense of Religion

By referring to religion as a category we don't mean to suggest that theological differences are unimportant and that all religion is the same. We merely affirm that making theological judgments is not our organization's purpose.

However, we cannot ignore the Conspiracy's attack on religion and our religious heritage. The Conspiracy targets religion for ridicule, infiltration, subversion, and eventually outright forcible suppression. The Illuminati itself was born as an attack on all the religions and governments of Europe.

Freedom First Society opposes this assault on our religious heritage. As did Alexis de Tocqueville, we recognize that individuals of strong, practicing religious faith make up one of our nation's vital layers of strength. Religious faith also strengthens the family, society, our culture, and our nation. And religion forms the foundation for morality and our laws.

When men lose their faith in God they are prone, particularly under the pressures of life, to compromise, lie, and appease — and they are more easily corrupted by an evil Conspiracy. Talented, self-centered opportunists with few scruples even make excellent targets for recruitment by the Conspiracy.

So it is within the non-sectarian focus of Freedom First Society to develop articles or even launch strategic campaigns that defend our religious heritage, as long as we can do so without getting involved in theological disputes, which may have lasted for centuries.

Examples of such leadership from the past include exposing:

- Liberation Theology that presents Christ as a Marxist leading his people to armed struggle against ruling authority;
- The Earth Charter movement with its sacrilegious "Ark of Hope";

- The New Age movement and the UN's promotion of a new world religion;
- The promotion of pantheism, specifically the worship of Mother Earth; and
- Communist domination of the National Council of Churches and the Council's origins in the Federal Council of Churches.[2]

Where the subversion gets too theological, individual church members must carry the battle. Nevertheless, we expect that our work will help enlighten our members and others as to the Conspiracy's strategy and tactics and help them to provide good leadership in their churches.

Religious Neutralism

Those who place limits on Christian responsibility, particularly regarding our nation's direction, will not likely seek membership in Freedom First Society.

However, it may happen that a religious member becomes frustrated as he recognizes the enormous challenge of stopping the Conspiracy. Then it can be a strong temptation to give up while deceiving oneself by saying, in effect, "I'll just get right with God and then God will do what needs to be done for me." Or to adopt the attitude that what is happening must be God's will and therefore all efforts to stop our nation's decline are fruitless.

This we would like to prevent. Perhaps, the best antidote to such demoralization is to understand thoroughly the opportunities available to make a difference (as well as recognizing our responsibility to do our best, with God's help). That is why we urge a regular review of the principles and ideas presented here — and why we plan to repeat these ideas to our membership as a matter of organizational life and to offer programs for strengthening our understanding of fundamental principles.

Several shades of religious neutralism prevent good people from effectively opposing their earthly enslavement at the hands of ambitious, evil men. This evil, of course, would purge the world of the religious values, worship, and evangelism that have marked the advance of Western civilization.

218

There are excellent *pragmatic* answers to the common variations of religious neutralism. But where the individual's convictions are based squarely on his interpretation of scripture, we can do little as members of Freedom First Society to persuade him otherwise, since we are not organized to provide leadership in matters of theology. On the other hand, members acting as individuals may achieve some success with theological appeals if they share similar religious convictions with a prospect.

Here are a few, mostly pragmatic, suggestions for rebutting three of the most common religiously neutralizing objections to effective action: pacifism, isolationism, and the demand for exclusivity.

Pacifism: "We Shouldn't Resist Evil. The outcome is in God's hands; resistance is futile. Moreover, resistance is anti-Christian — God lets Satan have charge of the Earth. Our sole job is to save souls for the hereafter. The best we can do is pray for God's favorable intervention."

Certainly, there are plenty of places in scripture where Christians are mandated to care for their fellow man — *in this world*. In fact, virtually every religion mandates some responsibilities in this world. For example, we have responsibilities to provide for our families. Few would rely solely on prayer to put food on the table, pay the rent, fix the family car, or limit a child's exposure to danger.

It becomes progressively more difficult to exercise substantial influence when we move from the family, to the community, to the state, and to the national level. To achieve such impact at those levels it is often necessary to link hands with others under sound leadership. But the principle of responsibility does not really change. Moreover, positive movements, such as the founding of our nation, have enjoyed success in the past. History does not show evil always coming out on top.

Nevertheless, an increasing number of deeply religious people are earning the apt description that "they are so heavenly bound that they are no earthly good." Certainly, the enemies of freedom must rejoice at the growth in this attitude, and it wouldn't surprise us to discover them helping to spread this attitude in devious ways. It's as effective at disarming a nation as complete demoralization.

Religious Isolationism: "True fundamentalists shouldn't work with the adherents of other religious viewpoints. We must not yoke

219

ourselves with those who do not share our precise religious convictions. Any program supported by non-believers or by those whose faiths are flawed by heresy is doomed to fail. Only a house built on pure foundations can stand."

Perhaps our nation's history provides the most compelling empirical evidence that such views are false. Most of what present day religious Americans still enjoy and understand to be good has been communicated to us in a national environment of mixed religious faiths. From the beginning, our nation was built on the principle that men and women of many different faiths could cooperate constructively in practical areas such as government and commerce, while still remaining true to their own beliefs.

***Exclusive* Focus on Our Religious Foundations:** "The answer is to focus *exclusively* on the long-term rebuilding of America's religious roots."

There is no question that rebuilding and strengthening our churches and religious roots is both an obligation and an essential investment in our nation's future. Yet if we focus *exclusively* on those tasks, we offer no resistance to what the enemy is doing *now* to destroy our religious roots and to make the future free exercise of religion impossible.

Does what *amounts to* pacifism in the face of such a threat make sense? Throughout history, men have always rallied to fight specific, imminent threats such as starvation, war, or tyranny with programs and leadership to address those problems.

Moreover, there is no evidence that any of the churches, as presently constituted, are inclined or able to add the full-time crusade of stopping this Conspiracy to their mission. Certainly, with so many different churches in America, none would be able to provide leadership to the majority of those who can be called upon to participate in this battle.

In the past, we have had little success in changing the minds of those who once embraced religiously neutralizing arguments. Our proper course is generally to move on and to build our educational army with others who have not become "conscientious objectors."

Our principal concern with the challenge of religious neutralism is to inoculate others from falling into this trap and to strengthen our own resolve against such arguments.

We should also recognize that sometimes those offering religious objections are merely seeking to justify their own inaction. They may be understandably reluctant to take on a new challenge, preferring instead to keep doing what's comfortable regardless of whether it is adequate for the task. In such cases, once a prospect gains greater familiarity with what the enemies and friends of freedom are doing, he may yet choose to dip his toe into the fight.

Religion is clearly a sensitive topic. And it is too easy when attempting to write about these topics from a common standpoint to say something with which the faithful would disagree. If we have stumbled in any way in our enunciation of principles and in our presentation of arguments, we just ask readers to seek the spirit behind our words.

ORGANIZE FOR VICTORY!

Chapter 19

Freedom or Global Slavery — The Choice Is Yours

*Once to every man and nation
comes the moment to decide,
In the strife of Truth with Falsehood,
for the good or evil side;
some great cause, God's new Messiah,
offering each the bloom or blight,
Parts the goats upon the left hand,
and the sheep upon the right,
And the choice goes by forever
'twixt that darkness and that light.*[1]

— James Russell Lowell (1819-1891)

I must study politics and war that my sons may have liberty to study mathematics and philosophy.[2]

— John Adams in a letter to his wife Abigail

Truth is not only violated by falsehood, it may be equally outraged by silence.[3]

— Henri Frederic Amiel (1821–1881)

We do not expect that every reader will be ready to accept what we have presented here regarding the plans and inroads of the Conspiracy. And some of that reluctance will be our fault. We simply have not had the space to establish our conclusions to the satisfaction of everyone.

However, as we have noted in the opening chapter, the evidence is overwhelming, and we have pointed the reader to much of that evidence. Conspiracy is not a theory — it is reality.

In fact, much of the Conspiracy's plans are openly discussed in its own journals. But it uses new world order jargon to obscure the intent from the casual reader, and it counts on a number of factors to keep busy Americans from catching on.

Such factors include the confusion caused by contradictory statements, the denials of political leaders we want to trust, the incredible scope and enormity of the evil, the Conspiracy's influence over broadcast news and commentary, and, in particular, apathy.

In that atmosphere, many Americans when initially confronted with our charges of Conspiracy will adopt one of two attitudes: 1) We must be mistaken — it can't be as bad as we say. Or 2) It's too late — nothing can be done about it. With either attitude there is no urgency to do anything. But neither of these opposing attitudes — blind optimism or hopeless defeatism — is worthy of a free people.

In fact, our situation is far more threatening than what we have been able to paint so far. And yet it is not too late to take responsible action to save the day. Before we proceed to recommend specific actions, let's take a brief moment to recap the threat and project what will happen if we do nothing.

The Looming Danger

The Conspiracy is moving rapidly to consolidate its new world order. But to do so it still must practice massive deception. One of its primary deceptions is gradualism — proceed in stages so that the end result is not universally obvious.

The example of boiling a live frog has often been used to illustrate the insidiousness of gradualism. If a frog is tossed into a pot of boiling water it will immediately jump out. However, if it is placed in a pot of warm water and the water *gradually* heated, the frog will never become sufficiently alarmed until it is too late and it no longer has the strength to escape. Or so we are told. We have never actually seen it done, but true or not, the analogy does illuminate the danger.

The Conspiracy is seeking to build a world government incrementally that it will totally control. A major milestone is to establish regional governments that can steadily accumulate unaccountable power over the member nations. Proposals for economic union — the Common Market in Europe and so-called "Free Trade" regions elsewhere — often provide the initial pretext. In North America, the pretext of promoting security has also been added (the Security and Prosperity Partnership of North America).

Economic union is designed to evolve under constant pressure and deception into political union.

This process is already well advanced in Europe. And the same process is underway in this hemisphere. The plan is for the authority of the NAFTA bureaucracies to become entrenched through precedent and then expanded to pave the way for a regional government that will eventually include all of North and South America. Through this strategy of regionalism, the U.S. is to be submerged in a world government totally controlled by the Conspiracy.

What this kind of regional union means is that the U.S. Constitution and Bill of Rights would be subordinated to a new level of government unaccountable to the people of these United States. Just as with the UN, such a government would not be firmly bound to any document, let alone to one that is presented to the people for their approval and ratification.

In a fully implemented union, republican principles would be gone. We would be merged with the worst dictatorships in this hemisphere. The socialists commanding those nations clearly disdain justice and fair play, and they certainly have no interest in preserving the superior opportunities, the property, and the standard of living of Americans. Rather than raising these governments up to our level, we would be lowered to theirs.

As Americans are exploited under this arrangement, we will undoubtedly be told that we really have no choice but to submit: We gave up our independence in exchange for the "benefits" of the Insiders' version of international law. We will be instructed that we *had to do so* in order to achieve peace and common prosperity and to deal responsibly with all kinds of global threats, such as terrorism and damage to the global environment.

Other Battlefronts
Of course, there are many other battlefronts. Here are a number and their status:

- Various crises — real or invented — continue to be used to centralize more and more unaccountable power in the Executive Branch. Vice President Dick Cheney, a former director of the

CFR, has been arguing that the president should have even more power and doesn't need congressional approval to initiate war.[4]

Not surprisingly, we have seen a willingness by numerous Insider-controlled administrations to send our sons to die on UN missions in no-win wars to help the Conspiracy build its new world order.

- Congress is being pressured into "harmonizing" our laws with the regulations of international bodies such as the World Trade Organization. Where the Senate has yet to approve subversive internationalist treaties, the administration in power proceeds to implement many of the provisions anyway, presuming that the treaties will eventually be approved or that the need for Senate approval will be forgotten.

- Our citizens are being conditioned to accept police state monitoring in the interest of preventing terrorism. Unbeknownst to Americans, the Executive Branch has cynically worked to create this "convenient" threat, through its earlier support of the Soviet Union and its long support of the pro-terrorist UN.

- The independence of our local police, which serve and are properly accountable to their law-abiding friends and neighbors, is steadily being subverted. If that agenda succeeds, the police in our communities will be totally controlled by Washington acting in service to the State. The formation of the Department of Homeland Security was the most recent step among several subversive strategies underway. The Insiders plan that eventually all our police would also come under *international* regulation and control.

- Already the cooperation between our top law enforcement agencies and those of the former Soviet Union are pushing up against our Bill of Rights. In recent years, the interrogation and torture of those suspected of helping terrorists, as well as the suspension of habeas corpus, has been hotly debated in Congress.

- The Insiders firmly intend to disarm all private citizens. That agenda is also proceeding incrementally. The United Nations naturally has the same agenda and is providing covering pressure for U.S. leaders to conform to UN policy.[5]

- Our nation's manufacturing and industrial bases have been decimated, as the Insiders have labored to convert the U.S., for the most part, into a service economy.

- One objective of the new world order is to make it impossible for nations, particularly America, to act independently. New *inefficient* economic dependencies are being forged. For example, lumber for the U.S. building industry is now being imported from the Far East, because regulation and lawsuits have effectively placed our forests off limits to U.S. mills.

   In the early 1980s, the U.S. Export-Import Bank extended credit to Red China to help build its steel factories.[6] The last of U.S. steel mills are closing down, and the U.S. is now increasingly and unnecessarily dependent on foreign imports for this critical component of our defense industry. Even textiles turn out to be a vital factor for national defense. And with the demise of our textile industry, America could easily end up relying on such nations as Communist China, Zimbabwe, and the former U.S.S.R. to supply cloth for such items as parachutes, tents, and uniforms.

- And it is no different with energy. The Insiders have long sought to control Americans by curtailing and regulating our access to energy and to have mass (easily monitored) transportation replace the independence of the private automobile. Everyone knows that gasoline prices have skyrocketed following the turmoil in the Middle East. Less understood is that the Insiders have conspired to ensure American dependence on Mideast oil.

- The Insiders continue to agitate for Senate ratification of the "Law of the Sea Treaty" (LOST) that would put the UN in charge of the "global commons" — a truly massive power grab, which the U.S. has resisted since 1982. LOST would give the UN an independent source of revenue — and help free the UN from its dependence on funding from member nations — an extremely dangerous development.

- Americans are being hammered from all directions with warnings of disastrous, *man-made* global warming. This purported crisis is being used to generate pressure on Congress to agree to draconian restrictions on remaining American industry.

- Our southern border is under attack by the open borders movement — an attack on the very essence of our nationhood.

- The Insiders have long sought to dumb down the masses (by encouraging illiteracy, social studies instead of basics, etc.), because an illiterate population dependent on managed news is easier to control.[7] The obvious flaws and failures of the government-run school system helped spawn the home school movement — a *temporary* setback for the Insiders.

  Imitating the worst totalitarian regimes of the past, the Insiders cannot tolerate any competition for loyalty (such as the traditional family). The federal government must gain total control of the education and development of our youth. And that is just one step toward the regulation of education worldwide by the UN's exceptionally subversive UNESCO.[8]

- It is no secret that decency is under daily assault. But the reasons why are not so obvious. Behind the opportunistic depravity there is an agenda to progressively push the limits — an agenda that has nothing to do with making a profit.

  The top planners in the Conspiracy chain have long realized that an indulgent society is easier to subdue. Those who might speak out about the transformation of values — for example, the drive to establish homosexuality as a socially acceptable lifestyle — face intimidation by being portrayed as intolerant religious relics of the past.

- The Insiders have also long sought to control Americans by setting up government as a gatekeeper to their medical care.[9] Rising medical costs, due largely to government regulation, provide the pretext for further government intervention and national health care plans.

  Socialized medicine will inevitably create scarcity and a need for some *non-market* mechanism to regulate who gets access to quality treatment and health-care facilities. The Insiders have already begun to establish quality-of-life guidelines for rationing health care. These guidelines are appearing in many of our nation's hospitals.

• The value of human life, highly regarded in traditional Western culture, is under attack by the same forces. To the abortion holocaust is being added euthanasia and assisted suicide.

And the Conspiracy is at work on many other battlefronts.

Of course, you will not hear this message on the nightly news. But the absence of a well spoken anchor telling us what to think does not make the threat any less real.

Moreover, decisive action is the most valuable precisely when the need is not obvious to most. We are truly facing an epic educational battle. And we are asking for your help.

Opportunity to Make a Difference
Even though the Conspiracy is well advanced and has enormous resources at its disposal, all we really have to do to stop and rout this Conspiracy is to organize to expose it. Robert Welch insisted that this was the path to victory and that opportunity was right before us:

> But the American giant still has many times the strength needed to arouse itself, shake loose from this whole smothering process, and to recuperate rapidly from the damage already done. It needs only to be made aware that *it is being murdered* and that *it is not suffering from the inevitably fatal ravages of natural disease.* We repeat in plain language, for probably the hundredth time: All it will take to stop this murder, *and the only thing that will stop it,* is sufficient understanding on the part of enough of the American people as to what is really taking place.[10]

Experience and logic both argue that Robert Welch had the right formula. He founded, led, and personally nurtured for more than two decades an organization implementing that formula. Although its achievements and influence were not generally recognized, The John Birch Society had, over several decades, amassed amazing influence for its size while recording numerous impressive victories.

All that had really been separating Robert Welch's followers from victory was the lack of sufficient resources, in particular more members, to implement his formula on a much larger scale. Mr. Welch regarded that as the overriding challenge.

The Conspiracy clearly came to share his assessment. Within two years of the founding of The John Birch Society, the Conspiracy launched a massive smear campaign to discourage patriots from giving The John Birch Society serious consideration.

Building an organization dedicated to exposing the Conspiracy will continue to be a difficult, but by no means impossible, challenge, even after Freedom First Society is well off the ground. But that's simply where the real battle lies.

The real battle is to uncover a core of patriots (within a society in turmoil) and appeal to both their intellect and their heart to embrace a plan for organizing more of their fellow Americans to preserve freedom.

Of course, Freedom First Society does not fight this organizational battle in a vacuum. The enemy also works constantly and cleverly to frustrate our efforts by diverting the attention of Americans, confusing them, and isolating them from genuine leadership. So we have the added challenge of always seeking better ways to gain the serious attention of busy Americans and get our message across to potential patriots.

In seeking those patriots, we must be willing to adjust our tactics, but not our principles, to the times and the technology available. And for that we must especially search for members with special leadership and communication skills. Our battle needs talent, dedicated talent, to help us reach the right Americans with more effective messages (it is the same challenge that our churches have).

Nevertheless, the most important qualifications for effective members are character, discernment, and determination. It's amazing the influence people of good character can achieve when they inform themselves, follow a good plan, work to persuade others, and offer them leadership.

Freedom First Society offers the right patriots an incredible opportunity to make a difference in this struggle. Through our organization, any one member's efforts can potentially ignite the kindling that leads to a major firestorm of activity and influence.

Through Freedom First Society, Americans can contribute their talents, time, and inspiration to this great battle at virtually any desired level. Membership also helps prepare volunteers for a variety of tasks. There is an especially great need for volunteer leaders to expand our base of chapters. Even those members who feel today that leadership is not for them can help *start* chapters and help ensure a chapter's success through their dedicated support.

Recommended Actions

If you are a prospective member, we suggest a few specific steps to start you on the exciting journey toward making a real difference. You have already completed the first step by reading this book.

If you recognize the opportunity, the next step is to join and get plugged in — add the force of your membership to our body. Just see the member who gave you this book or contact our headquarters to request an application. You should also continue your self-education by pursuing some of the recommended reading on our website, www.freedomfirstsociety.org.

As you inform yourself, you can begin to influence others. Share this book with a select few of your friends and neighbors with the end in mind of recruiting another new member into the active battle. And, of course, we encourage all members to interest others in visiting our website with the same objective.

The Choice Is Yours

It's now time to talk from the heart, not the head.

There is a battle going on to decide whether we and our posterity will continue to enjoy the fruits of freedom. Losing this battle would undoubtedly mean the suppression of the virtues and values of Western civilization, perhaps for generations. The suppressed values would include justice, freedom of speech and opportunity, freedom of religion, and many others, which most Americans take for granted.

For all but a favored, corrupt few, losing this battle would mean leading lives without hope — the lives of despairing slaves. Of course, that applies only to those who manage to dodge the purges, the terror, the pogroms, the relocations, the population reductions, and the famines.

Clearly, the battle won't go away if we should choose to ignore it — while we still can — or stay on the sidelines, until it *is* too late.

Who would not want to have a say in the outcome of this battle? What responsible American, if he is aware of and understands the battle, would want to be a spectator as our fate is decided?

Aside from concern about our personal fates, don't we have a responsibility to pass on to future generations the great heritage given to us through the often heroic sacrifices of others? Don't we have a responsibility even to improve on that heritage if possible?

Just as responsible men and women would not feel right about leaving a campsite in a mess for the next travelers, so we should not be content to allow a gang of criminals to steal our children's inheritance under our watch.

Okay, so we are not *content* to let it happen. But if we want to help *prevent* it from happening, then we have to get in the fight as serious players.

Useful participation does require some commitment. But with the initiative born of responsibility and foresight, the sacrifice can be far less than sending a loved one to fight, and possibly die, in a foreign land in a struggle that could have been prevented through early *volunteer* action. And if our nation continues on its course, future wars and battles may well be fought on our own land, not to defend national interests, but to enforce directives of the UN or some other world body.

Four-star Marine General Lewis W. Walt (1913-1989) served with distinction in three of our nation's wars (World War II, Korea, and Vietnam) and received many decorations for valor in combat. After retiring from active duty, General Walt wrote:

> For thirty-four years mine was a world of war and arms.... But I have learned as well as bled.... I have learned that wrong thinking, carelessness, greed, and apathy kill and maim, too.[11]

Although he did not have the understanding of the Conspiracy that

Robert Welch had, General Walt nevertheless spoke out against the direction of our nation (for example, he insisted the U.S. should get out of the United Nations and quit financing our Communist enemies), and he argued that specific decision makers were at fault:

> Neither monetary policy nor foreign policy nor military policy is fixed and unchangeable. Any or all can be changed simply by making a new decision. It is very important always to keep this in mind. The things we don't like — our military weakness, our constant edging toward a World Government, our inflationary economy, and our confused foreign policy — are all the products of decisions of specific individuals.[12]

General Walt also understood where responsibility must be found for a nation to remain free — in the people. Indeed, he warned that pressure for desperately needed change would have to come from the actions of responsible Americans:

> I think that the future of our country boils down to this simple proposition: either we as individual Americans will assume the responsibilities of citizenship or our nation, as the land of the free, will be destroyed.[13]

In response to the Conspiracy's attack on our nation, Robert Welch offered this inspiring call to action in the March 1961 *Bulletin*:

> Whether the drama of the Twentieth Century winds up as an unrelieved and horrible tragedy, or whether despite all of the suffering throughout its earlier acts the play closes with a happy ending, is still to be decided by the cast of characters — no matter what the nefarious playwrights behind the scenes have planned.
>
> Most important among these players on the worldwide stage are still the American people.... *Leadership* back onto the hard road of *freedom through responsibility*, and of *happiness through satisfied consciences*, is an opportunity we must not miss and a duty we cannot fail. Beyond any

233

question we have the chance to change the course of history — to change it infinitely for the better at one of the darkest crises of all of man's centuries upon this earth.

To fulfill that great promise we must moderately lament the sorrows and mistakes which brought us where we are; which put on our hearts this grief for the suffering of others, and in our faces the horror of the danger to ourselves. For without such consideration of and for the past, we would be poorly prepared for the future. But our epic undertaking is to prevent the even worse sorrows that otherwise are to come.

To that ennobling and energizing purpose we are called upon to give the best that is in us. We are fighting, against terrific odds, for the greatest stakes in history — universal human freedom against universal slavery — and we intend to win.

Yes, the stakes are huge. And we, too, intend to win. But we can't do it alone. Our hope for victory depends very much upon pulling other responsible men and women of character into this fight.

We are especially looking for:

• Patriots who believe future generations deserve to enjoy a legacy of freedom;

• Men and women who are unwilling to follow the herd into slavery;

• Parents who can't stand the thought of their children being indoctrinated by corrupt apostles of the glorious State; and

• Noble benefactors who wish to help America get back on course and climb new peaks — peaks in truth, justice, opportunity, personal freedom, responsibility, prosperity, and unfettered creativity, within a society that honors God.

And finally, we are searching for men and women who are serious about making a difference in this struggle as it moves rapidly toward its climactic finish.

If that description includes you, we welcome your application for membership. Freedom or global slavery — the choice is yours.

Appendices

Appendix A

On the Shoulders of a Giant — Robert Welch

How often has public calamity been arrested on the very brink of ruin by the seasonable energy of a single man? ... [o]ne vigorous mind without office, without situation, without public function of any kind ... I say, one such man, confiding in the aid of God, and full of just reliance on his own fortitude, vigor, enterprise, and perseverance, would first draw to him some few like himself, and then that multitudes, hardly thought to be in existence, would appear and troop about him.

— Edmund Burke[1]

It is not surprising that a biographer of Robert Welch would choose the above words of an 18th Century British statesman to introduce his work. Edmund Burke's optimism seems as though it were written to describe Mr. Welch's leadership in the freedom fight.

Robert Welch became most widely known for the organization he founded when he was 59 years old. But most of that attention came from those who supported what was happening to America and who were willing to distort the truth to stop what Mr. Welch was trying to do. Because of the strategy of his enemies to make him and his organization appear ridiculous, the public at large never had the opportunity to appreciate the stature of the man.

However, by age 59, Robert Welch had already amassed a substantial positive reputation and circle of influence, or he never would have been able to achieve the impact he did in so short a period of time thereafter. Later, one of his colleagues in the freedom fight, the much admired American poet and essayist E. Merrill Root, would write the following about his friend:

> As you meet him in his quiet office at Belmont, or as you see him in public at a meeting or a John Birch Society dinner, you feel a power. It is not what we call today

"charisma." Robert Welch does not have that as (on different levels) a John F. Kennedy did, or a Theodore Roosevelt, or a Patrick Henry. There does not at first seem to be a flair, a personal magnetism, a something that reaches out and grasps you. It is a quiet power. It affirms and insists, through convictions, through an amazing knowledge, through a goodness and integrity that seem almost to be tangible. It is not oratory. He is not a spell-binder. He writes clearly, often brilliantly or eloquently; he writes better than he speaks. Yet somehow, something fundamental in the mind and the man, a grasp of things as they are, a sincerity and integrity flow out of him and into his audience. His power lies in his goodness and his truth. I have felt this, I have seen this, and I bear sober witness to it.[2]

Fortunately for the country he loved, Robert Welch was a rare combination of scholar, businessman, and leader. He was also a genius with integrity and devotion to duty. Brilliance is common, but brilliance with absolute integrity and successful accomplishment in the world of affairs is very unusual.

But perhaps what set him so far apart from many of his contemporaries was that he took pains to understand what had to be done and then stepped forward and did it. He didn't just complain about the problem or dabble in a solution. When he finally saw clearly what had to be done, he committed his entire life to it.

That attitude was reflected in a poem he wrote decades earlier at age 20, entitled "At Twenty":

> If, fifty years from now, when I survey
> The scanty roll of things that I have done,
> I find a score of visions unfulfilled
> And victories I dreamed of still unwon,
> I'll doubtless see mistakes that I have made
> And places where I lost because I picked the losing side;
> But not a failure shall I find
> In the trail I've left behind,
> Where I might have won but didn't, just because
> I never tried.[3]

Growing Up

Robert Welch was born in 1899 on a farm in North Carolina. In his early years and through most of grade school, Robert Welch was homeschooled by his mother, Lina Welch. Young Robert was an exceptionally gifted student, and his mother encouraged him to use his intellectual gifts in what became a love affair with knowledge.

By age six Robert was proficient in elementary algebra. At age seven, he began the study of Latin. During the summer that year he read nine volumes of Ridpath's *History of the World* and thus began his love for history. At age 12 he won a DAR essay contest dealing with North Carolina history.

Robert *graduated* from the University of North Carolina at the unusual age of 16. He entered Annapolis at age 17 with a college degree for a brief, two-year Naval career (after two years he ranked fourth in a class of nearly one thousand cadets). By age 20 he had become a syndicated columnist of sorts with four substantial newspapers running his commentaries on the news in verse. And then he entered Harvard Law School.

Frustrated with the socialist views of one of his professors — future Supreme Court Justice Felix Frankfurter — Robert resigned from law school after two years to become an entrepreneur in the candy business.

Growing Influence

As a successful businessman, Robert Welch became involved in the National Association of Manufacturers (NAM) and through that connection developed a friendship with a number of prominent business leaders. For seven years Mr. Welch served as a member of the board of directors of NAM and for three years as a regional vice president.

For two years, Mr. Welch functioned as the energetic chairman of the Educational Advisory Committee of NAM. In that capacity, he came in contact with leading educators. For most of those two years he chaired bimonthly meetings across the country on the state of American education. Out of these discussions came a 32-page brochure widely distributed by NAM entitled *This We Believe About Education*.

The level of personal influence Mr. Welch achieved can be seen by the caliber of the men who respected him. When he formed the Council of The John Birch Society in early 1960, he invited a couple dozen men to serve on that body — all with character, but some especially influential in their own right.

Here is a list of *some* of the notable figures who accepted Mr. Welch's invitation to serve on the initial Council. Most had been close personal friends of Mr. Welch for many years.

- Hon. T. Coleman Andrews, former Commissioner of Internal Revenue of the United States.
- Hon. Spruille Braden, former U.S. ambassador to several countries, former assistant secretary of state. Expert on Latin American affairs.
- Colonel Laurence E. Bunker, a Boston lawyer and trustee. Personal aide to General Douglas MacArthur during the Japanese occupation and the Korean War.
- William J. Grede, president of Grede Foundries, Inc., Milwaukee. Former president of NAM and former president of the National Council of YMCAs. Member of board of directors of the Federal Reserve Bank of Chicago for 14 years.
- A. G. Heinsohn Jr., president of Cherokee Mills, Sevierville, Tennessee. Author of *One Man's Fight for Freedom*.
- Fred C. Koch, president of Rock Island Oil and Refining Company.
- Dean Clarence Manion, former Dean of Notre Dame Law School.
- W. B. McMillan, president of the Hussman Refrigerator Co., St. Louis, Missouri.
- Cola G. Parker, former president of Kimberley-Clark Co. and former president of the National Association of Manufacturers.
- Robert W. Stoddard, president of Wyman-Gordan Company, Worcester, Massachusetts, with additional plants in Illinois, California, and Bombay, India. Ph. D. from Yale.
- Lt. General Charles B. Stone, III U.S.A.F. (Retired). Succeeded General Claire Chennault as Commander of our 14th Air Force in China.

- Mr. Ernest G. Swigert, president of the Hyster Company, Portland, Oregon, with other factories in the Midwest, South America, and Amsterdam. Former president of NAM.[4]

Getting Ready for the Fight Ahead

Mr. Welch's political philosophy and concerns regarding current affairs developed at an early age. About 1934 he wrote an unpublished essay entitled "A Weight On My Shoulders," which included these thoughts:

> The glory that is passing in the America that I was born in; that was given to me by courageous and far-seeing men, many of whom died for that purpose; that I grew up in, went to school in, and loved more every year as I came to understand what a miraculous achievement it was as compared with any other social group at any place or any time in the history of the world; ... my America is being made over into a carbon copy of thousands of despotisms that have gone before.[5]

Mr. Welch felt a personal obligation to do what he could to pass on America's heritage of freedom to future generations. Following World War II, he began speaking publicly before groups on contemporary issues.

He also traveled extensively. Those travels included "two trips to England specifically to study the effects of the Socialist government; one trip round the world; and fairly extensive additional traveling in North America, South America, Europe, and Asia."[6]

During those trips he got to know world leaders such as Syngman Rhee, president of Korea, and Conrad Adenauer, chancellor of West Germany. Twice he met with China's Chiang Kai-shek. Following his 1955 visit to South Korea, President Rhee wrote him, "I must confess I did not know we had such a staunch ally and champion as you in America."

Robert Welch had published articles since he was 20. As an illustration of the diversity of his interests, in 1945 he published a children's book, *The Barnyard News*. But his writing soon took a more serious turn.

In 1951, Mr. Welch began giving a short speech entitled "Acheson and MacArthur" regarding our treacherous foreign policy in the Far East that helped betray China into Communist hands. The speech created quite a stir.

Henry Regnery got wind of the speech and suggested to Mr. Welch that they publish it as a book. Mr. Welch agreed and it became, with some enlargement, *May God Forgive Us!* General Albert C. Wedemeyer, who had commanded all American forces in China during some of the period described in the book, stated that it was "the most comprehensive and objective treatment of the complex situation in the Far East that I have read."[7]

Other books with significant reach and impact would follow. In 1954, Regnery published Mr. Welch's story of U.S. Army hero John Birch. Captain Birch was brutally murdered by our supposed allies the Red Chinese, while on a peaceful reconnaissance mission in Army uniform immediately following the end of World War II. The facts surrounding his murder were suppressed, even from John's parents, by a U.S. State Department eager to help the Red Chinese maintain a benign image before the American public.

Mr. Welch uncovered the story while "[a]ll alone, in a committee room of the Senate Office Building ... reading the dry typewritten pages in an unpublished report of an almost forgotten congressional committee hearing."[8]

In 1956, Mr. Welch launched *One Man's Opinion*, a magazine that shortly became *American Opinion*, when he invited others to contribute. The reach and respect of this publication grew as he assembled an impressive stable of writers and led his publication to take a hard-line in defense of Americanism and in exposing the Communist/collectivist conspiracy's influence on current events.

"As of January 1, 1957, Mr. Welch gave up most of his business responsibilities — and most of his income — in order to devote practically all of his time and energy to the anti-Communist cause."[9] Out of these efforts came his plans to launch a new organization to fill a vacuum of leadership in the freedom fight.

The John Birch Society

Mr. Welch had become increasingly involved in researching the causes of America's problems and in working to inform the

242

American public. He even sought to increase his reach by campaigning as a candidate in the Republican primary for Lieutenant Governor of Massachusetts. But he eventually realized that our nation's course would not be changed by giving speeches, publishing a magazine, or even attaining high political office. Something more was needed. And Robert Welch was determined to fill that need.

So in December of 1958, he called together a group of prominent men for a two-day meeting during which he analyzed America's problems and outlined his plans for a new organization — The John Birch Society. Mr. Welch had no intention of just adding another voice of opposition to the collectivist advance. He meant business every step of the way, and the goal he sought was victory.

While at the helm of that organization for a quarter of a century, Mr. Welch attracted and inspired those closest to him and a growing membership — "that multitudes, hardly though to be in existence" — through his leadership in the monthly *Bulletin*.

Although the story of those battles is not directly the subject of this book, much of Mr. Welch's leadership and wisdom imparted through those battles is. So the reader will find pieces of that story interspersed through the book's chapters. And Chapter 13, The Principal Challenge: Building Organization, particularly examines the challenges and successes of The John Birch Society under Mr. Welch's leadership.

Appendix B

Our Founding Principles

Purpose and Perspective

- **The purpose** of **Freedom First Society** is to defend, restore, and support the principles of freedom that made America great. We seek the opportunity for new generations to enjoy that heritage and to understand and value its underlying principles so they, too, can preserve the foundation for freedom and build constructively upon it.

- We recognize that at the time of our founding (2007) the most powerful and ruthless **Conspiracy** in the history of mankind **has a grip on world affairs** and is seeking rapidly to eliminate the last bastions of potential resistance to its world hegemony. This Conspiracy stands in opposition to the values of all of the great religions and seeks to infiltrate, undermine, and subvert all significant institutions for its satanic purposes. We are reminded of, and accept, the admonition: "**The price of liberty is eternal vigilance.**"

- We believe that the days of freedom are limited unless sufficient numbers of Americans can quickly be brought under strong leadership to expose this Conspiracy and force it to be routed. **The preservation of freedom will require major commitments** of time, influence, and money on the part of an increasing number of individuals to build the essential organization.

- Freedom First Society seeks value far beyond the immediate fight, because **the conditions for freedom must always be nurtured** and layers of strength built to ward off the next conspiracy against freedom or to prevent the erosion of those layers through complacency and lack of understanding.

Values and Insights

- Freedom First Society is particularly **guided by the insights and** experience of Robert Welch, as reflected in his writings and speeches.

- We thoroughly support the great Roman legacy — **the rule of law**, an immense contribution to protecting our rights over the discredited arbitrary rule of men.

- We subscribe to the principles of **a Republic** and the wisdom of **our Founding Fathers** who, with **the U.S. Constitution**, created the best, practical example of a Republic to date.

- We subscribe to **Americanism**, which is the novel concept that guided the birth of our nation — the idea that **government should be the servant of the people**, that governments are properly instituted to secure the people's God-given rights.

- And thus we support **the healthy distrust of those we entrust with power**. As Thomas Jefferson wisely counseled: "Confidence is everywhere the parent of despotism.... In questions of power, then, let no more be heard of confidence in man, but bind him down from mischief by the chains of the Constitution."

- We respect **the lessons of history**. History and reason both argue that indispensable supports for a free society include **widespread adherence to religion and morality**, the traditional family, as well as cultural elements of Western Civilization such as responsibility, truth, justice, initiative, and self-sacrifice.

- Although experience shows that freedom is the key to economic prosperity, the primary justification for defending freedom is not economic, but religious and moral. It is **man's God-given right to be free**.

- We subscribe to the principle, as stated in the Declaration of Independence, "that all Men are created equal, that they are endowed by their Creator with certain unalienable Rights." Thus we **vigorously oppose racism, anti-Semitism, hatred, and bigotry**, and recognize them to be destructive forces and motivations.

- We believe that foul and illegitimate **means cannot be justified by imagined good ends**.

Organizing Policies

- We seek to provide **monolithic leadership** to enable patriots to build an organizational body that will sufficiently inform Americans to rout the Conspiracy's influence, restore our Republic, and help rebuild our nation's layers of strength.

- Since we earnestly seek to preserve freedom, **our top priority must be to expose the Conspiracy**. Until that is accomplished, **any other focus must be regarded as a tangent**. We strive to be experts on the principles of freedom and to determine what its enemies are doing so we can identify for our members and prospective members the most effective strategies to defend our freedom.

- Freedom First Society is an **organization of volunteers**, whose very **lifeblood is the activity of its members**. We acknowledge that volunteers will differ in their abilities, opportunities, and even commitment to participate. However, each member should understand that preserving America is still his responsibility.

- Members are encouraged to develop their own understanding of the principles of freedom and to inform themselves of the threats to it. Members should understand, however, that this **self-education cannot be an end in itself**. The primary purpose for informing oneself must be to take effective action — to become an educating fire fighter.

- We agree with Edmund Burke: "**When bad men combine, the good must associate**, else they will fall one by one, an unpitied sacrifice in a contemptible struggle."

- For Freedom First Society to accomplish its mission, **an overriding responsibility of members** must be to **inspire other responsible individuals** to take an interest in what we offer and **help bring them into the organization**. Therefore, we seek the association only of responsible men and women of high character, capable of positively influencing others in the battle for freedom.

- Finally, we enthusiastically seek, in the words of Robert Welch, "**less government, more responsibility, and — with God's help — a better world**."

Appendix C

Not Just *Any* Organization

We are at a stage, Gentlemen, where the only sure political victories are achieved by non-political organization; by organization which has a surer, more positive, and more permanent purpose than the immediate political goals that are only a means to an end; by organization which has a backbone, and cohesiveness, and strength, and definiteness of direction, which are impossible for the old-style political party organization.[1]
— Robert Welch, 1958, *The Blue Book*

Only a very specific *type* of organization can hope to stop a powerful, well entrenched Conspiracy. In this appendix we will identify and explain the organizational attributes we believe are necessary for success. This is the mold in which we seek to cast Freedom First Society. Our discussion should benefit staff and volunteer members alike, as we all need a clear vision of what we are working to build.

The wisdom and accomplishments of Robert Welch form the foundation for our thinking. To establish that connection we have quoted liberally from his writings in what follows.

We will examine the necessary organizational attributes under a three-part framework: **I. A Solid Foundation; II. Strong Tactical Leadership; and III. Staying Power**.

I. A Solid Foundation

Since Freedom First Society must achieve enormous growth, building a quality foundation is especially critical. Without a strong foundation, erosion will offset gains, like building sand castles at the beach at low tide. So let's identify the building blocks of our foundation.

A. A Big, Inspiring Purpose
Men and women give truly dedicated support only to big goals and

plans, not small ones. Freedom First Society certainly has a worthy goal: Recognizing that history is always forged by the dedicated few, it aims to be a catalyst to change the course of history.

Mr. Welch embraced the maxim: "Not failure but low aim is crime." In the November 1965 *Bulletin*, he summarized his organization's immediate objective:

> Our first great undertaking, let us restate in other language, is to prevent the destruction of our whole material, political, and spiritual legacy; and to do our part towards preserving, for our children and their children, the once great country and humane civilization which we ourselves inherited.

B. Proper Positive Purpose
As we explained in Chapter 6, an organization needs a clear positive purpose to maintain a constructive course. Otherwise it may easily end up helping one evil to overcome another. And even the lesser of two evils is still evil.

C. A Focus on First Things First
Any organization that expects to reverse the decline of Western Civilization must focus on first things first. In the *Blue Book*, Mr. Welch ascribed our nation's decline to three diseases: the cancer of collectivism, the loss of faith (and faith-based morality), and a Conspiracy. He emphasized, however, that the most immediate threat to all we hold dear is the progress of an incredibly evil, well organized Conspiracy. He insisted that we must focus on overcoming this threat before it made sense to proceed with positive, long-range plans.

D. Commitment to Proper and Effective Strategy
The proper strategy for fighting a well entrenched Conspiracy that has not yet consolidated its power is to expose it and thereby unleash the power of American public opinion. If properly informed and led, public opinion will force officials to take appropriate action.

Exposing the Conspiracy, creating needed public understanding, and building a principled leadership force are the objectives of proper strategy. Mr. Welch explained it this way:

We believe that to this basic principle of exposure we have added the correct strategy of trying to inform and educate first a large enough body of influential citizens — and through them enough of the general public. (November 1964 *Bulletin*)

Merely getting the existence and the power of this Conspiracy widely enough understood is the very core of our problem, and the only practicable means of our winning the struggle. (December 1964 *Bulletin*)

Mr. Welch had no intention of just spitting in the wind by tasking his relatively small force with only *educating* a small segment of our fellow citizens. That would clearly be a losing strategy against a Conspiracy that has such tremendous resources for deceiving and confusing the American people.

Instead, Mr. Welch wanted his members to educate *and enlist* non-members in the campaigns and then recruit the best prospects. He consistently placed recruitment as the top agenda item. His strategic objective was *to build an organized force of sufficient size* so that, through national concerted action programs, that force could provide decisive opposition to the Conspiracy.

E. Commitment to Right Moral Means

Robert Welch saw his strategy as a unique form of opposition that the Conspiracy had not faced before:

And that is, a sizable body of men and women dedicated to the purpose of simply bringing out the truth.[2]

But in "simply bringing out the truth," Mr. Welch insisted, and so do we, that everything we ask our members to do in support of that strategy must be moral:

The Communists believe that any means may be used to attain their ends. Once this principle is accepted, all moral codes are replaced by a system of value judgments. For who decides which end is noble enough to justify how much foulness in bringing it about? Why the man who wishes to use the foul means to attain ends that appeal to him, of course. And even murder then needs no more defense than the ancient adage: De gustibus non est disputandum. (There is no disputing about tastes.)

[Our organization], on the other hand, believes that improper means are never justified by even the noblest of aims, and that means are as important as ends in any worthwhile civilization.[3]

We expect that many of our deeply religious members will agree with the principle that nothing good in the long run can come from the use of immoral means.

F. Organized for Action

Freedom First Society will have a monolithic structure not only to assure that the organization's principles are maintained, but also to ensure that the organization will always be able to give decisive leadership and not be tied up through internal disputes and dissention that plague parliamentary organizations.

Mr. Welch encouraged members to share their opinions with headquarters, but he was very careful to prevent his organization from becoming a debating society. The JBS in those days meant business every step of the way.

In order to offer clear, unequivocal, constant, and reliable leadership, authority within Freedom First Society will be managed so that the organization speaks with one voice. No loose association of *prima donnas* will do.

G. Organized to Promote Organizational Health

A membership organization that wishes to remain healthy — vigorously on track — must invest in its culture and its members. These are challenges best tackled through standing organized programs. They cannot be taken for granted or placed on some list of future projects, only to be pursued when the organization's leaders are not so busy.

Since member activity is the lifeblood of Freedom First Society, it is both necessary and prudent to take steps to promote member understanding, skills, and involvement.

Example: While every member has the responsibility to become informed and stay informed, Freedom First Society must be structured to encourage and facilitate that action among as many members as possible. Topics for study would certainly include the subjects in this book.

Mr. Welch was also quite adamant that something more tightly knit than a mere organization must be built. He addressed the matter at the founding meeting of The John Birch Society:

> And please note that I said body, not organization. There is a huge difference, as I hope to make clear in the morning. An organization is a collection of individuals or groups held together more or less loosely and more or less temporarily by a common interest or common objective. A body, in the sense I am using it because it is the closest I can find to a word to express my concept, is an organic entity.
>
> The Americans for Democratic Action is an organization. The Catholic Church is a body. The Republican Party is an organization. The Communist Party is a body, which can move and work and make itself effective as an entity.[4]

II. Strong Tactical Leadership

Tactics is a leadership area that generally separates the men from the boys. And it is an area where Robert Welch excelled and virtually all of his contemporaries missed the mark.

A. Courage to Use the "C" Word

Perhaps foremost for an organization to be effective in the freedom fight its leadership must have the courage and insight to tell the unpleasant truth about the Conspiracy. In particular, as we discussed in Chapter 10, the leadership must recognize the overwhelming tactical and strategic importance of exposing the Conspiracy's role in current affairs.

Mr. Welch had good relations with many other leaders involved in the freedom fight. But he saw a fatal weakness in the leadership they were offering. He agreed wholeheartedly with most of what they had to say. It was what they didn't say that distressed him. They were addressing symptoms of our decline rather than alerting Americans to the cause:

> It is this difference in approach to the Communist threat which today separates the men from the boys, and the realists from the self-deluding tilters at windmills, among the anti-Communist groups and leaders. It is so much easier and more comfortable to be welcomed by the *Insiders* as "loyal opposition," to be treated by the Liberals as "respectable opponents," and not to be subjected to all of the smears, undermining, and persecution which the Communists and their dupes and allies inflict on those who really stand in their way or endanger their progress. But these "respectable opponents" accomplish about as much toward saving their country under today's circumstances as King Canute did when he ordered the ocean waves to recede. — March 1969 *Bulletin*

The Conspiracy's agenda is seriously threatened only by exposing its influence at the top and the phony wrestling match it stages to confuse its potential victims.

What Americans need to understand is that revolutionaries have a grip on our own government — and that means a grip even on a "conservative," "Christian" president. Those revolutionaries *require* problems — war, hunger, unemployment, scarcity, you name it — to drive forward their agenda.

We will lose our country and our freedoms, while our men in uniform continue to die in foreign lands, unless many more Americans come to understand the reality that their own leaders — phony posturing notwithstanding — are part of the team orchestrating the crises.

If any organization expects to prosper under such aggressive and outspoken leadership, then it must take steps to ensure that the organization's members and supporters share this insight, as well. Robert Welch relied heavily on the monthly *Bulletin* for communicating this insight to members.

In 1968 Robert Welch developed a concise exposition of the

Conspiracy entitled *A Cross Section of the Truth*. He wanted members to use this particularly hard-hitting pamphlet to educate potential prospects for membership. However, in introducing the special project in that year's September *Bulletin*, he anticipated that some members would hesitate to do so:

> Some of our members will say of *A Cross Section*: "Oh, but it goes too far. It is all true, of course. But it will drive people away because it is too unbelievable. The public is not yet ready to be told such things." To which we reply: "Then when are we going to tell them? When we are hanging from lamp posts, and the public is also hanging from other lamp posts within listening distance?"

Mr. Welch understood that to be effective in the freedom fight, leaders and members simply must accept the responsibility of watchmen on the tower and sound the alarm. And Freedom First Society must develop a culture so that members and leaders will readily accept this responsibility.

Note: This does not mean that we can be unconcerned with our impact and ignore principles of communication. Our goal is to *persuade*, not to be able to say that "we told you so," after we lose our freedoms. Our goal is for people to wake up and respond to the danger, not roll over and go back to sleep. So we must strive to use good personal relations skills in approaching others and to present our warning credibly.

B. A Willingness to Take the Point

On strategic issues, leadership must be willing for the organization to be first — to take the lead, and thereby the heat. Experience shows that if the point is held strongly enough, then others eventually follow.

Many conservatives, and even some politicians, are emboldened to stand up and challenge Conspiracy-defined political correctness, once someone else has taken the lead and much of the heat. Excellent examples from the past include The John Birch Society's taking on the sacred cows of the United Nations and the U.S. Supreme Court (in the 1960s).

Those organizations and leaders who depend on the approval of other groups and politicians will not be able to hold the point. The point is often a lonely position, but a position that must be occupied if freedom is to be successfully defended.

C. Determination to Take the Offensive
Almost all opponents of the Communist/collectivist advance fail to take the offensive to roll back collectivist gains. Their posture is invariably defensive. They are willing to accept the accumulated damage done to our Republic as irreversible, while they attempt to fight off any new assaults. However, as Napoleon Bonaparte succinctly pointed out, "The purely defensive is doomed to defeat."

In his foreword to the May 1963 *Bulletin*, Mr. Welch addressed this serious defect in leadership:

> The truth of [Napoleon's] statement, especially in connection with any long drawn-out contest, is as obvious as that night must follow day. For when one party in a struggle fights only defensively, then any change which does occur in his position is always a retreat. There are never any compensating gains to offset those backward steps. Also, the initiative and the aggressiveness are always with the enemy; and the defender fights invariably on battlegrounds chosen by his opponent. Under such circumstances the gradual demoralization and ultimate defeat of the defender are inevitable.

We simply must make the enemy defend his gains and, ultimately, give up ground. Sound leadership will seek to *reduce* the size of government by forcing government to conform to constitutional limits. And sound leadership will not accept the perpetual subversion of our independence through continued membership in the United Nations.

D. Courage to Stand on Principle
The organization's leaders must have the courage, commitment, and understanding to rely on principle in navigating our course through a sea of confusion. In an age when arguments of expediency hold

sway in political planning, we must champion the twin guideposts of morality and the Constitution.

In the January 1963 *Bulletin*, Mr. Welch stressed that "basic moral principles must be the standard, and the *only* standard, by which the actions of others are judged and our own courses of action are determined."

On those occasions when there are differences of opinion within our own ranks, we urge everyone never to work on any project with which they disagree.

E. Resistant to Misdirection

Since so many Americans lack an understanding of basic principles, it has been easy for the Conspiracy to sow confusion among those reacting to the very problems it has created or exacerbated. As a result, well meaning Americans are constantly following false leadership and supporting programs of questionable, even negative, value.

Effective leadership must consistently steer clear of these traps and point them out to its members. Only in this way will it deserve a committed following.

Another type of frequent misdirection is merely to become bogged down in the inconsequential and forget what's important. The organization's culture must supply the necessary antidote. Leadership must implement ongoing programs to ensure that the entire organization — staff and volunteer — understand the objectives and remain focused on them.

F. A Focus on Quality Concerted Action

Sound tactical leadership will concentrate our smaller forces to attack vulnerable, strategic points in the enemy's defenses. We must pick a few good issues and confine our energies to those issues. As Mr. Welch explained in the June 1963 *Bulletin*:

> When you are attacking a huge, strong, and tremendously extensive wall, with a comparative handful of soldiers, you do not go throwing yourself and your men bodily against the whole wall, or in scattered attacks on long portions of it....
>
> If we really mean business ... then we simply must

concentrate on attacks which offer the greatest possibility of both success and effectiveness. Fighting the battle on all fronts is hopeless — and unnecessary. Combining all of our strength and determination into an attack at one point, when the opportunity offers, while carefully and patiently building up preparations for concentrated attacks on other vulnerable spots in due course, is the only strategy available to us that even makes sense under the circumstances.

III. Staying Power

No one should want to invest in building an organization that is not structured to withstand the expected storms. Weak support can easily buckle under the public heat that the Conspiracy can generate. And an organization with a weak structure is also susceptible to paralysis through internal dissension and schisms.

A. Ability to Grow Without Losing Focus
The organization must be able to maintain its focus and its principles through changes in leadership and over time. And especially it must be able to assimilate new members and staff and grow without losing its focus.

Flawed Approaches to Growth
Leaders of many organizations often seek to extend their influence by loosening up on their principles to admit a broader membership. But size alone is no measure of effectiveness.

It is critical to develop a following based on common commitment to fundamental principles of strategy. If necessary, prospective members must be excluded if they don't fit. An organization that is serious about its business can't allow individuals to join and bring along their pet causes.

Several decades ago, a memorable TV commercial for a bank claimed that "fifty percent of smart is knowing what you're dumb at." Leadership should not try to position the organization as expert on all issues or to divide its following over issues that are at most tangential to its objectives.

Opening your doors to tangential agendas and alliances may

appear to increase the organization's reach — in the short term. But in the long term, the organization, if it grows at all, will be ineffective.

Track Record of Quality

Initially, Freedom First Society must compile a track record of quality leadership — truth, responsibility, accurately analyzing Insider objectives, and an action program that is on target.

Quality is not only the key to short-term effectiveness, it is also the key to attracting the people that can help us grow and maintain the quality. And a growing, quality organization is what it will take to win. So leaders and staff must be committed to quality at every level.

To help inspire members to build the necessary organization in time, our leaders must strive for Freedom First Society to offer members something of high value they can't get anywhere else — the opportunity to really make a difference. And our program needs to be structured to allow each member to play as significant a role as his or her talents and dedication permit.

As we endure and grow, our monolithic structure will help the leadership pass on a tradition of quality and purpose. And our chapter structure will promote stability by inculcating our principles and understanding into new members.

B. Resistant to Outside Pressure

With so much at stake, any organization that shows signs of being effective will be subjected to pressures to compromise. The organization must be resistant to outside pressure so members can be confident it won't compromise on its fundamental mission and principles.

In 1963 Mr. Welch's organization was being subjected to a propaganda campaign of vitriolic attacks and distortion from many quarters, the likes of which has since toppled several governments. In the December *Bulletin* that year, Mr. Welch suggested why his organization had thus far been able to withstand those attacks:

It is the combination of underlying permanent purpose, and of a structure that was also designed for permanence, which gives us the strength that amazes both friends and foes. By being something far more soundly conceived, with far more worthwhile goals, than merely an anti-Communist or an anti-Socialist organization, we have been able to withstand all the attacks of the Communists and the Socialists.

We would add another factor. Mr. Welch had built strong member loyalty and toughness through his persistently refreshing appeal to and deep explanation of principle, particularly though the monthly *Bulletin* that each member received.

C. Resistant to Internal Disruption
The organization must be resistant to internal disruption of several varieties. One concern is maneuvering by staff or volunteer leaders. Such maneuvering can be deadly to any serious organization. Fortunately, clearly understood lines of authority within a monolithic structure discourage any such maneuvering by making it obviously ineffective.

Structure alone won't stop squabbles and dissension. But a monolithic structure provides a means for limiting the damage. In addition, leadership must constantly strive to inculcate proper principles throughout the organization to reduce any damage from those who would splinter our ranks by appealing to loyalty to a personality over principle.

Of course, a large voluntary membership organization can't be totally resistant to infiltration. The best deterrent is to make it obvious that infiltration doesn't pay. The monolithic structure and the development of a strong emphasis on principle can enable strong leadership to curtail the damage of those who would try to take the organization off course. A history of strong action should further discourage those who might otherwise try to divide the organization or inject other agendas.

In Conclusion
In March 1990, G. Allen Bubolz, as chief executive officer of The John Birch Society, shared his understanding and conviction as to the kind of organization required for success:

The success of The John Birch Society's education and action program is still the critical factor on which the future of Western Civilization turns. There is no other organized effort of any substance that has the vision, the resources, the experience, and the courage to confront conspiratorial efforts to build a worldwide socialist tyranny. As never before, America vitally needs our perspective and our leadership. *And that critical need can flow only from a focused action program that is both immune to political and economic pressure, and free from misdirection supplied by self-promoters, fools, conspirators, and cowards.*[5] [Emphasis added.]

There are three principal tasks to creating a *new* organization with the attributes we have discussed:

- The first task is to lay a solid structural foundation.
- The second is to build a culture during our early, formative years supported by standing programs that propagate these core values throughout the staff and membership.
- And the third task is to bring in talented people of character from the beginning.

This book is designed to help Freedom First Society with all three of these tasks as it strives to fill a huge vacuum in the freedom fight. The reality is that no organization has been adequately implementing these principles in recent years. Nevertheless, their implementation is absolutely necessary to achieve victory over the Conspiracy.

ORGANIZE FOR VICTORY!

Notes

Style notes: Throughout this text where quoted material indicates emphasis, the reader should assume that such emphasis is in the original unless otherwise identified as "Emphasis added." Also, Robert Welch is frequently quoted from his writings in the monthly *John Birch Society Bulletin*. For simplicity, this source is generally referred to as the *Bulletin*.

Introduction
1. Patrick Henry at St. John's Church on March 23, 1775, in Norine Dickson Campbell, *Patrick Henry: Patriot and Statesman* (Old Greenwich, Conn.: Devin-Adair, 1975), p. 128.

Chapter 1: A Fact, Not a Theory
1. Regarding structure, see, for example: John Robison, *Proofs of a Conspiracy,* original 1798 edition republished (Belmont, Mass.: Western Islands, 1967); and Carroll Quigley, *The Anglo-American Establishment* (New York: Books in Focus, 1981).
2. Robert Welch, *A Cross Section of the Truth* (pamphlet), 1968.
3. *JBS Bulletin*, October 1967. Prior to serving on the staff of the U.S. Senate for 25 years, Dr. Lucier had been the associate editor of the *Richmond News Leader*. He was also a frequent contributor to *American Opinion* from 1963 to 1966.
4. Ibid.
5. Ibid.
6. Carroll Quigley, *Tragedy and Hope: A History of the World In Our Time* (New York: Macmillan, 1966), p. 950.
7. Ibid., p. 952.
8. Quigley, *The Anglo-American Establishment*, p. 197.
9. John F. McManus, "Bill Clinton and Carroll Quigley," *JBS Bulletin*, October 1992.
10. Quigley, *The Anglo-American Establishment*, pp. 3, 4.
11. Ibid., pp. 4, 5.
12. Ibid., p. 5.
13. Ibid., p. 49.
14. Quigley, *Tragedy and Hope*, p. 953.
15. Ibid., p. 935.
16. Welch, *JBS Bulletin*, January 1971.
17. James H. Billington, *Fire in the Minds of Men: Origins of Revolutionary Faith* (New York: Basic Books, 1980), p. 94.
18. George Washington, letter to Reverend G.W. Snyder, October 24, 1798, *The Writings of George Washington from the original manuscript sources*, 1745-1799, John C. Fitzpatrick, ed. (Washington, D.C.: U.S. Government Printing Office), vol. 36, pp. 452-453.
19. George Washington letter to Reverend G. W. Snyder, October 24, 1798, quoted in Charles Callahan, *Washington: The Man and the Mason*, 1913 and Fitzpatrick, pp. 518-519.
20. R.M. Whitney, *Reds in America*, 1924 (Belmont, Mass.: Western Islands ed., 1970), p. 15.
21. William P. Hoar, "Andrew Carnegie," *American Opinion*, December 1975.
22. *Tax-Exempt Foundations*, Report of the Special House Committee to Investigate Tax-Exempt Foundations (Reece Committee), Eighty-Third Congress, 1954.
23. "Institute of Pacific Relations," Report of the Senate Committee on the Judiciary, Eighty-Second Congress, Second Session, July 2, 1952, p. 223.
24. Quigley, *Tragedy and Hope*, p. 954.
25. Schlesinger, Arthur M. Jr., *A Thousand Days: John F. Kennedy in the White House* (Boston: Houghton Mifflin, 1965), p. 128.

Chapter 2: Premeditated Merger
1. James J. Drummey, "The Internationalist," *The New American*, March 12, 1991. Dodd told his story several times, and it has been retold many times with slightly different wording. The story is also recorded in William H. McIlhany II, *The Tax-Exempt Foundations* (Westport, Conn.: Arlington House, 1980), pp. 62-63. McIlhany interviewed Dodd on June 25 and 26, 1976 and recorded the interviews. See note 1 and 29 on pp. 233-34 in McIlhany. Also, Norman Dodd in letter to Howard E. Kershner, December 29, 1962.
2. Fifteenth Report, California Senate Fact-finding Subcommittee on Un-American Activities, 1970.
3. William F. Jasper, "Silk Hats and Brown Berets," *The New American*, February 19, 1996.
4. George Racey Jordan, *From Major Jordan's Diaries* (Harcourt, Brace, 1952), p. 1.
5. Medford Evans, "The Emperor's New Bomb," *American Opinion*, October 1965.
6. Ibid.
7. Gary Allen, "The Unelected: How Do You Move Left From Here?" *American Opinion*, June 1968.
8. The Ickes diary was published posthumously in three volumes as: *The Secret Diary of Harold L. Ickes* (New York: Simon & Shuster, 1953-54). However, Simon & Shuster omitted the revealing passage, which had appeared earlier in

261

a magazine. The discrepancy is discussed by Westbrook Pegler, "Fair Enough," *The Billings Gazette*, December 11, 1953 (King Features Syndicate). The sanitized Simon & Shuster version of the events for July 16, 1935 appears on pp. 399-402 in volume I. In a "Publisher's Note" in that volume, Simon & Shuster promised to deposit the complete diary manuscript with the Library of Congress.

9. Sumner Welles quoted in "Target: Total Government," *The New American*, September 16, 1996.

10. Edward Mandell House, *Philip Dru: Administrator: A Story of Tomorrow — 1920-1935* (New York: B.W. Huebsch, 1912), Chapter VI, p. 35 in RWU Press edition, 1998.

11. Thomas W. Phelps, *Wall Street Journal*, July 1937, quoted by Westbrook Pegler, "U.S. Fascism Spawned in 1912," *Los Angeles Examiner*, August 26, 1954, p. I-25.

12. Zbigniew Brzezinski, "America and Europe," *Foreign Affairs*, October 1970, p. 29.

13. Brzezinski, *Between Two Ages: America's Role in the Technetronic Era* (New York: Viking Press, 1970), p. 72.

14. James Perloff, *The Shadows of Power* (Belmont, Mass.: Western Islands), p. 154.

15. Brzezinksi, *Between Two Ages*, p. 296.

16. Ibid., p. 295.

17. Leslie Gelb, "The Secretary of State sweepstakes," *New York Times*, May 23, 1976.

18. Jimmy Carter campaign booklet, *Why Not the Best?* (Nashville, TN: Boardman Press, 1975).

19. Chester Ward and Phyllis Schlafly, *Kissinger on the Couch* (New Rochelle, N.Y.: Arlington House, 1975), pp. 146, 150.

20. *Tax-Exempt Foundations*, Report of the Special House Committee to Investigate Tax-Exempt Foundations (Reece Committee), Eighty-Third Congress (U.S. Government Printing Office, 1954), pp. 176-77, quoted in Ward and Schlafly, p. 150.

Sidebar: Far Fewer Surprises!

1. Robert Welch, *The Politician* (Belmont, Mass.: Belmont Publishing, Library Edition, 5th printing, 1964), pp. xx, xxi.

Chapter 3: Betrayal of Allies

1. John Locke, *The Second Treatise on Government*, section 92 (New York: Liberal Arts Press, 1952), p. 52.

2. John Emerich Edward Dalberg-Acton (Lord Acton) (1834–1902) in John Bartlett (compiler), *Familiar Quotations* (16th ed.) (Boston: Little, Brown, 1992), p. 521.

3. Alan Stang, "How the Fabians Crippled Great Britain," *American Opinion*, March 1979. Also, Antony C. Sutton, *Wall Street and the Bolshevik Revolution* (New Rochelle, New York:

Arlington House, 1974), p. 25, 33.

4. Sutton; also see *Papers Relating to the Foreign Relations of The United States — 1918, Russia*, House of Representatives Document No. 1868 (Washington D.C.: U.S. Government Printing Office, 1931), Vol. I, pp. 374-376.

5. R.J. Rummel, *Death by Government* (New Brunswick, N.J.: Transaction Publishers, 1994), p. 82 in 2008 paperback.

6. See, for example: Julius Epstein, *Operation Keelhaul: The Story of Forced Repatriation from 1944 to the Present* (Old Greenwich, Conn.: Devin-Adair, 1973); Nicholas Bethell, *The Last Secret* (New York: Basic Books, 1974); Robert Welch, *The Politician* (Belmont, Mass.: Belmont Publishing, 1964); and Peter J. Huxley-Blythe, *The East Came West* (Caldwell, Idaho: Caxton, 1964).

7. See, for example: John T. Flynn, *While You Slept: Our Tragedy in Asia and Who Made It* (New York: Devin-Adair, 1951); Anthony Kubeck, *How the Far East Was Lost: American Policy and the Creation of Communist China, 1941-1949* (Chicago: Regnery, 1963); Freda Utley, *The China Story* (Chicago: Henry Regnery, 1951); and Robert H. W. Welch Jr., *May God Forgive Us* (Chicago: Henry Regnery, 1952).

8. Rummel, pp. 98, 99.

9. David Rockefeller, "From A China Traveler," *New York Times*, August 10, 1973.

10. *Wall Street Journal*, quoted in "Compromise or Collusion?" *The New American*, February 26, 1990.

11. Henry Kissinger, syndicated column, "China: Push for Reform, Not Rupture," *Los Angeles Times*, July 30, 1989.

12. Jay Ross, "Rockefeller: US business unhampered in Angola," *Boston Globe*, March 3, 1982, p. 36.

13. Evans-Raymond Pierre, "Genocide in Tibet," *The New American*, November 9, 1987.

14. Representative Michael A. Feighan, *Congressional Record*, August 31, 1960, p. 17407. [Also see Vol. 106, p. 18785.]

15. "Protest Over Berlin," *New York Times*, August 16, 1961.

16. Regarding *New York Times* coverage, see particularly articles by Herbert Matthews in the crucial years of 1958 and 1959. Regarding Smith complaint see "Correction Please!" *American Opinion*, July/August 1963; also re CIA involvement see John Martino with Nathaniel Weyl, *I Was Castro's Prisoner: An American Tells His Story* (New York: Devin Adair, 1963); and, of course, Earl E. T. Smith (U.S. Ambassador to Cuba, 1957-59), *The Fourth Floor: An Account of the Castro Communist Revolution* (New York: Random House, 1962).

17. See, for example: *Report of Senate Internal Security Subcommittee*, 1962; and Nathaniel Weyl, *Red Star Over Cuba* (Third revised printing) (New York: Devin Adair, 1962).

18. Anastasio Somoza as told to Jack Cox, *Nicaragua Betrayed* (Belmont, Mass.: Western Islands, 1980).

19. "Introduction to the Palace Guard," *The New American*, February 22, 1993.

20. Cyrus Vance statement, June 21, 1979, reported in *World Almanac's* "Chronology" of 1979 (published 1980), quoted in Medford Evans, "President Somoza Tells How Carter Betrayed Nicaragua," *American Opinion*, October 1980.

Chapter 4: The War *Against* U.S. Independence

1. G. Edward Griffin, *The Fearful Master: A Second Look at the United Nations* (Belmont, Mass.: Western Islands, 1964), p. 235.

2. Richard N. Gardner, "The Hard Road to World Order," *Foreign Affairs*, April 1974, p. 558.

3. Lincoln P. Bloomfield, Study Memorandum No. 7, *A World Effectively Controlled By the United Nations*, Institute for Defense Analyses (State Department contract No. SCC 28270, February 24, 1961), delivered March 10, 1962.

4. Alexander Hamilton, Essay No. 67, *The Federalist Papers* (New York: Mentor, 1961), p. 407.

5. Don Fotheringham, "War Powers," published on www.freedomfirstsociety.org, 11/2/2007.

6. James Madison, "Political Observations," April 20, 1795, quoted in *Works* 4:491-2. Reprinted as "The Most Dreaded Enemy of Liberty" in *Essays on Liberty*, Volume I (Irvington-on-Hudson, New York: Foundation For Economic Education, 1952), p. 88, taken from *Letters and Other Writings of James Madison*.

7. James Madison, letter to Jefferson, April 2, 1798, in *The Republic of Letters: The Correspondence between Thomas Jefferson and James Madison 1776-1826*, (James Morton Smith editor) Volume II: 1790-1804 (New York: W.W. Norton, 1995), p. 1032.

8. Abraham Lincoln, letter to William H. Herndon, February 15, 1848, in Philip Van Doren Stern (editor), *The Life and Writings of Abraham Lincoln* (New York: Random House, 1940), p. 310.

9. "Excerpts from Clinton's Speech on Foreign Policy Leadership," *New York Times*, August 14, 1992.

10. See, for example: "The New World Army," editorial, *New York Times*, March 6, 1992; "The Unsung New World Army," editorial, *New York Times*, May 11, 1992; Paul Lewis, "U.N. Chief Asks for Armed Force to Serve as a Permanent Deterrent," *New York Times*, June 19, 1992; "Help the U.N. Arm for Peace," editorial, *New York Times*, November 27, 1992; Bruce Russett

and James S. Sutterlin, "The U.N. in a New World Order," *Foreign Affairs*, Spring 1991; and Carnegie Endowment for International Peace and Institute for International Economics, "Special Report: Policymaking for a New Era," *Foreign Affairs*, Winter 1992/93.

11. Members of the commission who subsequently joined the Clinton administration include: U.S. Ambassador to the UN Madeleine Albright (CFR), Foreign Intelligence Advisory Board Chairman Admiral William J. Crowe (CFR), Under Secretary of State Peter Tarnoff (past president of the CFR), Assistant Secretary of State Winston Lord (past president of the CFR), Deputy Undersecretary for Global Affairs Jessica Tuchman Mathews (CFR), and Deputy Undersecretary of Defense for Policy Graham Allison (CFR). Morton Halperin (CFR) was nominated assistant secretary of defense, but withdrew while facing intense Senate scrutiny. A few months later, Halperin joined the administration in another position not requiring Senate confirmation.

12. Steven A. Holmes, "Clinton May Let U.S. Troops Serve Under U.N. Chiefs," *New York Times*, August 18, 1993.

13. Senator Trent Lott, October 5, 1993, in "Bill Clinton's Un-American Directive," *The New American*, November 29, 1993.

14. "Premeditated Merger," *The New American*, April 25, 1988. See also: "The Council on Foreign Relations," *The New American*, April 7, 1986; and G. Russell Evans, *The Panama Canal Treaties Swindle: Consent to Disaster*, Introduction by Admiral Thomas H. Moorer, USN (Ret.) (Carrboro, N.C.: Signal Books, 1986).

15. "X. The Review of the News," *JBS Bulletin*, November 1982. Also: Gary Allen, "Trade Trap," *American Opinion*, November 1980; and Gary Allen, "Ten Years Later Many Americans Are Calling it Conspiracy (Part II)," *American Opinion*, April 1983.

16. Antony C. Sutton, *National Suicide: Military Aid to the Soviet Union* (New Rochelle, New York: Arlington House, 1973), pp. 253-54.

17. Ibid., p. 258.

18. Senator William Armstrong, "Technology Transfer: Selling the Soviets the Rope," speech to U.S. Senate, April 13, 1982, *Congressional Record*, pp. S3386-89.

19. Chesly Manly, "U.S.-Red Bloc Links Questioned," *Chicago Tribune*, December 26, 1966, quoting dispatch from Stettin, Poland, in the Oct. 1 issue of *Die Pomersche Zeitung* of Hamburg.

Chapter 5: The Conspiracy's War on America

1. Testimony of Major General Lewis Walt, U.S. Congress, Senate, *World Drug Traffic and Its*

Impact on U.S. Security, Hearings before the Internal Security Subcommittee, September 14, 1972 (Washington, D.C.: Government Printing Office, 1972), Part 4, pp. 157-158.

2. Joseph D. Douglass Jr., *Red Cocaine: The Drugging of America* (Atlanta: Clarion House, 1990), p. 107. Also see: Harry J. Anslinger and William F. Tompkins, *The Traffic in Narcotics* (New York: Funk & Wagnalls, 1953); and Anslinger, "The Opium of the People's Government," in U.S. Congress, House Committee on Un-American Activities, *Soviet Total War: "Historic Mission" of Violence and Deceit,* Volume II (Washington, D.C.: U.S. Government Printing Office, September 30, 1956).

3. James J. Drummey, "Playing Games with Communists," *The New American,* October 9, 1989.

4. Douglass, pp. 1,2.

5. Mohammed Hassanein Heikal, *Nasser: The Cairo Documents* (New York: Doubleday, 1971), pp. 278-279, in "Drug War on the West," *The New American,* April 10, 2000.

6. Stefan T. Possony, *Maoist China and Heroin* (Taipei, Taiwan: China Publishing Company, no date), in Douglass, pp. 107-08.

7. Douglass, p. 71.

8. Ibid., p. 113.

9. Ibid., p. 144.

10. Ibid., pp. xiv, 33. Also, "Drug War on the West," *The New American,* April 10, 2000.

11. "Drug War on the West."

12. Ibid.

13. "China Invasion," *The New American,* September 1, 1997.

14. Charles Hutzler, "China, U.S. agree to cooperate on fighting drugs," Associated Press, June 19, 2000.

15. Ibid.

16. "U.S.-Red China: Police-State Convergence," *The New American,* July 17, 2000.

17. Michael Levine, *Deep Cover* (New York: Delacorte Press, 1990), p. 11.

18. Ibid., p. 15.

19. Lincoln P. Bloomfield, Study Memorandum No. 7, *A World Effectively Controlled By the United Nations,* Institute for Defense Analyses (State Department contract No. SCC 28270, February 24, 1961), delivered March 10, 1962, Chapter III: Assumptions.

20. Ibid., Chapter III and Chapter V: Principal Problems in Achieving a World Order.

21. Arnold Kunzli and Karl Marx, *Eine Psychographie* (Wien, Frankfurt, Zurich: Europe Verlag, 1966), pp. 703,712,715, quoted in Ray S. Cline and Yonah Alexander, *Terrorism: The Soviet Connection* (New York: Crane Russak, 1984), p. 9.

22. Claire Sterling, *The Terror Network: The Secret War of International Terrorism* (New York: Holt, Rinehart and Winston and Reader's Digest Press, 1981), p 14.

23. Ibid., pp. 249-50.

24. Ibid., p. 286.

25. Ibid.

26. Ibid.

27. "The Terror Conspiracy," *The New American,* February 27, 1989.

28. Ibid.

29. Donald H. Rumsfeld, "A New Kind of War," *New York Times,* September 27, 2001.

30. The National Lawyers Guild was cited as "the foremost legal bulwark of the Communist Party, its front organizations, and controlled unions" by the House Committee on Un-American Activities in *Guide to Subversive Organizations and Publications* (Washington D.C.: U.S. Government Printing Office, 1950), p. 121.

31. R.J. Rummel, *Death by Government* (New Brunswick, N.J.: Transaction Publishers, 1994), p. 9 in 2008 paperback.

32. John Barron, *KGB: The Secret Work of Soviet Secret Agents* (New York: Bantam Books, 1974), p. 12.

33. See, for example: Antony C. Sutton, *Wall Street and the Rise of Hitler* (Seal Beach, Calif.: '76 Press, 1976); and William P. Hoar, *Architects of Conspiracy: An Intriguing History* (Belmont, Mass.: Western Islands, 1984), Chapter XIII: Fascism and National Socialism.

34. Adolph Hitler, November 6, 1933 speech, in William Shirer, *The Rise and Fall of the Third Reich: A History of Nazi Germany* (Greenwich, Conn.: Fawcett, 1960), p. 343.

35. Ibid., p. 351.

Chapter 6: Foundations of Freedom

1. James Madison, "Who Are the Best Keepers of the People's Liberties?" 1792, *Writings,* Paul Ford edition (Richmond, Va.: William Byrd Press, 1964), vol. VI, p. 120.

2. *The New Americanism and Other Speeches and Essays by Robert Welch* (Belmont, Mass.: Western Islands, 1966), pp. 11-13.

3. Madison, Essay No. 10, *The Federalist Papers* (New York: Mentor, 1961), p. 81.

4. Robert Welch speech in honor of William Grede, "What is Americanism?" collected in *The Historical Significance of Robert Welch,* limited edition, 1993.

5. G. Edward Griffin, *The Fearful Master: A Second Look at the United Nations* (Belmont, Mass.: Western Islands, 1964), p ii.

6. Robert Welch, "My Concept of Freedom," opening statement at public debate with Norman Thomas, September 25, 1964, in G. Edward Griffin, *The Life and Words of Robert Welch* (Thousand Oaks, Calif.: American Media, 1975), p. 141.

NOTES

7. Gary Allen, "Tax or TRIM," *American Opinion*, January 1975.

Chapter 7: Economic Prosperity — A Fruit of Freedom

1. Henry Grady Weaver, *The Mainspring of Human Progress*, revised edition (Irvington-on-Hudson, New York: Foundation for Economic Education, 1953), p. 12.
2. Ibid., p. 14.
3. Ibid., p. 238.
4. Ibid., p. 13.
5. Ibid., p. 258.
6. Robert Welch speech, "What is Americanism?" collected in *The Historical Significance of Robert Welch,* limited edition, 1993.
7. Thomas Jefferson quoted by Robert Welch, *JBS Bulletin*, March 1974.
8. Roger Baldwin, 30th anniversary yearbook, published in 1935 by Baldwin's Harvard class of 1905, quoted in "XI. Protect Our Borders," *JBS Bulletin*, February 1989.
9. Hernando de Soto, *The Other Path: The Invisible Revolution in the Third World* (Harper-Collins, 1990). See also: Soto, *The Mystery of Capital: Why Capitalism Triumphs in the West and Fails Everywhere Else* (New York: Basic Books, 2000); and Soto and Francis Cheneval, *Realizing Property Rights* (Ruffer and Rub, 2006).
10. Gary Allen with Larry Abraham, *None Dare Call It Conspiracy* (Rossmoor, Calif.: Concord Press, 1971), p. 34.
11. Ibid., p. 33.

Chapter 8: First, Correctly Define the Problem!

1. Henry David Thoreau, *Walden* (1854), in *The Great Quotations*, compiled by George Seldes (New York: Pocket Books, 1970), p. 330.
2. John P. Foley (editor), *The Jeffersonian Cyclopedia: A Comprehensive Collection of the Views of Thomas Jefferson* (New York: Funk & Wagnalls, 1900), p. 274 (viewed online).
3. James Madison, "Who Are the Best Keepers of the People's Liberties?" 1792, *Writings*, Vol. VI, p. 120, in G. Edward Griffin, *The Life and Words of Robert Welch* (Thousand Oaks, Calif.: American Media, 1975), p. 315.
4. Apparently also said earlier in 1789, but reference here: John Adams, October 11, 1798, to the officers of the First Brigade of the Third Division of the Militia of Massachusetts, in Charles Francis Adams, *The Works of John Adams, Second President of the United States*, Vol. IX (Boston: Little, Brown and Co., 1854), p. 229.
5. Abraham Lincoln, quoted in Roy P. Basler (ed.), "Address Before Young Men's Lyceum of Springfield, Illinois, January 27, 1838," *The Collected Works of Abraham Lincoln*

(Piscataway, New Jersey: Rutgers University Press, 1953), Vol. I, p. 109.
6. Antonio Gramsci, *Prison Notebooks*, Volume I (New York: Columbia University Press, 1992), p. 137.
7. Richard Grenier, *Capturing the Culture* (Washington, D.C.: Ethics and Public Policy Center, 1991), p. xiv.
8. Videotaped interview of Norman Dodd by G. Edward Griffin, *The Hidden Agenda: Merging America Into World Government* (Westlake Village, Calif.: American Awareness, 1991).
9. Carroll Quigley, *The Anglo-American Establishment* (New York: Books in Focus, 1981), p. 49.
10. *Prison notebooks of Antonio Gramsci* in "Toward the Total State," *The New American*, July 5, 1999.
11. James J. Drummey, "Robert W. Stoddard: He Knew the Meaning of Freedom," *The New American*, November 25, 1985.
12. Robert Welch et al., "The Beginning of the End," *JBS Bulletin*, December 1980.
13. Edmund Burke, speech at County Meeting of Bucks, 1784, in John Bartlett (compiler), *Familiar Quotations: A Collection of Passages, Phrases, and Proverbs Traced to their Sources in Ancient and Modern Literature* (9th Edition) (Boston: Little, Brown, 1906), p. 411.

Chapter 9: Next, Assess Our Strengths and Enemy Weaknesses

1. *United States Army Infantry Journal*, 1939, in June 1972 *Bulletin*.
2. Robert Welch, *The Blue Book* (Belmont, Mass.: Western Islands, 1959), p. 160.
3. Charles Dudley Warner, *My Summer Is a Garden* (1870), in H.L. Mencken, *A New Dictionary of Quotations on Historical Principles From Ancient and Modern Sources* (New York: Alfred A. Knopf, 1942).
4. Ambrose Evans-Pritchard, *The Secret Life of Bill Clinton: the unreported stories* (Washington, D.C.: Regnery, 1997), p. 366.
5. Welch, p. 61.
6. See, for example: Francis Ivan Simms Tuker, *The Yellow Scarf: The Story of the Life of Thuggee Sleeman, or Major-General Sir William Henry Sleeman, K.C.B., 1788-1856, of the Bengal Army and the Indian Political Service* (J.M. Dent & Co., 1961); and William Henry Sleeman, *Rambles and Recollections of an Indian Official*, Chapter 13: "Thugs and Poisoners," paperback edition (Echo Library, 2006). **Note:** The fictional 1988 film *The Deceivers*, starring Pierce Brosnan, depicts the Thugee conspiracy, but alters the history of the main character. The term "Thug" comes from the Hindi word "to deceive" and refers to the skill of the Thugs in deceiving their victims.

7.

ntor-

ORGANIZE FOR VICTORY!

Chapter 10: Set Reasonable and Sufficient Objectives

1. Edmund Burke, speech at County Meeting of Bucks, 1784, quoted in John Bartlett (compiler), *Familiar Quotations: A Collection of Passages, Phrases, and Proverbs Traced to their Sources in Ancient and Modern Literature* (9th Edition) (Boston: Little, Brown, 1906), p. 411.
2. Eleanor Stables, "Border Fence Construction Not Moving Fast Enough for Rep. Hunter," *Congressional Quarterly*, July 11, 2007.
3. Liberal Republican Senator Hugh Scott (Pennsylvania), floor leader for the Nixon administration, boasted to a reporter: "We [Liberals] get the action and the Conservatives get the rhetoric." Quoted from *Battleline*, February 1970, in Gary Allen, *Richard Nixon: The Man Behind the Mask* (Belmont, Mass.: Western Islands, 1971), p. 1.
4. Marcus Tullius Cicero, speech in the Roman Senate (42 B.C.), in Warren L. McFerran, "Conspiracies," *The New American*, December 4, 1989. Although the statement has been widely attributed to Cicero, there is some doubt as to its authenticity. Wikipedia lists it as unsourced. Cicero was murdered the previous year (December 7, 43 B.C.), however, ancient historians often invented speeches for their characters or confused dates.
5. See, for example: Christopher Booker and Richard North, *The Great Deception: The Secret History of the European Union* (United Kingdom: Continuum International Publishing Group, 2003).
6. James Madison, in Charles S. Hyneman and Donald S. Lutz, *American Political Writing during the Founding Era: 1760-1805*, Vol. I., (Indianapolis, Ind.: Liberty Press, 1983), p. 633.

Chapter 11: To Restore Constitutional Government

1. Thomas Jefferson, *The Kentucky Resolutions* (1798), Bergh 17:388, in *The Real Thomas Jefferson*, p. 382. Also, Paul Leicester Ford (editor), *The Works of Thomas Jefferson*, Volume VIII (G. P. Putnam's Sons, 1904), pp. 474-75 (viewed online).
2. Chester Ward and Phyllis Schlafly, *Kissinger on the Couch* (New Rochelle, N.Y.: Arlington House, 1975), p. 151.
3. Carroll Quigley, *Tragedy and Hope: A History of the World In Our Time* (New York: Macmillan, 1966), pp. 1247-48.

Chapter 12: A Realistic Plan of Action

1. Robert Welch, *The Blue Book* (Belmont, Mass.: Western Islands, 1959), p. 160.

Chapter 13: The Principal Challenge: Building Organization

1. Thomas N. Hill, *JBS Bulletin*, March 1973.

Chapter 14: Organize, You Say?

1. Edmund Burke, *Thoughts on the Cause of the Present Discontents*, April 23, 1770, in *Familiar Quotations* (16th ed.) (Boston: Little, Brown, 1992), p. 330.
2. Robert Welch, June 5, 1964 speech "More Stately Mansions," *The New Americanism and Other Speeches and Essays by Robert Welch* (Belmont, Mass.: Western Islands, 1966), p. 122.
3. Rick Warren, *The Purpose Driven Church: Growth Without Compromising Your Message & Mission* (Grand Rapids, Mich.: Zondervan, 1995), p. 121.

Chapter 15: Member Opportunity and Responsibility

1. Edward R. Sill, "Opportunity," in Roy J. Cook (compiler), *One Hundred and One Famous Poems With a Prose Supplement* (revised edition) (Chicago: Reilly and Lee, 1958), p. 2.
2. Robert Welch, *The Blue Book* (Belmont, Mass.: Western Islands, 1959), p. 61.
3. G. Vance Smith, "The Chief Executive Officer Remarks ... ", *JBS Bulletin*, June 1994.
4. Hearing Before the Senate Subcommittee on Internal Security, Eighty-fifth Congress, Second Session (1958). Appendix IV to Part 2 (Washington, D.C.: U.S. Government Printing Office). Consists of a staff study by SPX Research Associates, "The Supreme Court as an Instrument of Global Conquest. (The Government Printing Office published Appendix IV as part of an expensive large document, so the SPX report was reprinted privately by Education Information, Inc. in Fullerton, Calif.)
5. Henry Willard Austin (1858-1912), "Perseverance Conquers All."

Chapter 16: Destructive and Neutralizing Tangents

1. Don Fotheringham, *Tangents: Neutralizing movements that undermine the work of patriotic Americans to preserve freedom* (revised edition) (Appleton, Wis.: The John Birch Society, April 2002).

Chapter 17: Presidential Politics

1. Theodore Roosevelt, in Robert Welch, *The Politician* (Belmont, Mass.: Belmont Publishing, Library Edition, 5th printing, 1964), p. v.
2. Samuel Pettengill, *Smoke-Screen* (Kingsport, Tenn.: Southern Publishers, 1940), p. 124.
3. Chester Ward and Phyllis Schlafly, *Kissinger on the Couch* (New Rochelle, N.Y.: Arlington House, 1975), pp. 150-51.
4. Carroll Quigley, *Tragedy and Hope: A History of the World In Our Time* (New York:

Macmillan, 1966), p. 945.

5. Peggy Noonan, "Ronald Reagan," *Time*, April 13, 1998.

Chapter 18: With God's Help

1. Alexis de Tocqueville, 1840, in *The New American*, December 22, 1986. Note: There is some question as to the authenticity of this beautiful statement often attributed to de Tocqueville.

2. See, for example, David Emerson Gumaer, "Apostasy: The National Council of Churches," *American Opinion*, February 1970.

Chapter 19: Freedom or Global Slavery — The Choice is Yours

1. James Russell Lowell, "The Present Crisis," 1844, in Geoffrey O'Brien (general editor), *Bartlett's Poems for Occasions* (Boston: Little, Brown, 2004), p. 443.

2. John Adams, letter to his wife Abigail, in James Truslow Adams, *The Adams Family* (Boston: Little, Brown, 1930), p. 37.

3. Tyron Edwards (editor), *A Dictionary of Thoughts* (F.B. Dickerson Co., 1908), p. 589.

4. See, for example, "Cheney's Law," PBS Frontline, broadcast October 16, 2007.

5. See, for example: Grenville Clark and Louis B. Sohn, *World Peace Through World Law*, Second Edition (Revised) (Cambridge, Mass.: Harvard University Press, 1962), pp. xxix, 225, 247-48, 256; and the website for the International Network on Small Arms (IANSA) www.iansa.org — which purports to be the voice of civil society, but which according to its own website has received funding from the governments of the UK, Belgium, Sweden and Norway, as well as from the Ford Foundation, the Rockefeller Foundation, the John D. and Catherine T. MacArthur Foundation, and the Samuel Rubin Foundation. IANSA helps supply the agitation (pressure from below) in support of the UN-led global gun control movement. Also see UN Secretary-General Kofi Annan, *We the Peoples: The Role of the United Nations in the 21st Century*, April 3, 2000.

6. See, for example, the signed determination of President Reagan in the Federal Register of September 9, 1982.

7. There are many books on this topic, but see, for example: Charlotte Thompson Iserbyt, *Back to Basics Reform ... or Skinnerian International Curriculum* (Bath, Maine: self-published, 1985); and her *Deliberate Dumb Down 3-D Proof Packet* of supporting documentation (1994); also by Iserbyt, *The Deliberate Dumbing Down of America: A Chronological Paper Trail* (Ravenna, Ohio: Conscience Press, 1999). Mrs. Iserbyt served as a Special Assistant in the Office of Educational Research and Improvement in the Reagan administration's Department of Education.

She was one of the first to blow the whistle on Outcome-Based Education (OBE).

8. See, for example, "A Global School Board," *The New American*, January 23, 1995 and "Schoolmarm to the World," *The New American*, April 3, 1995. Also see the two documents stemming from the World Conference on Education for All held in Jomtien, Thailand, March 1990: "World Declaration on Education for All" and "Framework for Action to Meet Basic Learning Needs." The six goal areas in the latter parallel closely the "Goals 2000" legislation signed into law by President Clinton in 1994. A more recent article: "UNESCO's Rotten Track Record," *The New American*, May 19, 2003 was written shortly before the Bush administration had the U.S. rejoin UNESCO after a 20-year absence.

9. See, for example: Robert Welch, "Medicine Leads the Way," September 1963 speech before the Section on General Practice of the Los Angeles County Medical Association, recorded on audiocassette by Gary Allen Communications (No. 320-A); Gary R. Handy, "Medicine Leads the Way," reprinted article from February 1976 *Bulletin*; and Elizabeth W. Wilson, "MediWhat? Compulsory Health Insurance," *American Opinion*, January 1966.

10. Welch, *In Plain Language*, pamphlet, 1969.

11. General Lewis Walt, U.S.M.C., Ret., *The Eleventh Hour* (Ottawa, Ill.: Jameson Books, 1979).

12. General Lewis Walt quoted in "They Paused to Remark," *American Opinion*, September 1979.

13. Walt quoted in "They Paused to Remark," *American Opinion*, September 1981.

Appendix A: On the Shoulders of a Giant — Robert Welch

1. F.P. Lock, *Edmund Burke*, Volume II: 1784-1797 (Writings and Speeches of Edmund Burke) (New York: Oxford University Press, 2006), p. 464.

2. E. Merrill Root, Introduction, in G. Edward Griffin, *The Life and Words of Robert Welch: Founder of The John Birch Society* (Thousand Oaks, Calif.: American Media, 1975), pp. xvi, xvii.

3. Ibid., pp. 66-67.

4. *The John Birch Society Bulletin*, February 1960. Note: Per Mr. Welch's intention, the Council was formed a year after the Society's founding. Its first meeting was held in Chicago on January 9, 1960.

5. Griffin, p. 132.

6. Robert Welch, *The Blue Book of The John Birch Society* (Belmont, Mass.: Western Islands, 1961), p. 167.

7. Welch, *Again, May God Forgive Us!* (Belmont, Mass.: Belmont Publishing, 1971), pp. viii, ix.

8. Welch, *The Life of John Birch* (Chicago: Henry Regnery, 1954), p. v.

267

9. "Postscript for the Second Printing," December 9, 1959, *The Blue Book*, p. 168.

Appendix C: Not Just *Any* Organization
1. Robert Welch, *The Blue Book* (Belmont, Mass.: Western Islands, 1959), pp. 95-96.
2. Welch, *JBS Bulletin*, July 1965.
3. Welch, *JBS Bulletin*, February 1970.
4. Welch, *The Blue Book*, p. 93.
5. G. Allen Bubolz, "Keep US Independent! — 1990," *JBS Bulletin*, March 1990.

Bibliography

Section I: There *Is* a Conspiracy

Barruel, Abbé Augustin. *Memoirs Illustrating the History of Jacobinism*. Fraser, Michigan: American Council on Economics and Society, 1995 (reprint of 1799 translation).

Bentley, Elizabeth. *Out of Bondage*. New York: Devin-Adair, 1951.

Billington, James H. *Fire in the Minds of Men: Origins of Revolutionary Faith*. New York: Basic Books, 1980.

Brzezinski, Zbigniew. *Between Two Ages: America's Role in the Technetronic Era*. New York: Viking, 1970.

Budenz, Louis F. *The Cry Is Peace*. Chicago: Henry Regnery, 1952.

— *The Techniques of Communism*. Chicago: Henry Regnery, 1954.

Burnham, James. *The Web of Subversion: Underground Networks in the U.S. Government*. New York: The John Day Co., 1954.

Chambers, Whittaker. *Witness*. New York: Random House, 1952.

Dies, Martin. *The Trojan Horse in America*. New York: Dodd, Mead, 1940.

— *Martin Dies' Story*. New York: The Bookmailer, 1963.

Evans, Medford. *The Secret War for the A-Bomb*. Chicago: Henry Regnery, 1953.

Hoar, William P. *Architects of Conspiracy: An Intriguing History*. Belmont, Mass.: Western Islands, 1984.

House, "Colonel" Edward Mandell. *Philip Dru: Administrator: A Story of Tomorrow — 1920-1935*. New York: B.W. Huebsch, 1912.

Hunter, Edward. *Brainwashing: From Pavlov to Powers (The Story of the Men Who Defied It)*. New York: Bookmailer, 1960.

— (testimony). *The New Drive Against the Anti-Communist Program*. Senate Internal Security Subcommittee. Washington, D.C.: U.S. Government Printing Office, 1961.

Ickes, Harold L. *The Secret Diary of Harold L. Ickes*. Published posthumously in three volumes. New York: Simon & Shuster, 1953-54.

Jordan, George Racey, USAF (Ret.). *Major Jordan's Diaries*. New York: Harcourt, Brace, 1952.

McIlhany, William H., II. *The Tax-Exempt Foundations*. Westport, Conn.: Arlington House, 1980.

Quigley, Carroll. *The Anglo-American Establishment*. New York: Books in Focus, 1982.

— *Tragedy and Hope: A History of the World in Our Time*. New York: Macmillan, 1966.

Robison, John. *Proofs of a Conspiracy Against All the Religions and Governments of Europe*. Belmont, Mass.: Western Islands, 1967 (reprint of 1798 original).

Romerstein, Herbert and Eric Breindel. *The Venona Secrets: Exposing Soviet Espionage and America's Traitors*. Washington, D.C.: Regnery, 2000.

Schaack, Michael J. *Anarchy and Anarchists: A History of the Red Terror and the Social Revolution in America and Europe*. New York: Arno Press, 1977 (reprint of 1899 original).

Schlafly, Phyllis and Chester Ward, Rear Admiral, USN (Ret.). *Kissinger on the Couch*. New Rochelle, N.Y.:

Arlington House, 1975.

Schlesinger, Arthur M., Jr. *A Thousand Days: John F. Kennedy in the White House.* Boston: Houghton Mifflin, 1965.

Seymour, Charles (ed.). *The Intimate Papers of Colonel House,* Vol. I, "Behind The Political Curtain: 1912-1915." Boston: Houghton Mifflin, 1926.

— *The Intimate Papers of Colonel House,* Vol. III, "Into the World War: April, 1917 — June, 1918." Boston: Houghton Mifflin, 1928.

Smoot, Dan. *The Invisible Government.* Belmont, Mass.: Western Islands, 1965.

Stang, Alan. *The Actor: The True Story of John Foster Dulles, Secretary of State 1953 – 1959.* Belmont, Mass.: Western Islands, 1968.

Whitney, R. M. *Reds in America.* Belmont, Mass.: Western Islands edition, 1970 (reprint of 1924 Beckwith Press edition).

Section II: Absolute Evil

The 46 Civilian Doctors of Elisabethville. *46 Angry Men.* Belmont, Mass.: American Opinion, 1962; originally published by Dr. T. Vleurinck, 96 Avenue de Broqueville, Bruxelles 15, 1962.

Ally Betrayed: Nicaragua. Alexandria, Virginia: Western Goals, 1980. (Foreword by Ambassador Earl E. T. Smith, U.S. Postscript by Ambassador Turner B. Shelton. Nicaragua Postscript by President Francisco Urcuyo Maliano.)

Barron, John. *KGB: The Secret Work of Soviet Secret Agents.* New York: Reader's Digest Press, 1974.

Bethell, Nicholas. *The Last Secret.* New York: Basic Books, 1974.

Braden, Spruille. *Diplomats and Demagogues: The Memoirs of Spruille Braden.* New Rochelle, New York: Arlington House, 1971.

Cline, Ray S. and Yonah Alexander. *Terrorism: The Soviet Connection.* New York: Crane Russak, 1984.

Dinsmore, Herman H. *All the News That Fits: A Critical Analysis of the News and Editorial Contents of the New York Times.* New Rochelle, New York: Arlington House, 1969.

— *The Bleeding of America* (third edition). Belmont, Mass.: Western Islands, 1977.

Dolot, Miron. *Execution by Hunger: The Hidden Holocaust.* New York: W.W. Norton, 1985.

Douglass, Joseph D. Jr. *Red Cocaine: The Drugging of America.* Atlanta: Clarion House, 1990.

du Berrier, Hilaire. *Background to Betrayal: The Tragedy of Vietnam.* Belmont, Mass.: Western Islands, 1965.

Epstein, Julius. *Operation Keelhaul: The Story of Forced Repatriation from 1944 to the Present.* Old Greenwich, Conn.: Devin-Adair, 1973.

Evans, G. Russell. *The Panama Canal Treaties Swindle: Consent to Disaster.* Carrboro, N.C.: Signal Books, 1986.

Finder, Joseph. *Red Carpet.* New York: Holt, Rinehart and Winston, 1983.

Flynn, John T. *While You Slept: Our Tragedy in Asia and Who Made It.* New York: Devin-Adair, 1951.

Gill, William J. *The Ordeal of Otto Otepka.* New Rochelle, New York: Arlington House, 1969.

Hamilton, Alexander, James Madison, and John Jay. *The Federalist Papers.* New York: Mentor, 1961.

Heikal, Mohammed Hassanein. *Nasser: The Cairo Documents.* New York: Doubleday, 1971.

Hempstone, Smith. *Rebels,*

Mercenaries, and Dividends: The Katanga Story. New York: Frederick A. Praeger, 1962.

Huxley-Blythe, Peter J. *The East Came West*. Caldwell, Idaho: Caxton, 1964.

Kubeck, Anthony. *How the Far East Was Lost: American Policy and the Creation of Communist China, 1941-1949*. Chicago: Regnery, 1963.

— *The Red China Papers*. New Rochelle, New York: Arlington House, 1975.

Lane, Ambassador Arthur Bliss. *I Saw Poland Betrayed: An American Ambassador Reports to the American People*. Indianapolis: Bobbs-Merrill, 1948.

Levine, Michael. *Deep Cover: The Inside Story of How DEA Infighting, Incompetence, and Subterfuge Lost Us the Biggest Battle of the Drug War*. New York: Delacorte Press, 1990.

Martin, David. *Ally Betrayed: The Uncensored Story of Tito and Mihailovich*. New York: Prentice-Hall, 1946.

Martino, John with Nathaniel Weyl. *I Was Castro's Prisoner: An American Tells His Story*. New York: Devin-Adair, 1963.

McCarthy, Senator Joseph R. *America's Retreat From Victory: The Story of George Catlett Marshall*. New York: Devin-Adair, 1951.

Mikolajczyk, Stanislaw. *The Rape of Poland: Pattern of Soviet Aggression*. Whitefish, Mont.: Kessinger Publishing, 2007. (Earlier hardback: New York: McGraw Hill, 1948.)

Morris, Robert. *Self Destruct: Dismantling America's Internal Security*. New Rochelle, New York: Arlington House, 1979.

Possony, Stephan T. *Maoist China and Heroin*. Taipei, Taiwan: China Publishing Company, no date.

Rowe, David N., Ph.D. *Ally Betrayed: The Republic of Korea*. Alexandria, Virginia: Western Goals, 1982. (Foreword by Major General John Singlaub, U.S.A. (Ret.), Postscript by Congressman Bob Stump.)

Rummel, R. J. *Lethal Politics: Soviet Genocide and Mass Murder Since 1917*. New Brunswick, New Jersey: Transaction Publishers, 1990.

— *Death by Government*. Transaction Publishers, 1994.

Schuyler, Philippa. *Who Killed the Congo?* New York: Devin-Adair, 1962.

Shirer, William. *The Rise and Fall of the Third Reich: A History of Nazi Germany*. Greenwich, Conn.: Fawcett, 1960.

Smith, Earl E. T. (U.S. Ambassador to Cuba, 1957-59). *The Fourth Floor: An Account of the Castro Communist Revolution*. New York: Random House, 1962.

Somoza, Anastasio as told to Jack Cox. *Nicaragua Betrayed*. Belmont, Mass.: Western Islands, 1980.

Sterling, Claire. *The Terror Network: The Secret War of International Terrorism*. New York: Holt, Rinehart and Winston and Reader's Digest Press, 1981.

— *The Time of the Assassins*. Holt, Rinehart and Winston, 1984.

Sutton, Antony C. *Western Technology and Soviet Economic Development, 1917-1930*. Stanford University, Stanford, Calif.: Hoover Institution, 1968.

— *Western Technology and Soviet Economic Development, 1930-1945*. Hoover Institution, 1971.

— *Western Technology and Soviet Economic Development, 1945-1965*. Hoover Institution, 1973.

— *National Suicide: Military Aid to the*

Soviet Union. New Rochelle, New York: Arlington House, 1973.

— *Wall Street and the Bolshevik Revolution*. New Rochelle, New York: Arlington House, 1974.

— *Wall Street and the Rise of Hitler*. Seal Beach, Calif.: '76 Press, 1976.

— *The Best Enemy Money Can Buy*. Billings, Mont.: Liberty House Press, 1986.

Timperlake, Edward and William C. Triplett II. *Year of the Rat: How Bill Clinton Compromised American Security for Chinese Money*. Chicago: Regnery, 2000.

Utley, Freda. *The China Story*. Chicago: Henry Regnery, 1951.

Welch, Robert H. W., Jr. *May God Forgive Us*. Chicago: Henry Regnery, 1952.

— *The Life of John Birch: In the Story of One American Boy, the Ordeal of His Age*. Henry Regnery, 1954.

—*The Politician*. Belmont, Mass.: Belmont Publishing, 1964.

— *Again, May God Forgive Us*. Belmont Publishing, 1971.

Weyl, Nathaniel. *Red Star Over Cuba: The Russian Assault on the Western Hemisphere*. New York: Devin-Adair, 1960.

Section III: Our Positive and Permanent Purpose

Allen, Gary with Larry Abraham. *None Dare Call It Conspiracy*. Rossmoor, Calif.: Concord Press, 1971.

Bastiat, Frederick. *The Law*. Irvington-on-Hudson, New York: Foundation for Economic Education, 1981 (first published in 1850).

Bowen, Catherine Drinker. *Miracle at Philadelphia: The Story of the Constitutional Convention, May to September 1787*. Boston: Little, Brown, 1966.

Griffin, G. Edward. *The Life and Words of Robert Welch: Founder of The John Birch Society*. Thousand Oaks, Calif.: American Media, 1975.

Hayek, Friederich A. (editor). *Capitalism and the Historians*. Chicago: University of Chicago Press, 1954.

Hazlitt, Henry. *Economics In One Lesson*. New York: Crown Publishers, 1979.

Kershner, Howard E. *Dividing the Wealth: Are You Getting Your Share?* Old Greenwich, Conn.: Devin-Adair, 1971.

Madison, James, Alexander Hamilton and John Jay. *The Federalist Papers*. New York: Mentor, 1961.

Martin, Rose L. *Fabian Freeway, High Road to Socialism in the U.S.A.* Belmont, Mass.: Western Islands, 1966.

Marx, Karl. *The Communist Manifesto*. Introduction by William P. Fall. Belmont: Mass.: American Opinion, 1974.

McDonald, Lawrence Patton. *We Hold These Truths: A Reverent Review of the U.S. Constitution*. Seal Beach, Calif.: '76 Press, 1976.

Mises, Ludwig von. *Human Action* (3rd. rev. edition). Chicago: Regnery, 1966.

— *Planning for Freedom and sixteen other essays and addresses*. South Holland, Ill.: Libertarian Press, 1952.

Nock, Albert Jay. *Our Enemy, the State*. Delavan, Wis.: Hallberg Publishing, 1983.

Weaver, Henry Grady. *The Mainspring of Human Progress*. Revised edition. Irvington-on-Hudson, New York: Foundation for Economic Education, 1953. (Originally published by Talbot Books in 1947.)

Welch, Robert. *The New Americanism and other speeches and essays by Robert Welch*. Belmont, Mass.:

Western Islands, 1966.

— *The Blue Book of The John Birch Society*. Belmont, Mass.: Western Islands, 1959.

Section IV: So What Is To Be Done?

Blumenfeld, Samuel L. *Is Public Education Necessary?* Boise, Idaho: Paradigm, 1981.

— *NEA: Trojan Horse in American Education*. Paradigm, 1984.

Booker, Christopher and Richard North. *The Great Deception: The Secret History of the European Union*. United Kingdom: Continuum International Publishing Group, 2003.

Chambers, Claire. *The SIECUS Circle: A Humanist Revolution*. Belmont, Mass.: Western Islands, 1977.

Evans-Pritchard, Ambrose. *The Secret Life of Bill Clinton: The Unreported Stories*. Washington, D.C.: Regnery, 1997.

Garrett, Garet. *The People's Pottage*. Caldwell, Idaho: Caxton, 1953.

Martin, Rose L. *Fabian Freeway, High Road to Socialism in the U.S.A.* Belmont, Mass.: Western Islands, 1966.

Powell, S. Steven. *Covert Cadre: Inside the Institute for Policy Studies*. Ottawa, Ill.: Green Hill Publishers, 1987.

Ray, Dixy Lee. *Environmental Overkill*. Washington, D.C.: Regnery Gateway, 1993.

Sleeman, William Henry. *Rambles and Recollections of an Indian Official*. Paperback edition. UK: Echo Library, 2006.

Tuker, Francis Ivan Simms. *The Yellow Scarf: The Story of the Life of Thuggee Sleeman, or Major-General Sir William Henry Sleeman, K.C.B., 1788-1856, of the Bengal Army and the Indian Political Service*. UK:

J.M. Dent & Co., 1961.

Welch, Robert. *The Politician*. Belmont, Mass.: Belmont Publishing, Library Edition, 5th printing, 1964.

Zoul, Louis. *Thugs and Communists*. Long Island City, New York: Public Opinion, 1959.

Section V: And *Organize* for Victory!

Crocker, H.W. *Robert E. Lee on Leadership: Executive Lessons in Character, Courage, and Vision*. Atherton, Calif.: Prima Publishing, 1999.

Gordon, Rosalie. *Nine Men Against America — The Supreme Court and Its Attack on American Liberties*. New York, Devin-Adair, 1958.

Griffin, G. Edward. *The Life and Words of Robert Welch: Founder of The John Birch Society*. Thousand Oaks, Calif.: American Media, 1975.

Hyde, Douglas. *Dedication and Leadership*. Notre Dame, Indiana: University of Notre Dame Press, 1966.

Kaltman, Al. *Cigars, Whiskey & Winning: Leadership Lessons from General Ulysses S. Grant*. Paramus, New Jersey: Prentice Hall, 1998.

Welch, Robert. *The Blue Book of The John Birch Society*. Belmont, Mass.: Western Islands, 1959.

— "More Stately Mansions" in *The New Americanism and Other Speeches and Essays by Robert Welch*. Belmont, Mass.: Western Islands, 1966.

Williamson, Porter B. *Patton's Principles: A Handbook for Managers Who Mean It!* New York: Simon and Schuster, 1979.

Section VI: Members in Action

Allen, Gary. *Richard Nixon: The Man Behind the Mask*. Belmont, Mass.: Western Islands, 1971.

— *Nixon's Palace Guard.* Belmont, Mass.: Western Islands, 1971.

— *Jimmy Carter, Jimmy Carter.* Seal Beach, Calif.: '76 Press, 1976.

Antelman, Rabbi Marvin S. *To Eliminate the Opiate.* (Volume I.) New York: Zahavia, 1974.

Fotheringham, Don. *Tangents: Neutralizing movements that undermine the work of patriotic Americans to preserve freedom.* Appleton, Wis.: The John Birch Society. Updated April 2002.

Hyde, Douglas. *Dedication and Leadership.* Notre Dame, Ind.: University of Notre Dame Press, 1966.

McGinnis, Joe. *The Selling of the President, 1968.* New York: Pocket Books, 1970.

Pettengill, Samuel. *Smoke-screen.* Kingsport, Tenn.: Southern Publishers, 1940.

Schlafly, Phyllis and Chester Ward, Rear Admiral, USN (Ret.). *Kissinger on the Couch.* New Rochelle, New York: Arlington House, 1975.

Welch, Robert. *The Neutralizers.* Pamphlet. Belmont, Mass.: The John Birch Society, 1963. Also on audiocassettes (2) No. 316. Gary Allen Communications.

Section VII: "And So, Let's Act!"

Beckman, Petr. *The Health Hazards of NOT Going Nuclear.* Boulder, Colo.: Golem Press, 1976.

de Tocqueville, Alex. *Democracy in America.* In two volumes. New York, Schocken Books, 1961.

Iserbyt, Charlotte Thompson. *Back to Basics Reform ... or Skinnerian International Curriculum.* Bath, Maine: self-published, 1985.

— *The Deliberate Dumbing Down of America: A Chronological Paper Trail.* Ravenna, Ohio: Conscience Press, 1999.

McCracken, Samuel. *The War Against the Atom.* New York: Basic Books, 1982.

Walt, General Lewis, U.S.M.C., Ret. *The Eleventh Hour.* Ottawa, Ill.: Jameson Books, 1979.

Appendix A: On The Shoulders of a Giant — Robert Welch

Griffin, G. Edward. *The Life and Words of Robert Welch: Founder of The John Birch Society.* Thousand Oaks, Calif.: American Media, 1975.

Welch, Robert H. W., Jr. *The Life of John Birch: In the Story of One American Boy, the Ordeal of His Age.* Chicago: Henry Regnery, 1954.

— *The Blue Book of The John Birch Society.* Belmont, Mass.: Western Islands, 1959.

— *The New Americanism and other speeches and essays by Robert Welch.* Belmont, Mass.: Western Islands, 1966.

— *Again, May God Forgive Us.* Belmont, Mass.: Belmont Publishing, 1971.